Chasing the Monsoon

'Mr Frater writes with infectious and enchanting enthusiasm, combining his interest in meteorology with an eye that captures idiosyncracies and motifs . . . A beautiful and remarkable book'
The Times

'One of the most remarkable travel books in recent memory . . . Frater's deftly engaging account finds greatness in a neglected theme – the profound relationship between people, culture and climate'
Newsweek

'A brilliantly amusing book... full of humorous perceptions about modern India and its inescapable links with the past'
New York Times Book Review

'Delightful . . . Frater's sophisticated wit and love for ordinariness make this journey a pure pleasure'
San Francisco Chronicle

'Altogether an endearing liquid discovery of India. In a genre that is ephemeral, this book is likely to survive because of its brilliance and its insight into how the monsoon makes India'
Economic Times (India)

'Alexander Frater's book is a wonderful amalgam of the beauty, strength, untamed power, frightening ferocity and the gentleness of the monsoon rains that nourish our lives and the life of the nation'
Financial Express (India)

'A travelogue that is as amusing as it is informative'
Indian Express

'Ranks with James Cameron's *Indian Summer* as a potential classic of travel writing on India'
India Today

ALEXANDER FRATER has contributed to various UK publications – Miles Kington called him 'the funniest man who wrote for *Punch* since the war' – and been a contracted *New Yorker* writer; as chief travel correspondent of the London *Observer* he won an unprecedented number of British Press Travel Awards. Two of his books, *Beyond the Blue Horizon* and *Chasing the Monsoon*, have been made into major BBC television films. One, *The Last African Flying Boat* (based on the former), took the Bafta award for best single documentary, while a programme for BBC Radio 4 (about his South Seas birthplace) was named overall winner of the Travelex Travel Writers' Awards. He lives in London, though, whenever time and money allow, is likely to be found skulking deep in the hot, wet tropics.

ALSO BY ALEXANDER FRATER

Beyond the Blue Horizon
On the Track of Imperial Airways

Tales from the Torrid Zone
Travels in the Deep Tropics

Alexander Frater

CHASING THE
MONSOON

A Modern Pilgrimage Through India

PICADOR

First published 1990 by Viking

First published in paperback 1991 by Penguin Books

First published by Picador 2005
an imprint of Pan Macmillan Ltd
Pan Macmillan, 20 New Wharf Road, London N1 9RR
Basingstoke and Oxford
Associated companies throughout the world
www.panmacmillan.com

ISBN 978-0-330-43313-6

10

A CIP catalogue record for this book is available from
the British Library.

Printed and bound in India by
Replika Press Pvt. Ltd.

For my mother

Acknowledgements

This book is largely an anthology of the information, advice, help, anecdotes and stories profferred by countless people throughout India. These, the voices of the 1987 monsoon, shaped and dictated my journey, and my debt to them is incalculable.

I must also express my gratitude to Y. P. Rao, the giant of Indian monsoon studies, whose classic book, *Southwest Monsoon*, I carried with me throughout. Though written primarily for other meteorologists, it became a personal touchstone, constantly consulted, not always understood, but teaching me respect for a phenomenon that seemed to grow more subtle and mysterious with every passing day.

Readers wanting a plain man's guide should seek out *The Monsoons* by P. K. Das, published by the National Book Trust of India. Dr Das, a sometime Director General of India's National Meteorological Office, has managed to make a difficult subject accessible and readable.

By far the most comprehensive study available is *Monsoons*, edited by Jay S. Fein and Pamela L. Stephens of the National Science Foundation, Washington D.C. Published by John Wiley & Sons, New York, it covers every conceivable aspect of the monsoon, running the gamut from its profound effect on Indian life and culture to the complex sciences governing its cause and effect. I drew much information and a real measure of enlightenment from this extensive work, and recommend it unreservedly to anyone with a genuine interest in the subject.

My thanks are due to Helen Simpson, whose researches at the India Office Library in London turned up so much invaluable material, and whose unflagging enthusiasm helped to sustain my own.

And, finally, I should like to thank my long-suffering family, without whose generous, good-humoured encouragement I could never have even contemplated this project. Writers less fortunate might have been expected to remain responsibly at home and get rained on in England instead.

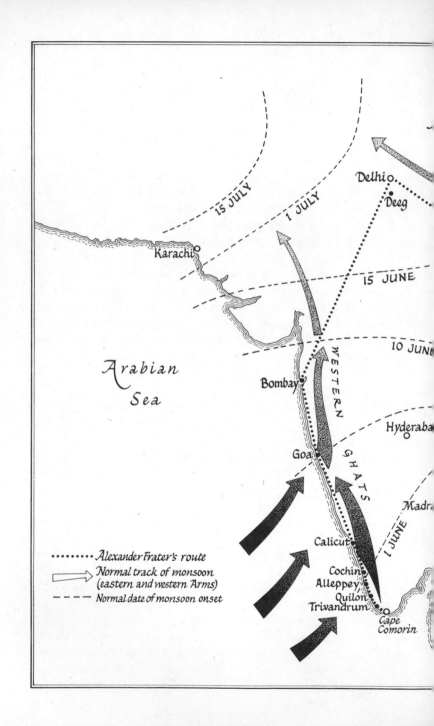

Arabian
Sea

Delhi
Deeg

Karachi

15 JULY

1 JULY

15 JUNE

10 JUNE

WESTERN

Bombay

Goa

Hyderaba

GHATS

Madra

Calicut

Cochin
Alleppey
Quilon
Trivandrum

1 JUNE

Cape
Comorin

.... Alexander Frater's route
⟶ Normal track of monsoon
(eastern and western Arms)
– – – Normal date of monsoon onset

HIMALAYAS

Gauhati ASSAM
MEGHALAYA Khasi Hills
        Shillong
        Cherrapunji

Varanasi

BANGLADESH

Calcutta

5 JUNE

Bay of
Bengal

BURMA

N

SRI LANKA

0   100   200   300 miles
0   500 km

Prologue

The first sounds I ever heard were those of falling rain. It was tropical, the kind that seems to possess a metallic weight and mass, and it began bucketing down as my mother went into labour at a small mission hospital in the South-West Pacific. It continued during the delivery and for some time after my birth, drumming on the galvanized iron roof, swishing through the heavy foliage outside.

The delivery was made by my father, the only doctor for a thousand miles in any direction. Several times a week he attended emergency calls by motor boat, often sailing great distances to reach patients in the remoter villages and settlements. The weather was thus of more than passing interest to him and, using a calibrated glass rain gauge and a creaking anemometer kept in the hospital garden, he measured and recorded it, noting down items like precipitation, hours of sunshine and wind speed and direction.

Years later, referring to these records, he told me that on the day I was born 2.1 inches fell in the space of seven hours and twelve minutes; it knocked flowers off trees and washed away topsoil; our little island was carpeted with fallen blossoms, damp and sweet smelling, the surrounding lagoon darkened by tons of deliquescent earth floating in suspension. The sea state had been moderate, the swell light.

Naturally I have no conscious recollection of these events but reckon they must have left a mark. I spent five years there before the threat of an impending Japanese invasion caused my mother, sister and me to be evacuated to Australia aboard an ageing, rust-streaked tramp steamer (which got under way through light air and a heavy pre-dawn dew) but during that period I experienced thousands of hours of rain and climatic extremes.

Tropical depressions moved in and out like trains, pulling their high precipitation, Force 8 winds and immoderate sea states behind them, and they always got a big welcome from me. The inevitable thunder and lightning overtures were exhilarating but I had been taught to observe them analytically, counting off the seconds between flash and boom at the rate of five to the mile, tracking the approaching storm, anticipating the foaming onset of the rain itself – comforting, cooling, charging the house with smells from the dripping garden; perhaps it was atmospheric electricity that sent mysterious squalls of frangipani and jasmine gusting through the rooms and lingering in fragrant air pockets long after the rain had gone. I liked the sense of privacy it invoked, the way towering curtains closed around the island and sealed it off from the rest of the world.

A picture hung beside my bed which accurately encapsulated all this. It was a framed, luridly tinted Edwardian print of a deluge inundating a range of steep grassy hills. Temples along the crests indicated that the landscape was oriental. In small forests lower down, tigers and naked pygmies with spears could be discerned. In some the tigers were avoiding the pygmies; in others the pygmies ran from the tigers. What made it remarkable, though, was the weight and density of the rain. Water fell torrentially from low, scudding cloud and sprang from the hillsides in countless foaming cataracts. Flapping sheets of water hung spinnaker-like in the air, more went surfing down the slopes. Its curious bottle-green opacity suggested that the artist – L. Geo. Lopez according to the signature – had placed his drowned landscape at the bottom of a lake.

This masterpiece, identified in a flowing intaglio caption as 'Cherrapunji, Assam: The Wettest Place on Earth', had been a wedding present to my parents. Its effect on me was so profound that afterwards, as a war evacuee in Australia, bouts of homesickness could be assuaged by simply willing it back again. In the mind's eye it had a dark iconic glow that dispelled even the darkness of my school dormitory.

My father admired the picture too. He called it a study of convectional turmoil. It was also a view of the Indian monsoon in the act of producing the world's heaviest rains; what L. Geo. Lopez had depicted here, probably without even realizing it, was the excessive precipitation you got when the upper tropospheric belt moved in over those lofty hills. 'Travelling, of course, on an oblique bias,' my father would say. He knew his stuff. The donor of the picture was an old Glasgow friend named Wapshot who worked in Cherrapunji as a Church of Scotland missionary, and their correspondence seemed to consist largely of exchanged weather information. Some of Wapshot's rainfall figures reduced even my father to silence. Thirty-five inches in a single day! Waterlogged earth made burials impossible so corpses were placed in vats of wild honey until the ground was dry enough to receive them. The honey tasted faintly of oranges and, according to Wapshot, lent the bodies a slick, eel-ike lubricity which made them very hard to handle.

My father often spoke of going to Cherrapunji. In meteorological terms he likened it to one of the Stations of the Cross and implied that a visit at the height of the monsoon, with his rain gauge, would be a kind of pilgrimage.

Two or three times a year, in season, we got a bravura climatic performance of our own. Hurricanes were usually presaged by a red moon, a purple dawn and oily green morning cloud. The sun – if glimpsed at all – would often be encircled by a halo, its open side announcing the quarter from which the blow should come. The barometer dropped so fast it almost fell off the wall. The sea became glassy and a curious stillness set in. Smoke rose from village fires in a structured, architectural way, forming pillars and but-tresses that supported a vaulted ceiling of heavy black overcast. From neighbouring islands the sounds of dogs barking and babies crying carried clearly. Small craft ran for cover. Storm shutters went up.

My father produced the hurricane flags which, traditionally, flew from a staff at the hospital landing – white for 'later' (twelve hours to go), yellow for 'soon' (six hours), black for 'imminent'. They were made of Admiralty-quality all-wool double warp bunt-ing, designed to withstand extreme conditions, and it was my job to hoist and lower them. The raising of the black flag was noted by those islanders in low-lying, exposed regions who later might have to climb to the tops of coconut palms, hack off the fronds and tie themselves on. Streamlined trees presented no obstacle to the wind; giant waves would surge by harmlessly below.

Only once did we experience the feared vortex, or eye of the storm, which passed overhead as precisely as an aircraft locked on to a radio beacon. Before the anemometer pole snapped like a sapling it was registering 130 knots, or double the maximum force on the Beaufort scale. A mill-race sea burst over the island, and the wind railed so deafeningly we had to communicate by lip-reading. It struck the house with heavy shocklike impacts that made it shudder and creak; during the most violent it felt like a ship under way, destabilized, rocked by small pitching movements, the roof flexing and tugging and warping its pitchpine rafters. Our anxiety about the roof was heightened by the fact that others were losing theirs; we saw four hundred square feet of Cambridge blue corrugated iron, previously the property of Mr Tallboys at Public Works, pass the end of the garden then make a steep climbing turn as it headed away south towards Australia.

And yet throughout all this I noted a special light in my father's eye. He may have been worried but he was exultant too. So was I. For dedicated fans of the weather this was great stuff, a classic performance witnessed from grandstand seats.

One evening in the wet season of 1941 he walked into the kitchen and told us the Japanese had bombed Pearl Harbor. It had been a day of moderate southerlies and partial cloud cover (castellated altocumulus) and he was as pale and shaken as I had ever seen him. He was angry too, his Scottish accent suddenly very pronounced. He knew it signalled the end of our life on the island though I was not to realize that for some time. Almost at once the rumours started – a planter on Malekula saw the Imperial battle fleet stealing by at dusk; a Yokohama-registered freighter had discharged hundreds of bicycles at Santo in readiness for the arrival of Tojo's infantry; a local Jap with a flourishing pepper garden on Efate was receiving coded invasion instructions from Tokyo on his crystal set.

My father supervised the digging of a trench in a yam bed behind the house. He called it an air-raid shelter but it soon became just another flooded pool. Purple lotuses took root and flourished. Frogs lived in it and so, curiously, did a species of newt which, our gardener assured me, had come down in a recent shower. The evaporative power of the South Pacific sun seemed to be such that, like a giant pump, it could suck live, wriggling matter straight up from the sea.

Finally, late one night, aircraft were heard overhead. Roused from our beds, we scrambled into the shelter where, too excited to notice any discomfort, I stared up as the sounds of pond life quietly croaked and splashed around me.

'There's only the one,' my father said after a while.

He knew what he was talking about, having seen aeroplanes overseas; out here they were unknown and this was my first encounter but, maddeningly, the sky was black and moonless. There were no stars either. Normally they shed a radiance of such intensity you could almost thread a needle by them but tonight high cirrocumulus obscured everything.

'It's probably a Zero,' my father said. 'He seems to be circling.'

From the grounds of the Residency three hundred yards away a fantastic swath of light suddenly sprang into the sky, ruler straight, with a confidence that seemed to indicate it was going to knife through the atmosphere and look for passing asteroids.

'Dickie's got his searchlight going,' my mother said, sounding surprised.

Dickie's searchlight wavered and juddered as Dickie got the hang of it but then, steadily, it began to comb the heavens and, all at once, we saw the plane – a tiny flicker of silver high overhead. Two immense explosions sounded from the Residency grounds. Dickie had hunted big game in Africa and now gave the intruder both barrels of his elephant gun. He missed. We heard the Jap fly away north, back to his carrier. The searchlight reeled in its beam, then went out.

And that was that. The rumours now had the urgency and authority of trusted intelligence and, three weeks later, my father put us aboard that weevil-infested tramp steamer and sent us to Australia. A large crowd came to see us off. Though the British and French governments had jointly administered the New Hebrides for half a century neither ever got around to building a school. When my mother arrived she addressed herself to the problem and started her own, organizing the erection of a thatched pavilion, sending the students into the forest to cut timber for their desks.

More than a hundred came to the wharf that early morning, the only natives in the islands who could read and write, and they sang us out to sea in the island way.

Among them was our larky old gardener, Moses, who had encouraged me to believe I was the reincarnation of a popular rain god. His conclusion, based on a reading of chicken entrails and a curious crab-shaped birthmark on my back, proved so appealing I didn't seriously question it as a viable career prospect. (That was left to an incredulous Bible Studies master at school in Melbourne.) It was hard to say goodbye to him.

On the way to Australia we passed through a big depression, the wind gusting at 50 knots, the waves tumbling and densely streaked with foam, blown spray making the air opaque. I was as sick as a dog but kept notes of the conditions and barometric readings so that I could send my father a really interesting letter.

Melbourne produced a new phenomenon – winter. Though the winters were, in truth, quite mild (a local radio station caused pandemonium when, as a joke, it reported snow falling over Collins Street) the sensation of coldness was strange and uncomfortable. I had never shivered before. Nor had I slept under blankets, their weight making me dream of lying in a grave with earth piled on top.

I witnessed lightning without thunder, the flash followed by an infinity of silence, hundreds of seconds fruitlessly counted off while the sky remained dumb.

The rain was cold, often thin, always mean. But a boy at school from the country's arid centre regarded it as a great novelty; where he lived they got none at all some years, and endured such heat that a match dropped on the ground would burst into flame. He loved this southern winter which filled him with health and energy. It probably did the same for me, though in the short term it served mainly to intensify my homesickness. When I complained of the cold to my father he wrote teasing letters asking after my husky dogs and wondering whether I was learning to like pemmican. Melbourne, he pointed out, enjoyed the same moderate temperatures as Oporto, Portugal, famous for its fine wines and benign climate; I wasn't so badly off.

He also gave me news of the island, occupied not by the Japanese but by the Americans. They had arrived first and were keeping the Japs safely holed up in the Solomons. A huge US Navy base now stood on Efate island, only a few hundred yards from his hospital, and he was being treated to unlimited fried chicken, fresh-ground coffee and giant steaks so tender you could almost cut them with a fork; his letters took on a note of wonderment; when he looked up from his desk he saw warships racing in and out of the harbour, fighter planes zooming everywhere, Catalina flying boats cutting creamy wakes in the sea only a stone's throw from his window. But he wrote of other things too: sunshine and precipitation, a rogue evening wind blowing puzzlingly from the south, waterspouts reported off Tanna, increased phosphorescence in our lagoon, an interesting rainbow featuring a fine secondary arc, its colours reversed and standing nine degrees outside the mother bow.

All this, however, unusually for him, was dealt with in a fairly cursory way. He appeared to be losing interest in weather matters. I detected more animation in the account of his first mint julep than of the hurricane – reported in an Australian paper – whose westerly vertex or 'cod of the track' had clipped our islands, and guessed that the Americans were taking him over. I was jealous of the way they always seemed to be popping in with food, drink and books, telling him jokes, inviting him to movies and shows; he saw the Andrews Sisters *live* at the base and had roast turkey at a Thanksgiving dinner. Turkey! In the South Pacific! And after he warned them of a dangerous uncharted reef spotted on one of his early motor boat journeys they revised the US Navy chart and printed his name right over that reef. It was registered and official. They had even put him on the map.

To a shy, impoverished young Scotsman raised to the ideals of service and sacrifice, taught to expect few rewards in this life (you got them in the next), the Americans must have seemed dazzling. Then I blamed them censoriously for the change in him but now I know he kept his letters light and entertaining because he was, in fact, having a very bad war. It wasn't glamorous. He didn't work under the enemy guns but stayed and dealt with the crises at home. A measles epidemic took the lives of countless native kids who, lacking any natural immunity, went down like ninepins. On island after island he diagnosed the rashes and the tell-tale Koplik's spots inside the cheeks, his launch laden with boracic lotion for their eyes and bismuth and opium for their bowels, sulphonamides and Epsom salts in case pneumonia followed. Mostly it was close behind.

Antibiotics remained undiscovered. The sulphonamides were his wonder drugs but, by modern standards, not exactly big workers of miracles; a lot of hope went down the needle with the serum. The most sensational thing about the arrival of penicillin was the way the Americans kept leaving crates of it on his veranda. In a letter scissored by the censor to look like origami paper he reported that it seemed to be okay for pneumonia, meningitis and boils but was no good for malaria. You had to inject 10,000 Oxford units every three hours and, like fish, it eventually went bad even when kept in the ice box.

A flu epidemic followed the measles, another measles epidemic followed that. At one point, he later told me, the island group's entire indigenous population seemed on the verge of extinction. It was a nightmare of Old Testament dimensions and it kept recurring.

And all the time Allied casualties were arriving at the mission hospital from battlefields in the Solomons. The Americans, whose own hospital was overflowing, sent him drugs and instruments and cases of bourbon. One morning Moses, our gardener, complained of a fever and curious lumps on his ears. My father diagnosed leprosy and injected him with Moogrol, but flu-like complications set in and he died within weeks. Soon afterwards a downed Japanese reconnaissance pilot admitted with burns pulled the pin off a concealed hand grenade while the matron, a rather dizzy Australian blonde named Molly – who had assisted at my birth – bent over him. My father had left them seconds earlier to scrub up for a cataract operation.

Meanwhile, back in Melbourne, I was getting acclimatized and beginning to enjoy such seasonal phenomena as wood fires and toasted waffles. My science master, of Portuguese extraction, confirmed that Oporto's climate was indeed similar to Melbourne's and known throughout Europe to be equable and pleasant.

No one else at school shared my interest in weather forecasting so, in time, I gave it up and turned my attention to other things.

*

After the surrender my father arrived in Australia ill, exhausted and in need of a long rest. He was also broke and immediately accepted a better-paid post as principal of the Fiji School of Medicine, an establishment offering islanders a four-year course in basic surgery, obstetrics, public health and tropical medicine. For practical reasons I urged him to include meteorology too; some day his students would be making their own motor launch trips to outlying atolls. His amused reply confirmed the disappearance of that old enthusiasm. In the New Hebrides isolation had bred self-sufficiency; the climate, capricious and unforgiving, turned him into a kind of obsessive player, constantly reading the game to stay ahead of a volatile opponent. But here in Suva, Fiji's busy capital, there were government experts with sophisticated instruments who did that for you. Their prognoses were read out daily on the radio but he listened with only half an ear. His epic small boat journeys were behind him now, and all he really needed to know was whether or not to take an umbrella to work.

He never again spoke of visiting Cherrapunji, the world's wettest place. Wapshot had died fighting the Japanese at Kohima, not far away, in a ferocious battle waged at the height of the monsoon. He now lay buried in the grass tennis court of the old Deputy British Commissioner's bungalow and I used to wonder whether he had been embalmed in honey too.

The British gave my father a medal which, along with his old Smart & Mason barometer, he left to me. The medal, in a small leather box bearing the legend 'MBE CIVIL', consists of a silver Maltese cross surmounted by a crown and suspended from a lobster-coloured ribbon, now faded to coral. An accompanying leaflet advises that it is a Fifth Class insignia of the Most Excellent Order of the British Empire; sometimes I wonder about the criteria used in these matters, and why the civil service awards committee sitting then reckoned he didn't merit a Fourth Class. It also asks that, when the holder dies, surviving relatives write to the Central Chancery of the Orders of Knighthood at St James's Palace, London, SW1, with the date of decease.

And this, when his time came, I duly did.

Chapter One

❈

In the autumn of 1986 a bizarre chain of events began leading me, via a desert oasis in Chinese Turkestan and a famous London teaching hospital, towards Cherrapunji in place of my father.

I had been travelling overland from Pakistan to Kashgar in western China. The three-day journey began on the newly opened Karakoram Highway, a 470-mile-long series of ascending passes that follow a spur of the ancient Silk Road up to the Chinese border. It took us through the Hunza, a secret, enchanted valley where fields of ripening buckwheat glowed pink in the evening light and luminous silk banners fluttered among the walnut trees, and past Rakaposhi, one of the world's loveliest mountains; with numerous lesser mountains marching away on either side she looked like an old music-hall star appearing with her chorus line. We stopped for apricots near a tiny ruby mine, worked only on demand, and a medieval fort where Silk Road travellers had paid their tolls; those failing to do so were fired on with garnet bullets from the embrasures of the wine-making room.

The journey along the massively pot-holed KKH was made at Formula One speeds, our vehicle swerving wildly to avoid the rock falls. Pakistan cannot afford the technology needed to stabilize perpendicular cliff faces, but it is richly endowed with sign writers and everywhere there were exquisitely painted notices warning of perils ahead. We crossed the shivery Khunjerab Pass and, 12,000 feet up, headed on across the frozen, dusty dome of China, the Kunlun mountains passing on one side, the Pamir on the other, the Karakoram swelling majestically before us – landscapes so vast that the human eye seemed unequal to the task of accommodating them; the huge messages sent to my brain kept getting sent back, sceptically, for clarification.

The road had a stony, corrugated surface which the drivers took very fast, slowing to ford streams but not for the long detours across eccentrically cratered yak pastures. Descending towards the Takla Makan Desert we entered a rubble-filled desolation rocked by earthquakes and blasters' dynamite. Here the road was still being built but in a very haphazard way, with several rival schemes apparently being tried out at once. Competing bulldozers kept wrecking the sections others had just cleared; gangs of obstructionist navvies ('All convicts,' muttered the driver) dumped rocks in places laboriously made rock-free by opposition gangs. Instead of imposing order on the landscape they simply added to its primeval confusion, filling the air with dust, danger and simmering resentment.

We tucked in behind the bulldozers pushing boulders and over-turned lorries in the same north-westerly direction that we were headed, and avoided lorries whose drivers teasingly attempted to push us into the riverbed below. Our own driver, wise to their game and expertly utilizing his four-wheel drive, always managed to scramble clear, crashing away over the jagged basalt with the vehicle's underside pealing like a bell.

The final stretch, on a wildly undulating switchback through the Takla Makan, was completed at 80 m.p.h. At Kashgar, aching and dust-covered, we ate melons; they could be bought for a penny and were available in such numbers that they perfumed the air.

Then, after several days in Kashgar, we turned round and did the whole thing again in reverse.

A week after arriving home in London I awoke one morning to find I had no feeling in my feet. The sensation was curious but not alarming; tight shoes, I thought, or the consequence of sleeping in an awkward position. Next day the numbness had risen to the knees, the day after that to the waist. I felt alarm but not panic. Perhaps it was a virus, an infection picked up out East, even a psychosomatic phenomenon, and I steadfastly resisted the idea that something might be seriously wrong. If you are creative enough you can raise that kind of resistance to the level of an art form.

A shaken incredulity set in when the numbness rose to the chest and spread to my hands, which began tingling as though tour-niquets had been tied around the wrists. The panic came later that day when it suddenly dawned on me that I was showing the early symptoms of multiple sclerosis.

My doctor displayed a level of professional detachment indicating there weren't too many laughs to come. Finally, he said, 'Yes, well I'm afraid it's pretty big.'

'How big? What have I got?'

'I don't know.'

'Is it MS?'

'I'm not sure. You're a bit old for that. It's fairly rare to get it after forty.'

'What else could it be?'

'Any number of things. I think you'd better see a specialist. With a bit of luck we might even get you to John Morgan-Hughes.'

He picked up the phone and called the National Hospital for Nervous Diseases in Queen Square, London. The admissions registrar listened then asked a question which was relayed to me.

Could I still get an erection?

'He's an Australian,' my doctor murmured.

I assumed this made it more of a routine social enquiry and tried to answer in the same spirit. The registrar said I should check in at nine o'clock the next morning. John Morgan-Hughes could see me and a bed would be ready.

My doctor, as I left him, said the National was probably the best hospital in the business, the flagship of world neurology. What I found was an echoing, ramshackle, turn-of-the-century building set in a small square beset by parking problems. Inside I noted the usual institutional smells of floor wax and frying, and the lift they directed me to was out of order. I sought directions from a builder who stood scowling up at an unplastered ceiling veined by exposed Victorian plumbing. 'Dunno, my son,' he said abstractedly. Wandering the corridors I passed an out-patients department filled with people in wheelchairs, twitching, shaking, racked by the palsy.

In the ward a young neurologist pondered me from a distance before approaching and asking me to take off my clothes. To neurologists initial impressions are important: aside from signs of obvious physical disability are there more subtle signals? Is the patient, for example, irritable, suspicious, hostile, depressed or inattentive? I was all of those things, and I was scared too. He stood beside my bed asking questions, thoughtfully brushing my limbs with cottonwool and lightly scratching them with needles. Holding a humming tuning fork to my feet – 'Can you feel that?' – he told me neurology was tougher than First Division football. 'I may give it up and go into blood,' he said. He was making notes. 'Haematology. You know? It's not nearly as élitist or competitive. Haematologists can spend time with their wives. Haematologists remember their children's birthdays.'

'What's wrong with me?' I asked.

'When we've cracked it we'll be straight round with the news,' he promised.

A young American examined me too. He came from Dallas, Texas, and said that for neurologists this place was Mecca. Running a well-sharpened pencil over the quadrants of my abdomen to test the reflexes he added, 'The faithful have come from a dozen countries. Maybe more. The next guy rostered to check you out is a Turk.'

'Have I got multiple sclerosis?' I asked.

He said, 'Hey, listen, man, where did you pick up language like that?' and drew his pencil point, briskly, across the soles of my feet.

The Turk was affable but rough with his needles. He made me stand on one leg and touch my nose with specified fingers then sat on the bed and wrote up his notes in Turkish.

'Will I live through the night?' I asked.

He said yes, if Allah willed it, no problem. A beautiful Chinese lady neurologist from Hong Kong noted the book I was reading and paused to talk perceptively about the work of its author, Bruce Chatwin. Then a Danish neurologist asked me to flex my hands and said, 'I think you can still hold a glass! After dinner you should visit the pub across the square. Two pints of best bitter. That is my prescription for you!' A grave young British registrar examined me kindly, kept his counsel and ordered certain tests. Then the consultant arrived, bustling in at the head of a squad of anxious-looking junior neurologists. John Morgan-Hughes, robust, well dressed, shrewd-eyed and exuding confidence, said good evening then whacked my knees with a little hammer.

'I've been talking to your GP,' he said. 'He tells me you've just been to western China in a jeep.'

'That's right.'

'What were the roads like?'

'Terrible.'

'How terrible?'

I gave him a brief summary of the road conditions and he nodded.

'Could this be relevant?' I asked.

'Quite possibly. But we're going to have to exclude a few other possibilities first.' He smiled, patted my hand and went to hammer the knees of the patient in the next bed.

That evening everyone in my ward got up and went to the pub. We bought each other drinks and talked of symptoms and treatments. A tanned, fit-looking young stockbroker spoke calmly of a brain tumour that would be removed in two days' time. Two men with MS talked animatedly about a new wheelchair so robust you could pile three people aboard and make high-speed runs down hills. A black youth said what he hated most about the National was the needles. 'I get nightmares about them. You had the myelogram yet? In the spine? They use *nails* on you, man.' At closing time we all reeled back to the ward where a pair of good-natured Filipino night nurses gave us cocoa and put us to bed.

Tests started next morning. They lasted, on and off, for ten days, the needles varying in size from electrodes stuck in my hands to a skewer-like bodkin used for the myelogram. As the radiologist pushed it between my third and fourth lumbar vertebrae I told him, through gritted teeth, that I knew what it felt like to be stabbed in the back. 'Oh really?' he said. He extracted a syringeful of gin-clear cerebrospinal fluid, replaced it with some radiopaque contrast stuff then, arguing with his assistant about the times of trains to Yorkshire, monitored its trickling intraspinal progress on the X-ray.

The myelogram makes you feel lousy for a week. I spent much of that period incarcerated in various scanners. Claustrophobic and womblike, they clicked and hummed and moved as they probed deep inside my neck; one, a £2 million monster using nuclear magnetic imaging techniques, was so precise it could home in on a swallowed penny and, if the doctor needed it, give him a magnified impression of the pendant dangling from the Queen's right ear.

The results, throughout, were being read and evaluated by some of the best minds in the field. They worked painstakingly, striking off the things I clearly hadn't got – multiple sclerosis among them – while growing increasingly interested in a rare congenital defect located at the top of the spine. They called it an Arnold-Chiari malformation and reckoned there might indeed be a connection with the road to Kashgar. Then that avenue of enquiry was abandoned. One of the scans had revealed a small spinal tumour and, all at once, I faced the bleak prospect of brain surgery. For several days I said my prayers, worried about insurance policies and, during visiting hours, saw my own turbulent feelings reflected in the eyes of my family. Also, for the first time in years, I dreamt of the Cherrapunji picture. Further deep scans, however, indicated that we were boxing with shadows. One sunny morning the grave young registrar, grinning from ear to ear, told me the tumour had magically melted away.

'What do you mean?' I asked.

'It was an optical illusion. A shadow on the scan!'

John Morgan-Hughes, attended by his white-coated courtiers, paid a final visit to hand down judgement. He said a severe whiplash injury in the Chinese jeep had exacerbated this Arnold-Chiari condition; a depending tonsil of brain in the lower cerebellum was now touching the top of the spine and causing the numbness and tingling. These might or might not go away of their own accord. There was no known medical treatment. I was handed a huge, unsightly orthopaedic collar and told to wear it when travelling in any form of transport. Meanwhile, I must avoid jeeps and bumpy roads; any further whiplash would put me in a wheelchair for life; a heavy fall could do the same. Finally, he had asked his colleague, David Grant, a consultant neurosurgeon, to look at my case. Surgery might be a solution, but only he could say.

Mr Grant appeared one evening after a long day in the theatre, went to the nurses' cubicle and sat motionless for an hour – I could see his silhouette through the frosted glass – reading my file with complete attention. Finally he came out, a trim-looking man with a disconcertingly level gaze, and said he wasn't going to recommend an operation. He could promise only a fifty-per-cent chance of success and no guarantee of any permanent improvement.

I thanked him and said goodbye to everyone in my National Health ward. Reflecting that I had received the finest neurological care available for less than a pound – the price of a few chocolate bars from an automatic dispensing machine near Out-Patients – I walked briskly to the Russell Square Underground station and caught the Tube home.

Depression set in a few days later. It began with shirt buttons and shoelaces, and the long, infuriating minutes needed to do them up; these trivial actions now required real effort and concentration, sometimes even assistance from my wife. The problem spread to the world outside and, though I took practical steps to minimize the humiliation (after a news vendor rolled his eyes at my arthritic fumbling for coins I learned to have them ready in advance), it made me feel clumsy and foolish. Some sort of sea change was taking place. I grew listless. Work became difficult. The numbness in the hands – flexing them gave a few seconds' relief – seemed to seep into my mind as well. Not a lot was going on in there. Once it had been a comfortable dwelling, so to speak, not so big perhaps but furnished with valued, familiar things. Now it was a cave, cold, dark, barely habitable; so, to all intents and purposes, I moved out. My attention span shrank. I drank a lot. One night I saw my doctor at a party. He walked over and said, 'That's your third whisky.'

'You bet,' I said.

'It's no cure, Alex. It may help in the short term but it can damage the nervous system. You're putting sand in your engine.'

'Okay,' I said, setting down the whisky and picking up an orange juice. After he turned away I added several fluid ounces of vodka to the orange and continued circulating, my engine sparking on all cylinders. Doctors! They had become the bane of my life.

Reality returned next day when a gale blew down the first crop of autumn leaves. At the National they had issued a stern warning about these. Leaves made slippery by rain were a major cause of falls, more hazardous even than snow and ice because they caught walkers off their guard. Now even a stroll on the common made me anxious. Employing an old man's shuffling gait I proceeded cautiously through a world booby-trapped and strung with trip-wires.

I wore my orthopaedic collar in the car, on buses and trains. It was a foam-plastic breastplate that extended from the lower lip to the clavicle and it made me look like a bulging pantomime frog.

Schoolchildren giggled, and staring adults glanced away, embarrassed, when I caught their eyes. On the day an elderly woman rose and offered me her seat I went home and threw it into the back of a cupboard. The damage it was doing to my self-esteem could be no worse than any physical harm that might be inflicted by its absence.

Several months after my discharge the National Hospital summoned me back for a routine final check-up. It was a dark March afternoon and the usual crowd of ill, distressed people and their sad-faced relatives had assembled in the out-patients waiting room. A woman appeared, pointed to a vacant seat beside me and asked if it was free. I noted smooth, cinnamon-coloured skin and striking features – a wide forehead, sculpted cheekbones, luminous green eyes. Her clothes were striking too. She wore a broad-brimmed Spanish riding hat, shiny knee-length boots and a very short skirt. It was gold and silky. Her legs were excellent.

Sighing, she made an unexpected gesture that encompassed the room. 'God!' she said.

'Not a fun place,' I agreed.

'Who are you waiting for?'

'No one,' I said. 'I'm a patient.'

'Oh?' She turned those fine eyes on me, her gaze slightly myopic. 'You don't look very sick.'

The voice was authentic upper-crust English but she wasn't. Englishwomen are never as direct as that. She listened closely as I recited a brief summary of my condition then opened a roomy leather handbag and produced a pack of small Swiss cheroots.

'Can we smoke?'

Half the people in the room were smoking and she offered one to me; lit by an old liquid-fuel Zippo, it tasted faintly of liquorice.

She said, 'My husband is here, you know. A patient like you. He's seeing a specialist and is supposed to meet me at three. Maybe he'll remember, maybe he won't.'

'What's wrong with him?'

'Migraines. He gets them every three years, almost to the day. It's something called the "cluster effect" and when he's going through a phase he becomes quite manic. A real *dingbat*. At the moment he's probably in there singing comic songs to the doctor.'

I laughed and I felt my spirits, which had recently acquired the density of marble, make a small but perceptible movement.

She told me her husband's name was Aloysius and that, in some quarters, he might be described as rich and useless. He dabbled in publishing but described himself first and foremost as a glider pilot. There was a small airstrip adjoining their house in Bombay and he spent much of his time quartering the sky above it. Once he had even held an all-India soaring record, won in foolhardy circumstances over the Western Ghats; the glider, buoyed aloft by storm-force monsoon winds, had gone so high they lost sight of it. At the time she was convinced he had been blown all the way to Burma.

She gave me her quick, short-sighted smile then, peering at my coat, leant forward and plucked a hair from the collar. 'Excuse me,' she murmured.

'I didn't know you got winds with the monsoon,' I said.

'Of course! They bring in the rains. You have never seen the monsoon's burst? In Bombay it is quite something. For months the city has been absolutely sweltering and then, usually on the afternoon of 10 June, huge clouds begin to build up over the sea. Soon your wind comes, so strong that it will sink any little boats that haven't taken shelter. The wind drops, it gets very dark, there is terrific thunder and lightning and then – the deluge! Suddenly the air is very cool and perfumed with flowers. It is a time of rejoicing. And renewal.' She frowned at me. 'It is also when I feel perhaps most truly Indian.'

Listening, I found myself recalling our island rains. I hadn't thought about them for years but now there they were, falling again tumultuously inside my head. The scene had a lens-like clarity that enabled me to see the cracks between the floorboards of our veranda, cobwebs in the ceiling, my father trudging up the path under his old broken-spoked umbrella. The light was soft and diffused. Fleetingly I felt the curious state of grace the rains always seemed to bestow, the way they washed away my sins – not literally, because I usually liked to stay indoors – and made apocalyptic lapses, for example mentally undressing the plump Golightly sisters in church (their half-mad father captained the schooner *Parsifal*) no big deal. Now I felt a small measure of that same comfort and peace and told her I had also been in rain like that as a kid. The old Cherrapunji picture came to mind.

Had she been to Cherrapunji? Did she know it? She gave me another of her intense, slightly unsighted looks. That place up in Meghalaya? No one went there now. It was off limits, an area of severe civil unrest, but her father had visited during his army days and seemed strangely affected by it. He called it unearthly. Naked hunters with bows and arrows lived silently in the forest and, walking in the mist one day, he stumbled upon an old British graveyard filled with people who had died by their own hand. It was written on the tombstones. She gave a little shiver and touched my arm. 'Did you have parties on your island when it rained?'

'Parties?' That hadn't been our style. 'No.' I was thinking of Wapshot.

'We did. We still do. In Goa. It's a kind of family reunion. A few days after the burst everyone flies off for a big monsoon thrash in lovely wet Goa. For me it's a high point of the year.'

I saw a small, neat-featured Indian with thinning hair ducking through the crowd, looking around anxiously. Something flashed in the buttonhole of his double-breasted suit which, as he spotted us and hurried over, turned out to be a tiny aeroplane made from mirror glass.

'Hullo!' he cried.

'Have they fixed you up?' she asked.

'They have given me suppositories,' he said, bending to be kissed.

'Which you won't use.'

'Exactly. I told the doctor they reminded me of small-bore ammunition and he said, "Oh! would you prefer a calibre more suited to the elephant gun?" I said tut tut, and this from a scion of the caring professions, shame on you. Give me a cigar, darling, I am gasping.' He threw himself down beside her.

She opened her handbag and said, 'This kind man has been keeping me company.'

'No hardship, I'll bet.' He gave me a warm, shy smile then held out a hand. 'Baptista,' he said. 'Isn't she beautiful?'

Mrs Baptista told him I was a patient here also.

He thumbed the Zippo ineffectually. 'This thing is hopeless. You'd be better off rubbing sticks together.'

'He has a gammy neck,' she said, lighting the cheroot for him.

'Yes? Tell you what, let's all jump in a taxi and go round to the Zanzibar. I could do with a daiquiri or three.'

'He hasn't seen his man yet,' she said.

'The neck is a very tricky area,' announced Mr Baptista. He lifted his head and gazed at the wheelchair cases parked around us. 'What's wrong with all these people? Are they neck cases too?'

'I don't know,' I said.

'They must give up parachuting. That is my advice.' He raised his voice and addressed everyone in the room. 'Look here, all this sky-diving nonsense will have to stop, you know.'

A profound silence followed. Mrs Baptista murmured, 'Aloysius, you're being embarrassing. We must leave at once.'

'First I will finish my cigar,' said Mr Baptista defiantly. Around us conversations were resumed in low voices. Two nurses watched us like hawks. He said to me, 'What were you two talking about?'

'The monsoon,' I said.

'Ah! It's a season you enjoy?'

I told him I had never experienced the monsoon. He said I should arrange to do so as soon as possible. What was my profession? A writer? Perfect! And what a coincidence! He was a writer too. Ignoring his wife's startled, peering look he said the monsoon was a phenomenon so nourishing and exalting that it had inspired artists for centuries. He spoke of monsoon ragas, classic compositions for voice or stringed instruments, and of exquisite miniature paintings depicting maharajas and their doe-eyed concubines joyously disporting themselves as the rains fell. (There were some good monsoon miniatures, stolen by the British, at the Victoria and Albert Museum.) Certain maharajas had even built ornately beautiful monsoon pavilions from which to observe the burst and swell of the rains.

And the poetry! Had I read Kalidasa? He was one of the Nine Gems of the Court of King Vikramaditya, *circa* 100 BC. He wrote *Meghaduta*, a book about clouds, and an epic work called *The Seasons* which, though more than 2,000 years old, remained an enduring favourite in India.

He declaimed:

The sky on every side is shrouded by rain-clouds
Which wear the beauty of deep blue lotus petals,
And here look like heaps of made-up eye-salve, and there
Possess the charm of breasts of women with child.

Mrs Baptista said, 'It's a terrifically sexy poem. And if you come you will see why. That meeting of the earth and the clouds is a kind of love-making.'

'The monsoon is a terrifically sexy time,' said her husband. 'Traditionally it is supposed to cast away all inhibitions. Affairs are embarked on and lovers taken. Many illegitimate babies are born the following March. Well, among the peasantry, at least, so I'm told. You don't see so much of it in middle-class Bombay.'

'You see some,' said his wife. 'And the rains rejuvenate. That's when Aloysius goes off for his massages.'

'South to Kerala State,' he said, 'for my annual monsoon cure. And Kerala, of course, is where it starts.'

'What starts?'

'The monsoon. On the first of June. Then it journeys all the way up India to the Himalayas. There's a rum little village called Cherrapunji. It's in the *Guinness Book of Records* as the world's wettest place. That's where the monsoon reaches its climax, so to speak.'

'We were just speaking of Cherrapunji,' said Mrs Baptista.

A nurse called my name. The doctor would see me now. We stood. Mrs Baptista buttoned her coat and straightened her hat.

I said, 'Is it possible to get to Cherrapunji?'

'No,' he said. 'There's trouble there. The locals are in conflict with the Indian government and Delhi has made it a restricted area. To a foreigner Cherrapunji would be off limits.'

Mr Baptista gave me his card. 'Call us when you are next in Bombay,' he said. His wife added, 'And if you are ever around in June you must come to our Goa party.'

'Look, you said the monsoon travelled up India from the south to the north. Is that right?'

'It comes, magisterially, on a wind from the south,' said Mr Baptista, 'which certainly carries it in a northerly direction. It is even supposed to get to the same places on the same days of the year. But sometimes, bewitched by its spectacular progress, we are inclined to forget that meteorologically the monsoon is a very complex affair. There are two arms, the easterly and westerly, which meet at —'

'How long does it take?'

He shrugged. 'It gets to Delhi on 29 June. So say a month to Delhi and then —'

'Mr Frater!' cried the nurse.

'Could you follow it?'

They both stared at me. 'Yes,' he said. 'I suppose so. If you met it at Trivandrum, where it enters India, and then ran with it, so to speak. Yes, you could do that.'

Mrs Baptista laughed. 'A race with the rains!' she said. 'From Cape Comorin to the Himalayas! That would be a lark!'

The neurologist waiting to examine me was the young Texan from Dallas. 'You're looking pretty chirpy,' he observed.

'I feel terrific,' I said.

'How's the neck?'

'I can live with it.'

That was the first time I had admitted such a thing, and I knew it to be true. He nodded, looking me over carefully. 'What have you been doing?' he asked.

'Not a lot. Trying to come to terms with it. Feeling sorry for myself.'

'And now?'

'Now,' I said, 'I'm going to India.'

Chapter Two

It was odd to be taking an interest in the weather again. Some
dormant cell seemed to have woken and fired up a whole constella-
tion of others which began rising above the mind's horizon with a
soft, nacreous glow. My reading, though, soon revealed certain
disturbing behavioural changes in the monsoon. During the past
two or three years it had grown capricious and spiteful. Some areas
of India were paid only fleeting visits, some no visits at all. This
wilfulness puzzled the weather men and frightened the politicians;
a failed monsoon could mean riots and lost elections. But most of
all it frightened the ordinary rural people whose crops and lives
depended on it. They, long accustomed to its ancient rhythms and
sturdy reliability, found its absence as shocking as, perhaps, a death
or madness in the family.

There were early indications, said the London papers, that it
would be temperamental this year too.

Further research revealed the kind of panic measures taken when
it didn't show up. The previous year in Bangalore, for example, the
city fathers paid a yogi to pray for rain. Seated on a tigerskin rug
beside the Bangalore Water Supply and Sewerage Board guest-
house the yogi chanted for 2 hours and 4 minutes while his
supporters chewed leaves and swallowed burning camphor. Afterwards he was able to inform senior Water Board officials – pros-
trated before him with offerings of coconuts – that the rain god
Varuna, though invisible to the naked eye, now approached them
'like waves of clouds'. The rain fell, all right, and torrentially, but
only over neighbouring Cochin. When the Bangalore city fathers
complained the yogi reminded them sharply who they were dealing
with: not only was he renowned for his ability to divert cyclones

but he had also been retained by the government as official blesser of their space programme. After India's first rocket crashed they choppered him to the launch pad of the second which, thanks to his vigorous intercessions, soared aloft without any trouble at all. So saying, he picked up his fee and drove away, leaving the city fathers many rupees poorer. It was a sad story, but a commonplace one.

I fretted over the monsoon in the airy Aldwych office of an attaché at the Indian High Commission. I told him further research also revealed that drinking the milk of a white cow might bless my venture. What did he think of that? He said, 'It is probably the most realistic course of action I can recommend.'

'Will they let me into Cherrapunji?'

He laughed. 'Your request is with our people in Delhi now. As you know, I'm afraid the auguries are not good.'

I decided to go to India late one night, after mulling over the known facts and tossing a coin.

So, thirteen days before the official onset of the rains over Bombay, my 747 descended through a drained, empty sky which had taken on the colour and shine of oiled teak. It was only 7 a.m. yet an engorged sun had already seen off any lingering nocturnal clouds, probably in puffs of steam, and made the air glassy. The Bombay earth seemed to smoulder. Countless small suburban fires – hinting mysteriously at spontaneous combustion deep underground – made dusty brown smoke which darkened and thickened the smog from the city. Into this soiled atmosphere we drifted, wheels down, flaps extended, licked and bumped by sinewy tongues of heat turbulence. On the ground the stinging light caused us to disembark squinting like lizards.

I felt deeply pessimistic. During the flight I discussed the monsoon's progress with several Indian passengers, each of whom offered a revised arrival date. These were based on privileged information from well-placed sources, and each was different. A steward proferred his own date, together with a day-old copy of the *Indian Express* which enlarged distressingly on the stories I had been reading at home.

Seven states still suffered from acute water shortages (some places hadn't had rain in four years) while countless thousand

Indians continued urgently and 'immediately praying for early onset of monsoon'. In Kerala, where I would travel the following day, tankers were supplying potable water to 12,500 assembly points as engineers installed 11,216 street hydrants. More than 500 tube wells and 400 bore wells had been sunk throughout the state, but still the poor went thirsty.

In parts of Andhra Pradesh water was being distributed only once on alternate days; reservoirs sprayed with aceto-emulsion to reduce evaporation dwindled anyway as they were drunk dry. In Madras each of the 180,000 families living in the Slum Clearance Board tenements was given a free plastic bucket but little to put in it; local train services suffered disruption when 'water-starved residents carrying empty pots' squatted on the tracks. In Rajkot, though, trains were commandeered to haul water to the city where enterprising local officials, using tractors and tank-mounted rickshaws, pioneered a home delivery service. In Palghat a gastroenteritis epidemic caused by water scarcity had claimed twenty-two lives. Wells were chlorinated and soft drink sales banned. The Excise Commissioner closed the toddy shops.

The taxi taking me to town was an ancient rust edifice held together with membranous layers of paint. They had been applied thickly by brush – you could see the marks – and I imagined a deep pot-hole suddenly rendering it down into a pile of flaky red dust. The road, its tar surface sludgy in the sun, took us past shanty towns where everyone seemed weighed down by invisible burdens. Even the beggars who worked the traffic lights, normally as agile and intrusive as monkeys, merely sauntered towards us.

The fan in my hotel room turned with the stolid thump and creak of a butter churn. I tried to phone the Bombay Met Office but kept getting a monosyllabic Hindi-speaking woman who, after the third or fourth time, adopted the strident tones of someone addressing a mass rally. I turned to the hotel switchboard for help and learned the Met Office had a new number. Nobody answered that at all; I was calling an empty building and wondered whether, with nothing much to forecast, they had all gone home. The girl at the hotel switchboard said yes, of course they'd all gone home. Today was a government holiday.

She had a nice intimate contralto voice and, more to keep her talking than anything else, I told her I was trying to find the whereabouts of the monsoon.

She said, 'Sir, it is in the South Andaman Sea.'

Above the bed hung a framed print of an alpine peak. Age had darkened the snow and warped the ice. 'What did you say?'

'They announced it on the radio this morning. Also in the paper. It is still very small and running late but definitely advancing. Do not fear, sir, monsoon is on its way!'

I told her she had the most beautiful voice in India, heard her startled laugh, then rushed to the door.

For the first time in months I handed small change to a news vendor without preparing for the transaction in advance. Standing beneath a brilliantly garlanded flame-of-the-forest tree I opened up the *Indian Express* and there it was, headed Weather Special Bulletin. 'South-West monsoon is advancing over South Andaman Sea and adjoining South-East bay as feeble current. The normal date of onset of the monsoon over the Andaman Sea is May 20. This year the onset over Andaman is lagging behind by a week.'

I returned to my room and dialled the Baptistas. A friendly sounding man said they were spending a few days in Delhi but gave me a number where they could be reached. All I got was silence faintly penetrated by a mysterious susurration, like air flowing over swallows' wings, the sound of countless distant, whispering voices. In reality they were all probably yelling for the operator, and eventually an operator told me the Delhi number was out of order. When I put the phone down it rang again at once. The switchboard girl said, 'Sir! Have you seen the *Afternoon Dispatch and Courier*? It has monsoon article in "Round and About" by Busybee! I am sending boy up with it now!'

She was gone before I could thank her. Like a gift the cutting came inscribed in spacious longhand with the words 'Every good wish from Miss Geeta Contractor, Tlphnst'. I sat down and began reading Busybee's breezy 500-word piece which, after welcoming the signs of activity in the South Andaman Sea, reflected, 'It is comforting knowledge. Comforting because it means that soon the torrid heat will dissolve in the cool waters of the rains, as the monsoon continues to advance and finally reaches our octroi nakas.'

What did that mean? I called Miss Contractor to find out but a brisk, matronly voice advised that she had just completed the early shift and left. Was there a message? I said no and returned to Busybee's text.

Once the monsoon advances into India it moves at great speed, causing large depressions, air pockets, raising storms, overrunning the last of the mango crop.

I have always been fascinated about the early monsoon bulletins. One morning it is at Kovalam beach, touching Trivandrum, by midnight it has moved many miles north-wards over the green coastal plains of Kerala. The next day it is in Cochin, blowing through the Chinese fishing nets, first the wind bending the palm trees to its will, then the rains. I have in the past chalked out their military advances along the coast. But the monsoon does not tarry. It gathers the clouds along the way and then, one early morning, they burst over Bombay.

Early next morning I would fly south to Trivandrum and, at Kovalam beach, find a room from which to witness its arrival. I slept fitfully, haunted by dreams of hot skies and a bright, flat sea. From across the horizon came a muted gong beat followed by Miss Contractor's voice speaking in the tones of an airport announcer. 'We regret to announce that your monsoon has been cancelled due to operational difficulties. You are entitled to voucher for complimentary refreshment while we await another. I am sending boy up with it now!'

Heading down the Western Ghats, a 600-mile-long mountain range rearing out of the Arabian Sea, the Indian Airlines A-300 Airbus passed through so many turbulent areas that the seat-belt sign, flashing on and off, seemed to be sending coded messages. Optimistically I took this to mean bad weather coming from the sea but a stewardess said it was due to heat coming off the land. 'I can read the bumps,' she assured me. It was cool in the cabin but glimpses of sun and shimmering red earth seemed to induce intense thirst in everyone with access to a window; fingers were clicked and flight attendants sent scurrying for cups of tepid water. Somewhere around here, I reflected, Aloysius Baptista had made his record-breaking glider ascent. The bony, reserved young man in the neighbouring seat suddenly offered me a tiny sachet of cologne-scented paper. 'For the face,' he said earnestly. 'It will make you feel very nice.'

He told me he worked in Dubai maintaining air-conditioners and was heading home for two months' leave. 'I am coming for the Id moon – the end of Ramadan fasting – and the monsoon. After two years in the desert I dream of it.'

'I hear it's on its way,' I said.

He smiled, exposing red gums and small, bitten-down teeth. 'Oh, yes. My mother has seen the pied-crested cuckoos. These are flying in from Africa just ahead of the rains. When they come the monsoon comes.' He hesitated. 'Also, I am getting married. There will be girls at the airport. In this plane are many Kerala men like me, working in the Middle East, and the girls will be there with their daddies to see what we bring.' He cleared his throat and counted on his fingers. 'I am bringing one Hitachi television, full colour, one Hitachi video recorder, one Aiwa stereo system with graphic equalizer and one Bendix spin drier.'

I stared at him. 'Who is the girl you're going to marry?'

'I am not knowing yet,' he said. 'But she will be waiting at the airport.'

As we approached Trivandrum a flight attendant announced an outside air temperature of 39 degrees Celsius. The aircraft coasted in over wide, muddy lagoons and an unending prospect of coconut palms. My neighbour swallowed and licked his lips. He said his heart was going boom boom. Pandemonium reigned in the small terminal. A viewing balcony above the customs hall was packed with wide-eyed girls and their sombre, watchful parents. This seemed as much of a seasonal phenomenon as the arrival of the pied-crested cuckoos, and jostling spectators peered through windows and clung to vantage points. The young men swaggered about. They hauled huge bales of merchandise off the baggage carousel and, constantly glancing upwards, summoned porters with rupee notes peeled off thick wads which they flourished aloft.

I lost my friend in the mêlée. I do not know how he fared but, when I left the terminal in a taxi, all the girls remained on the viewing balcony, staring down at their prospective husbands like bidders at a bloodstock sale.

I asked the driver to take me to Kovalam beach.

Always, in the latter part of May, attention starts to focus on Trivandrum, a sprawling, rackety, good-natured tropical city on the Malabar Coast. Its people are dark-skinned and notoriously pro-Communist. They are also loquacious, independent and always ready to engage strangers in coffee-house debate. They have the highest literacy rate in the country and, each day, read no fewer than forty local newspapers concerned with matters such as radical politics, the state of the world spice markets and – cheered on by their readers – the incompetence of central government in Delhi. This, together with ferocious chilli-spiked curries, is what Trivandrum is known for. But come the dog days of late May another aspect begins to impinge on the national consciousness.

An annual visitation by the Indian media has made Trivandrum's Meteorological Centre the most famous provincial weather office on the subcontinent. Built in 1840 by a maharaja interested in Western scientific disciplines, its hilltop location gives it extensive views over the Arabian Sea and lifts it a little closer to the sky. This lofty elevation enabled employees of the old Indian Meteorological Department, working in the days before radar or enhanced satellite imagery, to stand on their wide verandas and observe the monsoon's tumultuous approach through telescopes. From here, the most southerly of the meteorological centres, its arrival over India was formally announced or 'declared'.

There have been many changes in the country since, but that at least remains constant. The advent of the burst is still an event of imperial dimensions and Trivandrum continues to signal the news.

My trishaw's tiny two-stroke engine clattered and smoked on the gradients. The winding red earth road led past a reservoir with a glaring little god set in its concrete retaining wall, and the old Royal Observatory where between 1852 and 1869 John Allan Brown FRS, an enlightened Government Astronomer, helped establish Trivandrum as the foremost scientific centre in North-West Asia. Each year, usually between the fifth and seventh day of June, he would have noted the appearance of the Mirg, or monsoon star, and doubtless passed news of its ascendancy to his colleagues at the Meteorological Centre next door.

That was as airy and elegant as a small Spice Coast palace, its steeply pitched roof of weathered marigold tiles lustrous in the afternoon sun. A long flight of steps, also roofed, led to the veranda where several young men loitered. I explained my business and showed them my credentials.

'You are wishing to see Monsoon Officer?' asked one.

'Yes.'

He led me past a dim, cavernous room where rows of frowning clerks sat like examination candidates, the scratch of pens and rustle of paper audible as I passed, and halted beside a door marked 'Julius Joseph'. Then he drew himself up, cleared his throat and knocked smartly. We entered a shadowy, chart-hung little office cluttered with green filing cabinets.

Julius Joseph was on the telephone. He pondered my card, then nodded and waved me to a chair. He was small and intense with a clipped moustache and the flamboyant good looks of a 1930s movie star. Placing his hand over the mouthpiece he said, 'Won't keep you a jiffy.'

The young man, perhaps wishing to demonstrate how privileged I was to be here, murmured, '*Times of India* call ten minutes ago. Before that Cabinet Office in Delhi. PM *himself* wants to know. Everyone is most . . . anxious.'

He slipped out. Through the shutters I saw perspectives below of shimmering coral-coloured roofs and dense tropical gardens. A harassed, perspiring woman in an emerald sari put her head through the door and said, 'Sir, BBC are holding from London.'

Mr Joseph nodded and talked on in his quiet, slightly pedantic voice. 'At 8 a.m. it was cutting through upper Sri Lanka. Yes, forty miles north of Kandy. At present the outer extremity is flowing a hundred miles south of Cape Comorin. Well, two days, perhaps, maybe three. I cannot say for certain. The last satellite picture shows a low pressure area over the Andamans which may start to pull it back into the Bay of Bengal. That is potentially a little worrying. Yes. We are watching it carefully.'

He said much the same thing to the BBC, then hung up and sighed. 'I cannot afford to make false prophecies,' he said. 'This is a very volatile field. I speak as a scientist but people always listen with their hearts and emotions.'

I explained my interest in the monsoon, and the journey I planned to make in its company all the way up to eccentric, cloud-bound little Cherrapunji. He looked at me with disbelief. 'Good gracious!' he said. Then he asked if I possessed an entry permit. I said not yet, but Delhi had my application. 'That could be a problem for you,' he warned. 'Don't bet your shirt on getting it.'

'Will this low over the Andamans give you problems?' I asked.

He smiled. 'The whole system is made of cobwebs – a big sneeze could give me problems.' He hesitated. 'Do you understand it?'

'I've done a bit of reading.'

'The basic physics of the monsoon – the word comes from the Arabic, *mausim*, meaning "season" – have been known since the seventeenth century when Edmond Halley, Secretary of the Royal Society and the man who found the comet, produced a remarkable monsoon flow chart. Though the monsoon winds constitute one of the greatest weather systems on earth, and an enormous amount of research has been carried out since, many questions remain shrouded in mystery. It's like the human brain. We know it but we don't know it.'

The phone rang again. He picked it up and said, 'Yes, okay, I'll get them on the way home. No, it will be after eight. You know how it is now.'

He replaced the phone, picked up a pencil and, over the Rajasthan Desert on that morning's satellite picture of India, inscribed the words 'persimmons' and 'soda water'.

'The monsoon is a huge natural engine,' he said, 'driven by the temperature differences over sea and land; in summer the air over the land grows very hot. It expands and rises, so cool sea air must flow in to equalize the pressure. This differential heating sets up a massive aerial current from the Indian Ocean, south of the Equator. It heads for India, and the evaporating water it picks up from the oceans falls as rain when it reaches the land. This vapour condensation, though, releases latent energy which warms the air, pushing it upwards and allowing even more wet air to come in from the sea. But it also cools the land, always driving that heating and upward convection further into India. That is why the monsoon is a travelling phenomenon, always moving along that path you plan to follow. Are you with me?'

'I think so.'

'It is further complicated by the fact that it has two branches. The Arabian Sea one, which we get here, blows on to the Western Ghats and drops so much of its moisture that there is little left as it flows on over the rest of the country; only the airstream moving up the seaward side of the Ghats retains really heavy rain. The other branch comes in from the Bay of Bengal. It sets in at the same time – Cherrapunji gets its onset only a few days after we do – but is turned west by the Himalayas and falls over the Gangetic Plain. Calcutta's monsoon, in fact, arrives three days before Bombay's.'

'So each summer,' I said, 'India is embraced by these two great wet arms?'

Mr Joseph looked faintly pained. 'That,' he said, 'is the language of tabloid journalism. But, yes, in a sense you are right. The two currents eventually become one; indeed, when it approaches Delhi my colleagues there sometimes don't know from which arm their rains will come. We are talking about a very complex weather cycle here, with many factors coming into play. There is the warming of the Tibetan Plateau in the spring. There are trade winds from the Southern hemisphere. There is the onset of certain jet streams, including the crucial Somali jet which transits Kenya, Somalia and the Sahel, exits the African coast at 9 degrees north and heads for India, low-level, very fast. Another factor is that winds crossing the Equator are bent right by the Coriolis force, caused by the spinning of the earth, towards the inter-tropical convergence zone – the junction of the northern and southern trades. And, of course, there is the crucial business of the land staying warmer than the sea. That's really the key to the monsoon equation.'

There was a tap at his door. A bespectacled man in a checked shirt popped his head through. 'It's 4.45, sir. Time for launch.'

In a dry, stony garden another man stood holding an inflated latex rubber weather balloon with a metal canister and a foil square dangling beneath. Mr Joseph said, 'On Mondays, Wednesdays and Fridays we use imported balloons, on Tuesdays, Thursdays and Saturdays Indian ones; like the Indian weather, their quality is variable. All are filled with hydrogen. The canister contains a transmitter, an aneroid barometer, a thermister and hygrometer. This means our ground receiving station can record the air pressure, temperature, humidity and wind speed all the way up to 75,000 feet. That foil thing is for the wind-finding radar to track.' He added, 'Before the advent of balloons they used to do this with kites.'

He nodded and made a throw-away gesture with both hands. The balloon climbed slowly, rock-steady in the windless air, and I wondered whether this one would finally bring India the news it so feverishly awaited. Mr Joseph, as though reading my thoughts, said, 'What I want is evidence of a sustained westerly wind up there, with a 60-knot easterly jet stream blowing above it.'

'What happens to the balloon?' I asked.

'Eventually, at a height of between 25 and 30 kilometres, it bursts and falls into the sea. And bang goes another 500 rupees.' He stood with a hand shading his eyes. 'During the monsoon about forty weather stations throughout India releases four daily and, because of the expense, those flying over land carry a notice asking the finder to hand it in to the nearest police station. This is rarely done. The balloons sent up from Dum Dum airport in Calcutta carry pens, toys, cassettes and Met Office publicity stickers. That's supposed to induce people to hand them in but mostly, of course, they just keep the goodies and turn the canisters into cooking pots or water bottles. We've even found canisters in Assam carrying propaganda material from Taiwan intended for mainland China. There's quite an interesting little subculture growing up around weather balloons.'

Mr Joseph looked at his watch and excused himself. A man from All India Radio had come to do an interview for the national news. The Monsoon Officer spoke pragmatically: it might come in two days, it might come in a week; at the moment he hadn't enough evidence to be more precise.

'Is it possible,' asked the interviewer, slowly, 'that it may not come at all?'

As Mr Joseph pointed to his charts, emphasizing the Andaman Sea and the feeble nature of the current advancing across it, parrying the uncomfortable questions, stressing that few things in life are certain, I reflected that countless Indians would like to know what was really going on inside his head. He might be a middle-ranking official working quietly in the public domain but it was widely assumed – certainly by me – that he possessed a god-like inner eye somehow able to peer into the vaults of heaven itself. Tantalizingly, though, he remained non-committal to the end.

Later I chatted to one of his bright young assistants about the ground rules of monsoon forecasting. Rainfall before 10 May was not regarded as part of the monsoon. Five of Kerala's meteorological stations had to register 1 mm or more for two consecutive days before the monsoon could be declared; even then the declaration came only on the second day. Instability was an ever-present possibility; no one relaxed until the rains had reached 13 degrees north, or a third of the way up the Western Ghats. Sometimes advance warning of monsoon activity came from vessels on certain Indian Ocean shipping routes; ships also alerted them to the onset vortex which, some years, formed a few days in advance off the Kerala coast. That was a vital clue.

Finally, he counselled patience and urged me to stay out of the sun.

I thought this shockingly self-evident. Trivandrum roasted, the temperatures climbing to their annual apogee in an eruption of volcanic heat that felt as if giant magnifying glasses were focussing all the sun's rays directly on to the city. Soon, with a whoosh and a muffled whump, the whole place must spontaneously ignite.

Out at Kovalam beach the atmosphere was as close as the air in a locked room, the sea a motionless silver plain stippled with fragile pencil-thin fishing canoes. On the horizon ships slid by on rails, their smoke unravelling aft in low, lateral lines which sometimes closed and joined like hawsers on a suspension bridge. Large crows perched in the waterside coconut palms. Down on the beach a young couple bathed, the woman in a bright emerald sari, her husband in a woollen costume of a kind that had been fashionable during the Jazz Age. A small listless surf kept falling and turning soundlessly back on itself in a cloying way, like cream. The couple's black skins indicated that they were local, but the heat caused them visible distress and they soon abandoned the water for deep shade where, wearily, they anointed themselves with oil.

The monsoon hijacked every conversation. People kept seeing signs. One man told me he had observed partridge feather clouds, another sparrows bathing in the dust. Both were considered propitious. A hot wind blew fitfully. Someone said it was called the *loo*.

I hadn't known sun like this before. It penetrated the crown of the head and imploded in the brain so that you got dazzle inside as well as out. Even the smallest movement activated the sweat glands. They soaked clothes and flooded shoes; walking became a mushy business, like treading grapes. The temperature was 42 degrees Celsius but felt higher. One of the local papers warned that such heat caused severe stress and urged its readers to change their underwear – which should be made from the lightest natural fibres – several times a day.

The stress was taking its annual toll. On 29 May a scolding husband drove his 32-year-old wife to suicide at the village of Vilappilsala; according to the *Indian Express*, she 'hanged herself at the end of a sari from a tree-top'. On the same day, at Kottayam, rival political parties clashed violently during a local election, one claiming that gangs of unruly Marxist workers had 'affixed the electoral ink marks to female index fingers while distributing the hand-imprinted bindi'. The complaint had been made by a vociferous 'nine-woman squad' but stoutly denied by the Marxists. At the groundnut oil town of Amreli, a clash between cart-pullers and shopkeepers left two dead and nine injured. In Attingal a man named Nirmal Kumar was stabbed to death by his neighbours. Four died during Punjab riots and, in Bihar, a massacre claimed forty-one victims.

'All is normal,' a man remarked to me in a coffee house. 'But those who survive the days must then survive the nights. They are the worst. Sleep becomes so difficult we dream with our eyes open.'

Chapter Three

❀

31 MAY

I awoke during the night and pressed the light switch. Nothing happened. Sweat made my eyes sting. It seemed to be flowing directly into the sockets, flooding them like twin pools; the ceiling, if discerned, would doubtless be opaque, the view of a fish perceiving the sky.

I sat up and remembered an entry from *The Travels of Ibn Battuta AD 1325-1354*. 'The heat was intense,' it said, 'and my companions used to sit naked except that each had a cloth round his waist and another soaked with water on his shoulders; this would dry in a very short time and he had to keep constantly wetting it again.'

Working by torchlight I pulled a sheet from the bed, held it under a tap, wrapped it around me and sat on a chair, thinking of the monsoon, bidding it get a move on towards this dark and airless coast. In my mind's eye it had become a fabulous aerial machine lit by exploding beacons of lightning and driven by great rain-making engines, booming with thunder and storm-force winds. It was out there, lurking somewhere south of Cape Comorin and, musing on that, I suddenly remembered something.

Near the Cape – where the subcontinent dwindles to a pebbly south-facing beach before falling away into the sea – I once glimpsed a secluded residence the size of a minor palace.

The sighting had been made several years earlier from a 747, enabling me to ascertain that it appeared to be the last house in India, and to note that it was white, with a roof of orange tiles and a large tree-filled garden containing several large pools. We had been seven miles high but the clarity and calmness of the air – still carrying a fiery hint of early morning colours – revealed even reflections in the pools. A friendly Bengali stewardess brought breakfast and identified the Cape. 'Yes, that is the place where India ends,' she told me. 'There all our troubles come together and are finally drowned in the ocean.'

Looking down at the house I was seized with curiosity about its inhabitants. Who were they? What were they like? How did it feel to live at the confluence of three seas and two great trading coasts, the Malabar and Coromandel? And to observe, regularly, a famous local phenomenon: the full moon and setting sun entering and exiting simultaneously from the same patch of ocean? I determined one day to make my way there and drop in for tea.

If the monsoon was still running late I would go tomorrow. Soaking the sheet again I went to sleep sitting up and awoke just before dawn, feeling unexpectedly refreshed.

The sky had a strange ivory pallor and seemed to give off isolated gusts of smoke, as though the last of the old season's cloud was being burned off like stubble. I walked past a small, empty seaside palace owned by Trivandrum's elderly Maharaja, its lofty stone tower occupied by crows that kept up a sustained clattering noise, and found a crowded bus going to town. The driver, head buried in the engine, shouted that it would leave in five minutes. I boarded and sat squashed up against a bony, worried-looking man wearing wire spectacles. He asked me the time, sighed and said, 'Sod this for a game of soldiers.'

I laughed and got a quick smile in return.

'I am knowing your vernacular from several Church of England chaps who were out here sinking wells,' he said. He gave me a sideways glance. 'Monsoon is late, bus is late, I am late. I am *two days* late, actually. Always this is so. For my wedding I did not show up at all. I am thirty-three and still a bachelor – of Arts, not Hearts!' As the driver clanged the bonnet shut and scrambled aboard my companion suddenly exclaimed, 'Another day will really make no difference!' and jumped off. The bus started and went lurching up a hill. By the roadside gaunt women in saris were breaking rocks with pickaxes. At the Trivandrum bus terminus I caught a motorized rickshaw up to the Meteorological

Centre. The young men lounging in the portico said Mr Joseph
was busy.

'He is declaring monsoon!' they exclaimed.

'Yes, but for which day?'

They gave me knowing smiles. One took my card, knocked at a
door marked. 'M. S. Rajagopalan, Director' and went in. A
moment later he emerged, beckoning. Mr Rajagopalan received
me standing up in an agitated state, my card in his hand.

'I cannot buy equipment!' he said. 'I do not have authority.
Only Madras has authority for all this kind of thing.'

I stared at him. 'What kind of thing?'

'Telescopes.'

'*Telescopes?*'

Mr Rajagopalan sat and eyed me warily. 'Aren't you wishing to
sell me one? It says here the Observer.'

'That's a newspaper. I'm a journalist. And what I wish to do is
speak to someone about the onset of the monsoon.'

This caused him to throw up his hands exasperatedly and cry,
'Look, look, monsoon is *coming*! Everyone is going around saying it
is late but it will be here Wednesday, Thursday latest. This will be
confirm by satellite picture coming through at 1.15 today. Speak to
my expert, Mr Julius Joseph. But not now. Come back this afternoon. We are all frantic at the moment.'

We both then became aware of the fact that, at the moment,
he had absolutely nothing to do. Plainly nonplussed, he pulled a
year-old copy of *The Economist* across his desk and went zipping
through the pages like someone consulting a first-aid manual
while a companion lay dying of snake bite. I slipped out and, on
the wide, airy veranda, talked for a moment to a small, lithe,
dark-faced meteorologist who bubbled with enthusiasm for his subject.

He said, 'The difference between our weather and the weather in
Europe is the difference between the poor man and the millionaire.
European weather is the poor fellow. His habits are predictable, his
movements restricted. Each day he will follow the same routine,
taking morning coffee in the same restaurant, trudging off to a
tedious job, going home to his bored wife. Indian weather, though,
is extreme, wilful, fast-moving and wholly unpredictable. It's the

millionaire – the sort who will impulsively jump on a plane and fly off to London for lunch.'

I laughed and asked if he was referring to the precocious nature of the monsoon.

'Perhaps certain aspects of the monsoon,' he said. 'The way a major thunderstorm can appear from nowhere in forty-five minutes and dissipate again in thirty. But the monsoon itself is a creature of such grandeur and complexity that it defies comparison with anything.' He smiled and touched his heart. 'This is where it starts. When Delhi call us, in the days leading up to it, they often ask how we feel. Being a man on the spot is very important. Predicting the burst is not just a matter of dry figures and charts. As it approaches you begin to feel elated, even slightly intoxicated. Maybe it has something to do with charged particles in the air; I don't know. But only the foolish forecaster ignores his emotions.'

The trishaw took me back to town and a small florist's shop on Mahatma Gandhi Road where, in a room extravagantly banked with tropical flowers, I met an affable, open-faced young man named Babu Varghese.

I had been given his name in London. Mr Varghese also ran a travel business, Tourindia, and knew Kerala better than anyone; if you needed help or advice he was the chap to see. Now he sat with a friend, and both looked sad. The friend, Peter, a keen-eyed writer of short stories in Malayalam, the language of Kerala, had brought news of the death of another friend, a Malayalam film director named John Abraham.

'He fell from the balcony of his flat in Calicut last night,' said Peter.'It was quite high up – the third floor, I think.'

'Had he been drinking?' asked Mr Varghese.

'Apparently, yes.'

'John drank a lot.'

'They seem to think that was the reason. He somehow toppled over.'

Mr Varghese gave me a cup of nutty black Kerala coffee as Peter paid for a wreath – an expensive arrangement of jasmine and orchids normally afforded only by doctors and spice merchants. When he had gone Mr Varghese attributed this to the buoyancy of the Malayalam short story market. 'Our top writers make good money,' he remarked. He settled back in his chair. 'How can I help you?'

I told him of my general interest in the monsoon and a more immediate interest in the last house in India. Mr Varghese said, 'Yes, I know the place. It's a hotel. I can take you there in my car. Shall we go tomorrow?'

When I thanked him he smiled. 'It will be nice for me to get out of town a bit. And please call me Babu. Keralans do not like to stand on ceremony.' He glanced at his watch. 'What are you doing now?'

'Nothing much.'

'If you are free we could visit a friend of mine – a sword-fighting doctor whose work is very much dependent upon the rains.'

But Babu's car, an elderly Hindustan Ambassador with a seven-horsepower engine, would not start. As the driver, an intense, small-boned man in a safari suit, opened the bonnet to take a look, Babu said that the ubiquitous Ambassador, by far the most commonly sighted vehicle on Indian roads, was in fact a precise copy of the old 1950s-designed British Morris Oxford. 'It's heavy and quite underpowered,' he said. 'The engine's about the size of a coconut.'

'This engine *is* a coconut,' said the driver unexpectedly, getting back in. He tried again and, moments later, nursed the Ambassador past a downtown temple where statues of snakes lay coiled among the roots of a banyan tree. The heads of the snakes were dusted with yellow turmeric. Two teenage girls touched one, placed their fingers to their own foreheads, then walked chatting through the door of a shack bearing a sign saying:

Photostats
Cute & Crisp Copies in Secs

We drew up beside an anonymous-looking two-storeyed building. Babu said it was the Kalarippayat Centre and conducted me into a small consulting room containing a desk and a couple of chairs. Wisps of woodsmoke drifted through the door from an ante-room behind. We heard murmured voices and the scrape of heavy metal cooking pots, then a fit-looking man in his fifties bustled in and smiled at us. He was lean and bespectacled, with an aquiline nose and a manner combining pastoral gentleness and high intellectual confidence.

Babu jumped up. 'This is C. V. Govindankutty Nair,' he murmured. 'The *gurukkal*, or master, of the Kalarippayat Centre.'

'Hullo!' said Mr Nair.

'His father was master before him,' Babu continued, 'and his son will succeed him as the next master.'

Mr Nair grinned. 'You are thinking nepotism is alive and well in South India! Well, it will be less confusing when you have observed what we do here. But first things first. Coffee or tea?'

A shy, middle-aged woman brought us coffee the colour of stout with a frothing white head to match. Mr Nair cocked an eye at me. 'Do I detect a slight problem with your neck?' he enquired.

I stared at him. 'Well, yes,' I said.

'Perhaps the result of a motor accident?'

Mr Nair listened closely to a summary of my condition but offered no particular comfort. 'Spend a month with me and I would have you in a condition of exceptional good health and high spirits,' he said. 'But I cannot mend you.'

'It is done with massage,' said Babu.

'A course of massages using an infusion of oils,' said Mr Nair. 'And the burst of the monsoon is the correct time to start. That is the period when body and mind heal best. To a European it may sound like quackery, but I promise it works.'

He stood and beckoned us into the ante-room, a small boiler house smelling of herbs with a fire smouldering on a blackened stone hearth. An old man painstakingly poured sesame oil from beer bottles into a giant iron cooking pot. Two women sat on a bench, one nursing an ulcerated arm wrapped in a stained bandage. 'The dispensary,' said Mr Nair. 'These ladies are awaiting treatment.' From somewhere nearby I could hear grunts and the clashing of swords. 'What you are going to see may lead you to suppose I specialize in sports medicine, but my practice is fairly general. People come to me with rheumatic complaints, bad backs, muscular atrophy -- that is a wasting condition – and for general overhauls of the body. We call that a *sukha chikilsa*, and the monsoon provides the most ideal conditions.'

He led us down a passage and the gladiatorial noises grew louder. Someone cried, 'Unngghhh!' The reverberating clang of metal striking metal sounded like a multi-car motorway pile-up. Mr Nair continued, 'The *uzhichil*, or massage, should be done early in the monsoon by the master himself. He rubs medicated oils into the patient with his feet while supporting himself from ropes.'

'The Indian rope trick!' said Babu.

We entered a small, sunken circus ring where two men in loincloths, torsos gleaming, were attacking each other with heavy swords. They moved very fast and precisely, cutting, parrying, thrusting, ducking and whirling. One combatant, in his mid-twenties, kept rocking his teenage opponent back on his heels with a series of fast, crashing blows that made the boy yelp and show the whites of his eyes. Mr Nair called out a peremptory command and the two, exchanging deep bows, immediately desisted and went to their corners.

'The older one is my son,' said Mr Nair.

I watched the son throw down his sword, pick up a cane quarter staff and begin swishing it through the air like a fly swat.

'This is Kalarippayat, a form of martial arts founded by the gods – well, travelling Japanese monks, probably – to protect Kerala. A century ago training was compulsory for every youth in the land, male and female alike. It was a crucial part of their education, as important as learning to read and write. They used it to settle disputes and often fought to the death so the British banned it. But combatants were still killing each other as recently as the 1930s.'

A dozen youngsters stood along the side of the arena, watching intently. Two adult white Americans were waiting to fight, a man and a woman in loincloths, the woman with a length of cotton gauze bound around her breasts. She was pretty and very sexy. I smiled at her and got the kind of impersonal, measured look that indicated she was sizing me up for a blow to the skull.

Mr Nair, nodding at the children, said, 'The discipline will give them great poise and confidence in later life. Eight is the ideal áge and the burst of the rains the ideal time. Youngsters should start at the outset of their eighth monsoon. First, for seven days, they get their feet massaged in a mixture of ghee and castor oil – done by me hanging from my ropes – then they begin training. They learn about balance, body control, the importance of watching your opponent's eyes. Always the eyes! Never the hands! They learn the techniques of fighting with the long staff, quarter staff, dagger, sword and shield.'

The son and his teenage opponent returned to the arena carrying quarter staffs, knelt in gestures of respect, then engaged each other in furious close combat. Mr Nair said, 'Once we fought with curved wooden prods which were absolutely lethal. If you jabbed at any one of 108 pressure points on the body you could cause death or unconsciousness; there are 64 fatal pressure points, as a matter of fact. The British also banned the prods and the pressure points, and were right to do so.'

I confessed that I still didn't understand what all this had to do with the monsoon.

Mr Nair said, 'After the rigours of the summer the body is run down and exhausted. But then the rains come and offer, each year, the chance of rebirth. They nourish and sustain. Suddenly the body has the potential for strength and growth. That is the moment to treat it for chronic conditions – and to train it to achieve standards of physical excellence such as you see here today.' He smiled at me. 'There is no mystery about it. This knowledge is as old as India.'

The combatants, their duel concluded, touched Mr Nair's feet and then four tiny shrines containing oil lamps set among flowers. I went to talk to the Americans, an intense couple from Arizona who told me they planned to go home and start their own Kalarippayat workshop.

'I can handle the sword and the quarter staff,' said the woman, 'but I don't like the spear and I don't like the mace.'

'What's wrong with the mace?'

'You bludgeon people with it. It's a mugger's weapon. It also weighs a ton.'

'Application of the mace below the waist is prohibited,' said the man.

'Arizona is definitely not ready for the mace,' said the woman.

A well-fed, well-dressed, middle-aged man tapped my elbow and enquired about my interest in all this. I took him to be a retired fighter who had done well in the law or accountancy, but he turned out to be the proprietor of a Kerala nursing home whose patients would arrive, with the rains, from all over India.

'What's wrong with them?' I asked.

'They're a bit run down, perhaps. Tired, stressed. Maybe over-weight and over-indulged – the usual problems of the rich. The Kerala monsoon cure, or special treatment, has become very fashion-able, though ironically it's based on theories devised 5,000 years ago. Ayurvedic medicine was banned by the British, who thought it a product of superstitious heathen minds and ordered all the books to be burned; a few, thank God, escaped the flames. What intrigues people today is that it works, and nothing unpleasant happens. There is a diet, and regular massages with a substance rendered from boiled rice, or certain powders, or oils mixed with herbs and the saps of medicinal plants. These oils require extensive preparation and cost a great deal of money; our treatments do not come cheap.'

'But why is the monsoon so important?'

'Well, for a start,' he said, guardedly, 'it brings equable tempera-tures, neither too hot nor too cold.'

'You could get those with air-conditioning.'

He gave me a quizzical, faintly sorrowful look, then shook his head and turned away to watch the Americans.

Down in the ring they were facing up to each other, circling warily with quarter staffs at the ready. They clashed, the woman pressing home her attack with blazing eyes. Clack-clack went the staffs. 'Hey!' said the man, jumping back and looking startled. 'Come *on*!' she yelled.

Arizona, I reflected, may not be ready for the mace but was it even ready for her? I said goodbye to Mr Nair, who stood watching intently with folded arms, and accompanied Babu back to the car.

He said, 'This isn't really fighting, you know. It's too formalized and controlled for that. They're performing a kind of martial ballet, a series of exercises designed to test them physically and mentally. Fitness, health and discipline! That's what it's about.'

'And it all relates to the monsoon.'

'Oh, yes,' said Babu. 'The monsoon is absolutely crucial.'

*

He dropped me in Press Road before returning to his office; more wreath orders would be coming in for John Abraham. We arranged to travel down to Cape Comorin early next morning and he drove off, clanking engine trailing a veil of blue smoke. The flame-of-the-forest and flamboyant trees were massed with incandescent flowers which, when the burst came, would fall and carpet the streets like hot coals. I walked past the Ladies Fancy Centre and, near the Swopna Tourist Home, found a small coffee shop serving excellent toasted cheese sandwiches.

There I remembered the nine lepers banished by my father to a tiny island a mile or two from our own. He visited them a couple of times a month but, due to the risk of contagion, I was not allowed to accompany him. Now I recalled their regular appearance in canoes after heavy rain. They would come drifting out of the still blue air, the canoes making no mark on the water, and pass within a hundred yards of our house with their hands raised in salutation. 'Give them a wave,' my father would command. They were always too far off to see the leonine features and eaten-away limbs that really interested me, but now, for the first time, I wondered why they always chose that moment to venture forth. Pondering the apparent link between health and the monsoon I reckoned the atmosphere may have induced a sense of well-being so profound that they were inspired to take a little exercise.

Would the monsoon's burst be as beneficial to me? Did it really release some subtle analeptic substance able to make one whole again? Was it good for necks?

The waiter brought my bill and, while counting out rupee notes, I asked him whether he believed in the healing qualities of the rains.

He was a small, spindly, unshaven man, but he spoke firmly and without preamble.

'If certain basic rules are followed, yes. The general rule for rainy season is moderation; avoid chill, physical exercise, sunshine and sexual intercourse. Always eat according to your *dosha*, or bodily constitution. On hot, windless days you may require food sweetened with honey, on cold and stormy days just boiled winter rice and a little clear soup; drink coconut wine in small quantities, and rainwater mixed with honey. Take regular massages with gingili oil on a table carved from *kaanjiram* wood; massages on soles of feet promote sound sleep and good vision. Do not sleep during the day, and do not read; it strains the eyes. Keep amused by watching life go by in the streets. Wear garlands and live in house free from damp. Do all these things and, by the time of the Goddess Parvati's festival in September, you will feel new man.'

I called on the editor of one of Kerala's forty daily papers. He said, 'This time, just before the burst, is very trying for everyone. Crops are finished, commodities are down, incomes are down, even our circulation is down. There is little advertising and fewer people can spare the coins to buy a newspaper. My staff and I await the rains just as eagerly as any farmer.'

At the Meteorological Centre a couple of local journalists stood outside the office of Julius Joseph who, they told me, was in conference. One said, 'If you are wanting to talk to Joseph you'll have to join the queue.'

'What's the latest word?' I asked.

'Two days. And they are saying this year it will be very vigorous monsoon.'

In a bookshop on Mahatma Gandhi Road I examined shelves filled with anthologies of Malayalam short stories. Babu had been right about their popularity; they were almost as plentiful as cook books and obviously selling in the same quantities. Then my eye fell on a large blue volume entitled *Southwest Monsoon* by Y. P. Rao, Director General of Observatories, India Meteorological Department. Rao's *Southwest Monsoon* was a classic text, very hard to come by. The haughty, fine-eyed girl at the cash desk said it had probably belonged to the estate of some deceased meteorologist; occasionally her boss bought up dead men's libraries. I dipped into it on the bus back to Kovalam. Y. P. Rao's preface said the south-west monsoon had been the subject of intensive study for over four centuries and, as proof of this, his chapter headings covered aspects as diverse as Onset and Withdrawal, Flow across the Equator, Air Masses, Orographic Effects, Cloud and Rainfall Characteristics, Balance of Mass, Radiation, Angular Momentum and Numerical Modelling.

That evening, dining on curried seer fish, I tried to plumb its mysteries. Sheet lightning played across a starless black sky and the waiter, wiping sweat from his forehead with the backs of his hands, complained that he couldn't see the new moon of Ramadan, lost among the towering cumulus congestus tops like a gold ring in a snow drift.

'Berson and Deacon have shown the occurrence of heavy rainfall during monsoon (June–July) is more frequent at certain epochs of lunar synodic cycle,' Rao's book said.

'What do you think it means?' I asked the waiter.

He peered over my shoulder. 'Tonight is First Bright of waxing moon and start of Bright Fortnight in which rains will come.' He poured me some water. 'Or maybe he mean monsoon's Lunar Mansions. These told astrologers when clouds would become pregnant and burst. In old days astrologers always made the monsoon forecasts. My uncle says they were very accurate. He says they should be employing a few at the Met Office now.'

The lights went out. He muttered, 'Perhaps moon is still Dark Waning after all', and hurried off to fetch a candle.

1 JUNE

Babu picked me up at the crack of dawn. He said the run to Kanniyakumari, the little township on the very tip of Cape Comorin, would take four hours assuming the elderly Hindustan Ambassador was up to it; he and his driver spoke worriedly about an impending axle problem.

The sky flared with the colours of coral and claret, the cool air carried a fragrance of lemons. As we turned on to the Cape road by Kovalam beach, one of the finest in India, Babu complained that it suffered a seasonal infestation of ageing European hippies – the kids who had flocked to the ashrams in the 1960s and, due to a combination of inertia and poverty, never made it home again.

'There are many nudists and drug-takers,' he said, severely. 'During the season ganja is as easy to buy as bananas. Some is grown locally, in a forest garden run by a very violent American woman. Ganja is another big monsoon crop and, after the harvest, it is brought out in gunny sacks by young white people who do it to finance their travels through India. The police do nothing because the woman is a psychopath. They are scared of her.'

Now the beach, out of season, was an empty, crescent-shaped sweep of bright sand rimmed by heavy surf. In need of something to jolt us awake, we paused at a tea shop filled with tobacco smoke and the clamour of voices raised in debate. On every beach the forty Malayalam newspapers were being read aloud, quoted from, argued over.

'They are Marxists to a man!' yelled Babu over the din. 'Kerala being a Communist state these people pay more attention to Moscow than to Delhi and they make Rajiv Gandhi very, very nervous.'

A beaky, bespectacled man, overhearing this, shouted in my ear, 'Gandhi and the Congress Party are *finished*! Congress is like a dinosaur – still twitching in the outer extremities but totally brain dead! No signals have been received from that brain for many moons!'

Back in the car Babu said, 'If you had been a Russian they would have thrown a spontaneous party in your honour. I have been caught up in such functions. They can be long and very exhausting.'

The road ducked inland. Small villages appeared among the coconut groves and, in each, lines of women stood quietly with buckets and pots, awaiting the water tanker. Many of the pots had been burnished till they glittered and their owners, in vivid, gorgeously coloured saris, looked like guests bringing gifts to a wedding. 'It is very bad now,' said Babu. 'Many of them are thirsty. If the rains do not come very soon – and I mean within the next few days – the situation will be critical.'

In each village children were going to school, some very small and plainly apprehensive, all scrubbed and spotless; the girls wore flowers in their long plaited hair. 'June the first!' said Babu. 'The first day of school *and* the monsoon! When I was a kid it usually arrived at about 8 a.m., when we were on our way, soaking us to the skin.'

He handed me a creased copy of the *Indian Express*, and pointed to a front page item. It said:

About 57 lakh youngsters will make their way to schools in the State today marking the beginning of yet another school year.

Among the 57 lakh will be around 6.2 lakh tiny tots entering the new world of understanding and the new plane of relationships.

The reopening of schools traditionally coincides with the onset of monsoon in the State. But the summer is still persisting and the rains, which usually form the backdrop for the dampened spirits of the young, are expected only one or two weeks hence.

'One or two weeks!' I said.

'That is the opinion of their education correspondent,' said Babu. 'You can't expect him to know about meteorology as well.' He retrieved his paper. 'Our parents would fret and watch the sky, urging us to leave in plenty of time. We, of course, planned it so that the burst would catch us fair and square. When it came the road would be full of dancing, yelling kids, shouting in the wind and rain. We eventually got to school wet through, almost drunk with excitement, and the teachers would implore us, "Settle down! Settle down!" But they were just as exhilarated and those first hours back at school had a quality of shared happiness that was almost transcendental.' He smiled at the memory. 'With the monsoon roaring away outside even algebra could seem like a celebration of life.'

We halted beside a sunken, grassy courtyard containing mossy stones and a small temple. Babu handed coins to a child with a wizened face who applied dabs of sandalwood paste to our foreheads and then called to a hidden colleague. Seconds later three volcanic bangs and a wild rush of smoke scared the wits out of me.

'They are just crackers,' said Babu, 'to bless our journey and bring us luck with the matter of the axle. It is obligatory to stop here. The number of crackers you buy depends on the skill of your driver; a very good driver requires only two, a really bad one a dozen or more. Though buses do not stop, passengers always throw coins out as they pass, and crackers are lit for them also. The service operates twenty-four hours a day and during that period they will let off 7,000 crackers.' He signalled the driver onward. 'On the way home we must buy more as a gesture of thanks for our safe deliverance.'

Now we entered a gentle landscape with smoothly sculpted hills to one side, to the other a chain of deep pools connected by stretches of broken water splashing over pebbles; the paddies, gardens and copses between were all complementary shades of green. Close your eyes slightly and it was like peering through lenses of opaque Roman glass; open them and the tropical light gave definition to every leaf and palm frond.

Babu talked about the monsoon. He said that three years earlier a big prayer ceremony was held in Trivandrum. It took place during the pre-monsoon dry period and, by tradition and decree, began with the lighting of a fire. (The priests charged with the task followed ancient procedures by rubbing sticks, but took so long they were taunted by the local press. 'Still No Flame!' mocked the headlines. They finally achieved combustion on day three.) The procedures also ordained that the blaze should be doused by rain, and this aspect had aroused considerable interest abroad. Several Western scientists were present, including an observer from NASA.

'The week wore on,' said Babu, 'and nothing happened. Huge crowds came to pray beside the fire. The atmosphere was very devout. The wife of the chief priest sat with her hands clenched, her fingers pressed hard into her palms, and could not open them until the rains came. This penance meant that everything had to be done for her – she had to be fed, her teeth cleaned and so on. But the skies remained absolutely clear and the weather continued baking hot. Towards the end of the week people started complaining, so the priests went to work.'

I laughed.

He gave me a solemn look. 'I was *there*,' he said. 'I saw everything they did. The fire had been lit in a large wooden pavilion and, when special mantras were chanted which caused the flames to jump ten feet, the building itself began blazing. Forty fire engines were parked nearby because of fears that the whole of Trivandrum would burn. The priests began throwing certain things into the fire. It started giving off smoke, very thick and pungent, which grew into a stupendous column thousands of feet high. Then, out of the smoke, sailed many eagles. The sky grew dark and, quite soon, torrential rain began to fall. Within minutes it put the fire out and everyone went home.'

'I don't believe a word of that,' I said.

He shrugged. 'People called it a miracle, but a hundred special herbs, leaves, spices and aromatic woods known only to the *nambi*, or chief priest, were used. Burned in the proper order they produce rain. The Western scientists certainly thought so. They spoke of curious chemical reactions to the substances in the fire.'

'And the eagles?'

He gave his slow, faintly mocking smile. 'All that smoke flushed thousands of tiny birds from the trees. The eagles were there for no noble or holy purpose, my dear Alex. They had simply come to lunch.'

Odd noises began issuing from the underside of the car. At the next village we consulted the blacksmith, a heavy-set, uncommunicative man who sucked his teeth as he gave the axle a few desultory bangs with a mallet. We proceeded cautiously and, approaching the outskirts of Kanniyakumari, I began seeking my house. But Kanniyakumari proved to be a shabby little town, its only sizeable buildings a few gaunt hotels and one or two ornate temples. Otherwise I saw only rows of souvenir stalls selling peanuts, painted shells and packets containing sands of three colours taken from adjacent beaches facing the seas that meet at the Cape: the Arabian, the Bay of Bengal and the Indian Ocean.

Two hundred yards off the toe of India stood the rocky islet on which, in 1892, Swami Vivekananda meditated before embarking on his evangelical crusade in America. Rusty little iron ferries bucketed back and forth, packed with the honeymooners and pilgrims who flock here to immerse themselves in the three seas at the Kumari Ghat. For newly-weds the dip promises happiness, for sinners absolution and a new beginning.

We saw the spot where Mahatma Gandhi's ashes, brought by train from Delhi, were dispersed in the tide, and watched people of all ages pick their way across the tiny, stony beach to launch themselves valiantly into giant breakers that had rolled up, without interruption, all the way from Antarctica. Later, with luck, they would observe the business of the setting sun and waxing moon sharing the same oceanic quadrant. Several hundred people sat on the sea wall, staring south into the late afternoon sky. It was a bruised, feverish red, flaring like the aftermath of an explosion, and it induced a sombre mood among the spectators. The air was very still.

'There's your monsoon,' said Babu, also peering at the sky. 'It's not very far away.'

Walking through the bazaar past temples dressed, like liners, with strings of coloured lights I realized that mine was the only white face in town. The voices around spoke in all the dialects of India and, not for the first time, I was struck by the notion that I was just one alien among many. This seemed to be a nation of millions of foreigners, a bewildering accretion of mutually exclusive tongues, gods and cultures the governance of which, shaky although it might be, appeared nothing short of miraculous.

I was approached by a number of naked sadhus, rough-looking customers who began demanding money with menaces. Babu, shooing them off, led me towards a large, graceless building called the Kerala State Guest House where, in a squalid dining room reeking of stale grease, he summoned a cook and demanded tea.

Then, beaming, he said, 'Well! This, I think, is your place.'

I laughed in disbelief. 'It can't be!'

'It must! It's the last building in India.'

'But my house stood in a big garden among trees.'

We sought the advice of a fellow tea-drinker, a wiry, keen-eyed physician from Cochin who sat with three high-spirited, middle-aged women in peacock-blue saris. The stories they exchanged made them speechless with laughter. 'Ripping!' cried one. I took this to be a reunion of schoolgirl hockey players but the physician said they were just his sisters on holiday. 'They're triplets,' he added. He summarized my problem thus: 'You first saw the house from a plane? Your problem is one of perspective, the difference between bird's eye and worm's eye views. In a helicopter you would find, probably, that it lies only a mile or two out of town.'

We chatted about the rains. When I mentioned Trivandrum's great fiery prayer meeting the physician smiled. 'Yes, yes, but there is really no need to go to all that trouble. If you break tender young coconuts on a statue of Shiva as the priest chants certain mantras you will get rain. Within twenty-four hours. Absolutely guaranteed.'

Babu, plainly worried by the dying light and ominous red sky, seemed anxious to be off. I was secretly pleased that the house had not yielded up its identity too easily; it gave me an excuse to return.

*

Two hours later, in profound darkness, the driver spoke quietly. Babu grunted and twisted round in his seat. I saw a flicker of light among the trees on the left, then an answering flicker from the right. Signals were being exchanged with torches. The noises beneath the car were now very pronounced, a metallic grinding that grew then subsided again. The driver had slowed almost to walking pace.

'He thinks we have a breakage,' said Babu, finally. 'He wants to stop. I told him this is not a good place.'

'Why not?'

'There are no repair shops,' he said.

'There's somebody out there.'

'I can see.'

He gave the driver a peremptory order and we picked up speed again, bumping along with a crabbing motion and a sound like a hacksaw slicing through tin.

'Are there bandits on this road?'

'It has been known,' said Babu.

He remained silent until, much later, we reached the sanctuary of the cracker temple. When the child appeared he gave him a spilling handful of coins and, as the explosions marked our safe deliverance, turned and grinned at me in the gunflash lights. 'Worth every anna!' he said.

2 JUNE

The wind woke me before dawn. It came from the south-west with a curious singing note, steady and melodic. A deeper accompaniment was discernible in the background which, at first, I took to be breaking seas. Thinking they were breaking outside my window I went to investigate but found only the wild thrashing of coconut palms.

I returned to bed but couldn't sleep. The monsoon seemed to be on its way and my journey in its company could commence. The fact that it had finally made its move was one worry less, but new doubts began to assail me over the travel arrangements. An eccentric monsoon, starting and stopping at whim, perhaps making unscheduled diversions, would make life very complicated. And what was happening about the Cherrapunji permission? I made a mental note to call Delhi but then, remembering I would have to use the Indian telephone system, immediately cancelled it. That problem could be faced nearer the time.

Dawn revealed a deep cumulus overcast and flayed, streaming coconut fronds. The crows had been blown away (even now they were probably hurtling backwards, wildly cawing, over Goa) and replaced by flights of brown sea eagles. These had taken up station fifty feet above the brow of the cliff beyond my window, ranged along it like sentinels, perfect flying machines hanging almost motionless as they waited for fish in the boiling sea below.

Half a mile out men waited for fish in fleets of flimsy, high-prowed canoes which, later today, Julius Joseph would order ashore; spinning like compass needles they kept vanishing beneath the huge swell and reappearing, dizzyingly, far from where they started. Periodically a sunbeam touched the dark sea and ignited it in a wild, irradiating flash.

The bay below my hotel had become a white tidal race, the waves surging up the beach and over the road. A foolhardy cyclist venturing on to the road with a milk pail was knocked flat. Hoisting the bike shoulder-high he staggered on, pail in the crook of an arm, surf surging about his ankles. The coast, running north for many miles, lay semi-obscured under an opaque ribbon of spray which, touched by those sunbeams, briefly glittered with a rainbow luminescence.

'Monsoon coming!' said the waiter at breakfast.

'When?'

'I think this afternoon.'

I nodded, unsettled by the behaviour of my watch, a 25-year-old Swiss Omega which, ever since I had owned it, lost precisely $4\frac{1}{2}$ minutes a day. Nothing could apparently be done about this; a droll Zurich expert to whom I once showed it said the $4\frac{1}{2}$-minute lapse lay so deep in the mechanism it was more a matter of metaphysics than watchmaking, accessible to God perhaps, but not to him. This morning, though, routinely checking it against my undeviating electronic alarm clock as I strapped it on, I noted with astonishment that it was running eight minutes *fast*. Such a bewildering development, I decided, must have been caused by charged particles or a strange force field moving up in the van of the burst.

Still preoccupied I walked to the village through salvoes of flying vegetation, bought a paper and took shelter in a coffee shop. 'Monsoon Due in 48 Hours' proclaimed a front page headline. The story, filed in New Delhi and dated the previous day, said:

> Though there have been some pre-monsoon showers in certain parts of southern India in the last few days, south-west monsoon is likely to break out in its normal run along the Kerala coast in the next 48 hours.
>
> Giving the information on the basis of satellite imagery of monsoon conditions, Dr N. Sen Roy, Additional Director of the Meteorological Department, said once the monsoon breaks out of Kerala it would spread to the neighbouring Karnataka, Andhra Pradesh, Tamil Nadu and other States in the next week.
>
> UNI adds from Trivandrum: Conditions are becoming 'favourable' for the onset of the south-west monsoon over Kerala and Lakshadweep during the next three days, meteorological sources said here today. It said that isolated heavy rain was likely to occur over Kerala during the next 48 hours.

If it arrived here today – or tomorrow – when might it be expected in Cochin, my next stop on its route? Julius Joseph must now be one of the most sought-after men in South India but, even so, I would soon need a word with him. A voice said, 'Well, well, sod this for a game of soldiers!' and my bespectacled friend from the bus parked himself on the bench opposite, grinning.

I was pleased to see him. 'What are you late for this time?' I asked.

'Nothing. I am taking day off. All it will do is make me one day later for all things for which I am hopelessly late already.' He laughed and placed a dog-eared school exercise book on the table. 'Today I am sitting here writing.'

'Writing what?'

'A short story, sir. That is my trade.'

I said I had once written short stories too and we talked happily of the problems of finding good beginnings, credible endings and themes that lent themselves to the subtle brush strokes of miniaturists like ourselves. He told me he admired the work of Maupassant, Chekhov, John Cheever, William Trevor and Rabindranath Tagore.

The Trivandrum bus would be leaving in a few minutes. I finished my coffee and asked what story he would be working on today.

'It is based on a true incident,' he said. 'About local farming village with bad water shortage. A dozen girls went into the paddy fields with a priest, took off their clothes and danced naked. The girls are doing this quite willingly, you understand – it is traditional dance to bring rain. But nudity is illegal in India so police are coming along and arresting them.'

'And did they bring rain?'

He smiled and tapped his nose. 'Read the story! I am giving it twist in tail!'

Aboard the bus I opened the paper again. Water shortages remained very much in the news. The Andhra Pradesh government had begun transporting water in special trains, with celebrations attendant upon the departure of the first, *aarti* being offered and coconuts broken as the fifty-tanker 'rake' set off. And here, by way of a contrast, was a report about the Delhi authorities going under water to look for shipwrecks near Lakshadweep. 'Archaeologist S. R. Rao said that the search for treasure-carrying vessels would be taken up only after the monsoon.'

The mood at the Meteorological Centre was like that in a theatre before the curtain went up on an important first night. People moved with quickened tread and an urgent sense of purpose. Mr Rajagopalan, the Director, came pacing by with furrowed brow and hands clasped behind his back, the leading man mentally rehearsing his lines. He didn't remember me, and looked startled when I interrupted his reverie. 'We are talking hours and minutes now!' he declaimed. 'Hours and minutes!'

Julius Joseph stood outside his office, speaking to an attentive young assistant. The lines of worry had vanished from his face; he suddenly looked as relaxed as someone back from a long holiday. 'Tell them to be here at four o'clock for an official announcement,' he said.

'Yes, sir!' said the young man, rushing off.

'That's for the local media,' said Mr Joseph, smiling. 'To put them out of their misery.'

'So today's the day,' I said.

'Undoubtedly – though, as is customary, we will not formally announce it until tomorrow. We think it will arrive between 3 and 3.30. This morning the wind was gusting at 40 knots from the south-west – the classic prelude to the burst.'

'When will it get to Cochin?'

'Tomorrow.'

'Maybe I should get up there tonight.'

'Through a great barrage of rain and wind? No one would take you. My advice is to wait and watch its arrival here. And the best place for that will be out at Kovalam beach. It should be quite a spectacle.'

His secretary, wearing a burst-day sari of rain-cloud-coloured silk, called to him. Delhi was on the line! Mr Joseph sighed and hurried away.

I set off for the florist's shop in Mahatma Gandhi Road, noting that an electric mood had come over the city. People stood in groups on street corners, talking animatedly and looking at the sky. The traffic moved faster and more eccentrically than usual, and the thin wheeping sound of police whistles filled the air. Then, on impulse, I asked the trishaw driver to take me to a hospital. 'A traditional hospital,' I added. 'South Indian.'

He nodded, unsurprised. 'We go to Ayurvedic Teaching,' he said.

The matter of the watch still puzzled me. Now, following that and almost as weird, the stiffness in my neck and hands had been replaced by a faint tingling sensation. It was pleasant, even exhilarating, providing the kind of lift you might get from tiny cardiac implants dispensing cold gin. These two factors had to be connected. Perhaps they pointed to a course of treatment, even a cure.

The hospital stood in a tree-filled garden, a large, airy building suffused with the heady smells of a spice bazaar. A friendly woman in a white coat sat at the reception desk. She listened to my tale of whiplashed necks, stiff hands and fast watches without ceasing to smile, though I noted a little tension appearing behind the eyes. I was asked to take a seat. One of the doctors would see me shortly. The corridors were full of stunningly pretty trainee nurses and lounging male patients wearing nothing but breechclouts, their heavily oiled skins gleaming like varnished mahogany. The heavily oiled women, presumably, had remained in the seclusion of their wards.

Several battered Ayurvedic medical journals lay on a nearby table. I leafed through them, learning that victims of cholera or acute gastroenteritis were given intravenous drips of coconut milk. Powdered seeds of bastard teak could, if eaten daily with gooseberry juice, ghee and honey, turn an old man into a youth.

A 22-year-old college student had been cured of chronic headaches by being purged with *gandharva hastadi* castor oil, then, each day before lunch, swallowing an ounce of *pippalyadi arishtam*. He took a tablespoon of *chavana prasa* and a cup of milk before bed and, on rising, had unconcentrated *ksheerabala* oil applied to the head; on twenty-one occasions the oil had also been administered nasally.

I saw how these head applications were done. A shiny, well-built young man came by in a wheelchair, pushed by one of those flashing-eye child nurses, a small leather crown set atop his shaven scalp. The receptionist said he suffered from migraines.

'The hat contains a tank which we are filling daily with oils of cider and concentrated milk extracts. The mixture is absorbed naturally and, quite soon, he will be getting better.'

The doctor who saw me was a busy, plump, middle-aged lady with beautiful skin. Though interested in the accelerating watch – 'I heard of town hall clock that once chimed thirteen times during monsoon burst' – she offered little comfort.

'I am not denying there may be force fields and charged particles in the atmosphere today,' she said briskly. 'Only a physicist could tell us that. And if such things exist it is possible they may be affecting you. But I doubt they could help us make you better. Perhaps we could ease the symptoms, but our methods are very slow. Take pain, for instance. We don't treat pain, we treat only the cause. This can take many weeks. Even we Ayurvedic doctors sometimes suffer pain ourselves and would gladly kill for an aspirin! We too become impatient. But nothing must be allowed to interfere with the natural healing process. So you will need plenty of time.'

'I must go to Cochin tomorrow,' I said.

She shook her head. 'You Westerners! Always demanding instant results. Look, I am trying to tell you, we work in different areas. Factors like the time of your birth, the influence of your father and mother, are important to us. You would consult holy men as well as doctors. We use leeches for blood-letting. This is not Harley Street, or your famous National Health Service.' She glanced pointedly at her watch.

I stood. 'Is it gaining much?' I asked.

She gave a small, gurgling laugh, unexpectedly sexy but, by the time I had reached the door, was already calling for her next patient.

At the flower shop Babu, in a state of some excitement, asked if I would like to meet Kamala Das. He had called her and she was prepared to see me at 5 p.m. 'We must take flowers, but what kind would she like?'

I stared at him. 'Babu, I haven't the faintest idea what you're talking about. Anyway, I'll be out at Kovalam watching the burst.'

He looked dismayed. 'Kamala is one of India's greatest poets. In 1984 she was nominated for the Nobel Prize for Literature and she lives here, in Trivandrum. She understands better than most what the monsoon means to us. And I thought it might be interesting for you to sit and talk while the first rains are falling.'

'My word!' I said.

He smiled. 'Come back after your burst. We will go together. Meanwhile, I shall sit and ponder the matter of the bouquet.'

A line of spectators had formed behind the Kovalam beach road. They were dressed with surprising formality, many of the men wearing ties and the women fine saris which streamed and snapped in the wind. Their excitement was shared and sharply focussed, like that of a committee preparing to greet a celebrated spiritual leader, or a victorious general who would come riding up the beach on an elephant; all they lacked was welcoming garlands of marigolds. As I joined them they greeted me with smiles, a late guest arriving at their function. The sky was black, the sea white. Foaming like champagne it surged over the road to within a few feet of where we stood. Blown spume stung our faces. It was not hard to imagine why medieval Arabs thought winds came from the ocean floor, surging upwards and making the surface waters boil as they burst into the atmosphere.

We stood rocking in the blast, clinging to each other amid scenes of great merriment. A tall, pale-skinned man next to me shouted, 'Sir, where are you from?'

'England!' I yelled.

The information became a small diminishing chord as, snatched and abbreviated by the elements, it was passed on to his neighbours.

'And what brings you here?'

'This!'

'Sir, us also! We are holiday-makers! I myself am from Delhi. This lady beside me is from Bangalore and we too have come to see the show!' He laughed. 'I have seen it many times but always I come back for more!'

The Bangalore woman cried, 'Yesterday there were dragonflies in our hotel garden. They are a sign. We knew monsoon was coming soon!' She beamed at me. 'It gives me true sense of wonder!'

More holiday-makers were joining the line. The imbroglio of inky cloud swirling overhead contained nimbostratus, cumulonimbus and Lord knows what else; all riven by updraughts, downdraughts and vertical wind shear. Thunder boomed. Lightning went zapping into the sea, the leader stroke of one strike passing the ascending return stroke of the last so that the whole roaring edifice seemed supported on pillars of fire. Then, beyond the cumuliform anvils and soaring castellanus turrets, we saw a broad, ragged ban of luminous indigo heading slowly inshore. Lesser clouds suspended beneath it like flapping curtains reached right down to the sea.

'The rains!' everyone sang.

The wind struck us with a force that made our line bend and waver. Everyone shrieked and grabbed at each other. The woman on my right had a plump round face and dark eyes. Her streaming pink sari left her smooth brown tummy bare. We held hands much more tightly than was necessary and, for a fleeting moment, I understood why Indians traditionally regard the monsoon as a period of torrid sexuality.

The deluge began.

She relinquished her grip and went scampering back into the trees, chiding her clerky husband for not raising his umbrella fast enough. The umbrella, raised, almost lifted him off his feet before being blown inside out. The rain hissed on the sea and fell on us with a buzzing, swarming noise. The air was suddenly fluid and fizzing. As a child in the islands I once attempted to walk across the lip of a waterfall. I slipped midway over and the plunge to the pool below seemed to take for ever; the sensation I felt then, of being cocooned inside a roaring cataract of falling, foaming water, was very similar to the one I felt now.

Elated, I made my way slowly back to the hotel. Water sheeted off the hillside, a rippling red tide carrying the summer's dust down to the sea. I changed and persuaded a taxi driver to take me to the flower shop. He muttered and sighed and asked for many rupees. But passing through Kovalam I spotted a place offering traditional Ayurvedic massages and, on the spur of the moment, asked the driver to wait.

The masseur, a lugubrious brahmin with small, muscular hands, bade me strip and lie on a table. For twenty minutes he rubbed me down with thick, spicy gingili oil, pausing every few minutes to walk to the window and spit into the streaming rain. The procedure was soothing and faintly soporific and, afterwards, I felt an inexplicable sense of well-being. The masseur, though, remained wary when questioned about this. All he would say was, 'There are three places on body you cannot massage – gent's penis' (he called it 'pennies'), 'lady's chests and face of both sex; face massage make muscles go slack and give wrinkles.'

Babu, wearing a tie, his hair combed for Kamala Das, awaited me with purple orchids in a basket. The axle of his car had been repaired and we set off through flooded, gurgling streets strewn with flamboyant and flame-of-the-forest blossoms knocked down by the rain. Some were carried along in the gutters, making them resplendent, more lay heaped and scattered across the pavements; beneath their shiny umbrellas the passers-by moved across this glowing, lambent surface like fire-walkers. Many shops and offices had closed, their workers awarding themselves an unofficial public holiday.

I told Babu about the massage. 'Yes, I know of that man,' he said. 'He is quite good. But did he bless the öil before he rubbed it on?'

'I've no idea,' I said.

'He is supposed to hold each application cupped in his hand for a few seconds while he offers it to the gods. With you being a foreigner, though, he probably didn't bother. If an Indian had caught him just pouring and slapping it on he would have complained.'

He handed me Volume 1 of Kamala Das's *Collected Poems* and I leafed through it in the waning light. The poems were moving and very fine, with the monsoon a recurring symbol of, it seemed to me, sadness, wistful regret and tenderness. In 'The Time of the Drought' she had written:

> *When every night my littlest child awakes and*
> *Limpets to my side, I am heavy with unshed tears,*
> *I am the grey black monsoon sky*
> *Just before the rain . . .*

And, in 'A Souvenir of Bone':

> *How often*
> *Have I wished as a child to peel the night like old*
> *Wallpaper and burn it, to hold at monsoon time*
> *The wounded wind in my arms, to lull it back to sleep.*

But when, half an hour later, I put the sadness theory to her she crisply dismissed it. 'Nonsense!' she said. 'It's the most beautiful time! It means rejuvenation, greenery, new growth. It's nothing less than the reaffirmation of life.'

We sat drinking tea in a lofty blue room piled with books. The house was rambling and comfortable, the sounds of the dripping garden audible through the open shutters. A small, bespectacled woman with a teenager's complexion, Kamala Das wore a vivid blue sari with great panache and I reflected that she must have been a great beauty.

She continued, 'The monsoon's arrival is quite magnificent. It comes towards you like an orchestra and, not surprisingly, has inspired some of our loveliest music, ragas which evoke distant thunder and falling rain. For centuries our artists have painted monsoon pictures and our poets serenaded the monsoon; I am simply in that tradition.' She smiled and said, 'What I would really like to talk about, however, is the forests – or, rather, the lack of them. Some friends will be joining us shortly. They share my concern and I hope you will listen to them. The problem is inextricably linked with the monsoon so should be relevant to your researches.' She gave me a keen, questing look. 'I gather you plan to travel up India in its company?'

'That's the idea,' I said.

'You may find it an unreliable, even treacherous, companion. These days it has become very elusive. It is often late. Deforestation is one of the reasons for this. Trees help to make rain. Forests seed the passing clouds. Before they cut them down the monsoon was always scrupulously punctual. My grandmother planned everything around it – washing the clothes, drying the grain, visiting relatives – in the certain expectation that it would arrive on the appointed day. The rains were heavier then. Within minutes of the burst small rivers had formed around our houses in which we children sailed paper boats. The monsoon was part of our lives, like sleep. We watched the world being reborn around us while the rain seeped into the house's foundations, making it creak and wobble. In the last two weeks of July we picked ten sacred herbs that grew in the puddles, took them inside and blessed them.'

'It was always the morning we went back to school after the long Ramadan holiday,' said Babu. 'My parents made a terrible fuss. They were scared of chills and implored me to stay out of the rain. But how could I?'

'Parents are much more enlightened now,' said Mrs Das. 'Children are encouraged to go out into the rain to enjoy this "gift from heaven". Also, on a practical note, it helps them build up a resistance to monsoon complaints.' She cocked an eye at him. 'But morning? I distinctly remember it coming during the early afternoon, at about two. We always had an early lunch and hurried through the washing-up so that we could enjoy the spectacle. And when it arrived each villager would crack a raw egg, swallow the contents, fill the empty shell with sweet oil and swallow that too. They believed it did them a power of good.' To me she said, 'One aspect you should look into is health. The monsoon cure is big business in Kerala these days.'

I told her of my attempt to find a cure that morning. I also told her about my watch.

'Your watch may have been accurate. Perhaps we have all gained eight minutes without realizing it. As for your cure, I would send you to a place near here where your physician prays before an oil lamp and shrine dedicated to Dhanwanthari, the god of medicine; occasionally mantras are chanted also, the chief reason being that the *sound* is beneficial to the patient. Then his four assistants place you in a large wooden tub filled with warm medicated oil. Different types may be prescribed. Women wanting shiny skin, for example, have a particular red oil with a very sweet smell. The assistants massage you for an hour. (A curious thing about the massage is that it improves the vision; half-blind old men have been known to throw away their spectacles.) You get only bland food, to cool the system, and you may not go into the sun. This goes on for twenty-one days and takes years off your age. My father had it regularly because he wanted to stay young. He died at eighty-four and, apart from his white hair, he had the appearance of a forty-year-old.'

To me Babu said, 'But you must always do exactly what the doctors tell you.'

'Oh, goodness, yes,' said Mrs Das. 'Last year two rich socialite girl friends of mine flew down from Bombay for the monsoon cure. But each evening, as soon as their physician left them, they came over here to carouse. They'd sit with me, chain-smoking and drinking scotch until dawn (they were a damned nuisance, actually), then sneak back to be in their rooms when the physician returned at 9 a.m. But after twenty-one days a terrible thing happened. They began to age. They became wrinkled old hags, their youth and beauty gone for ever. When I last heard they were at home in Bombay awaiting plastic surgery.'

Mrs Das's anti-deforestation committee arrived, shaking and furling their umbrellas, half a dozen courteous young people and an intense, middle-aged man referred to as the doctor. They took tea and before commencing their meeting, put the problem into perspective for me.

They said India was once a sylvan country. When Alexander the Great invaded in 327 BC he encountered dense, close-canopied, almost impenetrable forests. But peasants were already pursuing a slash-and-burn policy and, after the Emperor Ashoka came to power, the reforms proposed in his Rock Edicts included the planting of 'useful trees' along roads and on military camping grounds. The Marathas and Gonds planted mangoes beside their marching routes.

Trees play a crucial role in the monsoon cycle. By seeding clouds they encourage the rain to fall; by trapping it they help recharge the aquifers and hold groundwater in store for the common good. Some water, rising with the cell sap, is returned to the sky by transpiraton through the leaves. A well-stocked teak forest gives off the equivalent of 1,000 mm of precipitation. Great rain forests act on the atmosphere like tropical seas; they supply it with water vapour and help replenish the rains.

By and large India is a natural tree-bearing country. Though it nas 5 million hectares of eternal snow, most of its soil groups will support something – oaks and conifers in slightly acidic higher-altitude soils, sandalwood in coarse, shallow soils, casuarina in deep coastal sands, rosewood on riverine alluvium, babul, neem and palas in alkaline soils, bamboos just about anywhere.

Many Indians, though, have never visited a forest and are perhaps unaware that ever widening man-made gaps in the canopy will allow heavy rains to wash away the herbs, grasses and leaf-mould carpeting the floor. Then the soil itself is washed away leaving the underlying rock exposed. Silting and flooding follow. Some of India's most tragic floods have been caused by denudation of forests once so thick that tigers lived in them.

'We have reached the stage now,' said Mrs Das, 'where only 4 per cent of the state of Kerala lies under forest. Within a short time, due to private greed and public indifference, we could be another Ethiopia. So I go to the villages and hold sapling-planting seminars, mostly with the women. I start with a prayer – one should *always* do that in India – and then I say a few words about the hardness and injustice of life and we have a little cry, and then I get on to the subject of trees. And they understand. They really do.'

'A thick forest,' said the doctor, 'traps and keeps its rainfall. It seeps through the floor into the subsoil and feeds the streams during the rainless period. Forests are great natural reservoirs. But today with so many gone, 80 per cent of the monsoon rainfall simply runs away into the sea. This means that if next year's monsoon fails, or is late, there will be intense personal suffering. Once again people must go thirsty – and hungry. There will be a 40 per cent drop in our agricultural output and that affects people right down the line, from the State Treasury to the humblest peasant.'

Suddenly the lights went out, came on again and then, for several minutes, flickered weakly and erratically. Mrs Das gave a loud, contented laugh. 'That is the monsoon!' she cried. 'Just as I remember it. All is back to normal!'

I took a taxi to my hotel and, at the Admiral's Bar, watched the onset of night and toasted the monsoon in Indian whisky. The rain had eased but the wind, if anything, blew with even greater force. The straining flags hoisted over the bar gave off reports like cracking whips. The day didn't fade, exactly. The black sky just kept assuming deeper shades of black until, suddenly, it had blacked itself out entirely. The roaring white water down in the bay gave off an eerie luminosity, while the long, winding band of spray heading north, following the precise contours of the coast, glowed like a ghostly motorway.

An elderly Indian wearing a club tie and blue blazer stood staring out at all this, beer in hand. He said, 'Spray of such magnitude goes whirling right up into the atmosphere, you know. Indeed, there is evidence to suggest that a salt particle may lie at the heart of every raindrop falling on the earth.' He waved his glass. 'In general it's the hills that get the rain, with the southerly and westerly aspects getting the most. The wettest aspect is at eight o'clock on the compass.'

'Yes, indeed,' I said.

He nodded and walked away. I found a sheltered corner and opened an anthology of travellers' tales from nineteenth-century India. One, entitled 'The Monsoon along the Madras Coast', was very sad. It concerned Captain B—, commander of a large, well-found sailing ship who, on a day not unlike this – 'the surf rolling upon the beach with terrific violence, causing its roar to be heard for several miles inland' – put into Madras with a cargo of teak from Tenasserim. Late in the afternoon the wind abated and, ignoring local advice, he moved close inshore so that he could begin floating off his timber at first light. During the night, though, the gale returned and what came ashore at first light was not the timber but the ship. Huge waves carried it up the beach to within twenty yards of the road and then pounded it so vigorously that the thousands who came to witness the fate of the fool who failed to take their advice were soaked to the skin; the vessel itself became a ship-shaped penumbra of whirling spray. As for poor, obdurate Captain B—, he 'was from that time on a broken man. He quitted Madras soon after and went to Rangoon where he died, without relations or friends to cheer his last moments.'

After dinner I packed in readiness for an early morning start. I planned to catch a bus to Quilon and then a ferry through the maze of inland waterways that led to Aleppey and, ultimately, Cochin. If the burst was travelling at its advertised 10 m.p.h. then I should catch up with it somewhere among those muddy inland creeks and, provided the ferry could maintain that speed, reach Cochin in its company. Outside the rain had returned, merging with the steady, sonorous noises of the wind and sea. The monsoon was on song tonight and I wondered whether, eventually, a distinctive voice would emerge; if it got away from me at Cherrapunji, for example, would I recognize it from afar as it went prowling around some remote Himalayan valley?

Y. P. Rao had devoted several pages to the onset over Kerala. My eye lit on an entry stating that the five- to sixteen-day interval between the first appearance of easterlies blowing past Aden and the monsoon's arrival at Kerala had been pointed out by Sutcliffe and Bannon in 1954. Though Y. P. Rao appeared to discount the Aden easterlies as a reliable means of predicting the burst date I knew that the area was a fountain of famous and formidable winds.

Aden, before its revolution, had been a bunkering stop for vessels heading up the Red Sea to the Suez Canal. I called there in 1959 aboard a ship laden ten to a cabin with young Australians off to seek their fortunes in the Old World, but suddenly realized I could remember nothing about Aden at all. I habitually retain at least some recollection of every place I have visited but now, for Aden, there was just space.

Had the forces affecting me and my watch also affected my brain? The watch had now resumed its routine daily deficit, but Aden had imploded and vanished into itself like a dead star.

In bed I tried to claw back some small vestige of Aden's colour, light, sensation or smell. Nothing. I recalled the ship, the people, the parties and each of the other places we stopped at. But Aden was gone, leaving only a faint aftertaste of boredom and heat. Was the monsoon emptying my mind of dross? Had other tacky, trivial things also been rubbed out? I tried to imagine what they might be and realized I would never know. But the idea of undergoing a puja, or spiritual cleansing, at the hands of the monsoon was not unappealing.

I drifted off to sleep still hoping for glimpses of Aden, but seeing only mile-high cirrus streamers driven by those huge winds east around the Horn of Africa.

Chapter Four

⚜

3 JUNE

I awoke early, to silence. Incredulous, I realized the rain had stopped. So had the wind. I looked up at a shining pink sky, empty but for a benign sun and a few fluffy strawberry clouds. The coconut fronds hung limp as ribbons. The sea eagles had flown away.

It was a beautiful day.

I dressed, packed and paid my bill. 'Where's the monsoon?' I asked the cashier.

He shrugged. 'Gone.'

'*Gone*?'

'Yes, sahib.' He counted out my change.

'Gone where?'

Another clerk proclaimed, 'Monsoon is here in paper', and handed me his *Indian Express*. He added, drolly, 'It has gone into journalism.'

A front page report, dated the previous day and sent from Trivandrum, formally announced the monsoon. It had set in 'almost on schedule, bringing relief to the drought-hit people of the State. Moderate to heavy rains had been reported from most parts of the southern districts during the last 24 hours.

'*Warning*: A strong westerly wind at a speed exceeding 60 km per hour is likely to lash Kerala coast during the next 48 hours.'

Worried that we might be dealing with a break monsoon in which, for periods of up to twenty-one days, rogue jet streams impound the rains, I used the cashier's phone to call Julius Joseph.

He wasn't there, but a duty officer offered reassurance. 'Fine weather like this after burst is not unusual. Monsoon is an oscillating current, remember. Don't worry, in Cochin you will get wet on schedule!'

The monsoon made its first visit to India during the Miocene epoch between 600 million and 800 million years ago. The cause seems to have been the mighty 'uplift' of the Himalayas and the Tibetan Plateau – a process begun several million years earlier when the northward-moving Indian subcontinent collided with the Asian Plate. Seabed sediment was analysed for tiny opaline skeletons called diatoms and single-celled marine plants known as radiolaria (described by Tom Pedersen, a University of British Columbia marine scientist, as 'the signature of the monsoon') which are brought to the ocean surface by the monsoon wind and allowed to sink again when it has passed. Core samples dating the winds indicate that the earliest blew during the Miocene epoch, when the Himalayas had achieved a height commanding enough to beckon them in.

The Quilon minibus joined the honking early morning traffic and headed north, huge, pewtery puddles making the road ahead look like a draining estuary. I was sad to be leaving Trivandrum. With its low red roofs, shadowy gardens, winding lanes and contentious, voluble, newspaper-mad citizens, I thought it a most agreeable place. The driver said the airport would be closed, during the final fitful showers of the monsoon in September, for a big thanksgiving procession. 'Our old maharaja, carrying a sword, will lead a long line of people down to the sea for a ritual bathe. He follows traditional route, which happens to pass straight across main runway.'

'What happens to the planes?'

'They must divert or circle. There is no problem. He owns all the airport land and, before agreeing to the airport, insisted that one day a year his procession would have unrestricted access. Even the control tower is decked with flowers.' He lit a Scissors cigarette. 'Maharaja also owns a lot of land in the south. Two years ago his tenants at Kanayakumari suffered from bad drought. So he went there, knelt in a paddy field and prayed to Vishnu. He said to Vishnu, "Why are you doing this to me?" One hour later – torrential rain! He is very devout old gentleman, popular with everyone, even the gods.'

At Varkala, less than an hour away, pure mineral water sprang from the lofty red cliffs by the beach. Quilon lay only a dozen miles to the north. The bus station, a muddy square clamorous with the din of revving engines, blaring horns and yelling drivers, was only a few yards from the ferry landing which, by contrast, consisted of a stretch of greensward planted with coconut palms and invaded by squadrons of tiny blue butterflies. In a small, open-sided waiting pavilion a young woman sat drowsily sunning herself, her fibre suitcase emblazoned with a sticker saying SUCH SWEET THUN-DER. I asked where one bought tickets for Aleppey. 'From office in godown,' she said, gesturing towards a small warehouse behind us. I went in. It was very dark, piled with strong-smelling sacks of copra. I spied a glass-fronted booth inhabited by an unshaven, pot-bellied man, and asked for a single on the ten o'clock to Aleppey.

He passed it over, yawning.

'Is it leaving on time?'

A further yawn engulfed him, turning into a minor seizure that shook his wattles and made his eyes water.

'No.'

'How late will it be?'

He snorted thunderously to clear his nasal passages. 'Five hours,' he said.

'Five *hours*!'

Nodding, he turned away, his role in the matter concluded. I went back to the waterside pavilion and told the young woman about the delay.

'I know,' she said. 'It is stuck on mudbank somewhere. These ferry skippers are drawn to mudbank like moth to candle.'

I asked her what the words on her suitcase meant. 'It is advertising slogan,' she said. 'For BOAC jetplanes. My uncle worked for them once.'

'It's certainly very seasonal.'

She frowned. 'By seasonal you are meaning Christmas?'

'No. I mean monsoon.'

She said, 'Ah!' and turned her face back to the sun.

Well, I had certainly passed time in worse places. It was a resplendent morning, the waters of Lake Ashtamudi shining before me, the venerable red-roofed town behind washed by the rain and giving off the wholesome smells of the staples in which, for centuries, it had profitably traded: coffee, cashews and coconut products. The Phoenicians, Persians, Greeks and Romans all sent vessels here, their galleys surging east before the monsoon wind; during the eighth century fleets of sea-going junks brought Chinese merchants who took up residence in the town; later, ambassadors were exchanged between Quilon and the Court of Kublai Khan. (By the sixteenth century it seems to have entered the decline evident today; the contemporary historian Samuel Purchas included a reference to Quilon in his anthology of travellers' tales. At 'Coulam, a small Fort of the King of Portugals . . . they lade onely halfe a ship of Pepper'.) I watched a country boat slip by, creamy patchwork sail slapping in the small breeze, laden to the gunwales with coir doormats and bars of yellow laundry soap. It had a rearing dragon prow – perhaps some lingering relic of Chinese influence.

A small yellow Swaraj Mazda lorry drew up and discharged six bare-chested young men clutching spades and pickaxes. A portly, bespectacled supervisor descended from the cab. He wore dark trousers and a cotton shirt, the line of pens in his pocket arranged as precisely as shells in a cartridge clip, and carried a large red book of the kind used to register births, deaths and marriages. Moving with magisterial gait he led his labourers to the centre of the grassy landing and bent to prod the earth with a finger. A pen was selected, an entry made in his book. Finally he stood back and nodded.

The men began to dig.

I strolled over, noting that the lenses of the supervisor's tortoiseshell spectacles were as opaque as glass paperweights. When the sun caught them the huge, owl-like eyes vanished into unfathomable pools of light, and his only response to my greeting was a glittering nod. The hole began to take shape. It was perhaps a foot across, circular with vertical sides, the dimensions giving not the slightest clue to its purpose.

I was joined by some men from the town, our numbers soon swelling from a handful to several dozen, all watching the work in hand with close interest. Eventually the supervisor, clearly accustomed to commanding the attention of large audiences, rocked back on his heels and allowed that bright, raking gaze to move slowly across the tops of our heads. I thought he might be about to make a short speech of welcome or explanation, but he simply sighed and turned back to the hole.

'For what are they looking?' enquired a whiskery man beside me.

I said I didn't know.

'Treasure?' surmised a youth. 'Oil? This will be a well, perhaps.'

A perceptible sense of companionship began to form. The whiskery man, who had keen but oddly discoloured eyes, told me his passion was philosophical discourse. When he challenged me to define the nature of truth his companion, who was tall with a military bearing, said, 'Before defining nature of truth we must define nature of God. Can we define either?'

Several voices cried, 'Yes! Yes!' and began defining both. As the conversations around us grew diffuse and general the military-looking man told me he was a Syrian Christian in the mixed nuts business. His church and people had been in Kerala for nineteen centuries and still chanted the same litany their spice-trading forefathers brought with them.

The whiskery man once worked as a ship's purser. 'I was on small 2,000-ton steamer,' he said. 'Mostly Indian coastal work but sometimes Middle East too.'

'Did you ever go to Aden?' I asked.

'Aden? Of course.'

'What's it like?'

'Define the nature of Aden!' said the military-looking man, winking at me.

At that moment the supervisor, possibly irritated by the hum of animated talk and concerned that he was losing our attention, raised an arm and snapped his fingers, producing a startling report. The labourers sprang backwards and, in the hush that followed, he approached the hole and peered into it. What he saw caused him to make not one but two entries in his book with pens of different colours. The labourers placed a metal awl in the hole and began boring even deeper.

One of our number finally approached the supervisor and asked what the hole was for. He returned to say it had something to do with the water table; levels needed to be ascertained due to the monsoon's onset. 'That fellow is from Baroda,' he added, pulling a face.

The ship's purser said, 'Aden is city built in a crater. It is a place of rock and dust. The men are thieves, the women unfriendly. They sell you bad fish; it can poison you. Their dates are small and without taste. The harbour dues are high. The nature of Aden is the nature of a bad dream. It should be expunged from memory on waking.'

I said I'd been there and could remember absolutely nothing.

He nodded. 'Your mind is working for you. Do not fight it!'

The volume of talk and laughter grew. A policeman appeared, plainly worried that ours was becoming a riotous assembly. A vendor of snacks arrived and did good business. A drinks vendor came hard on his heels, offering tea and coffee from a wheeled stall. An itinerant barber planted his stool nearby and touted for custom. He was followed by a young man claiming to be from the press. 'What is going on here?' he demanded, pushing through.

He was told and stayed on to watch. The nut merchant remarked that, if our numbers continued to grow at this rate, we would have to elect an MP and send him to Delhi. The purser told me that world cashew prices were going through the roof. 'They are edible gold!' he said. 'If you have spare capital invest in a nut garden!'

Then, quite unexpectedly, the supervisor from Baroda yelled, 'Stop!' In the ensuing hush he crouched intently by the hole, made a three-pen book entry of essay length, then ushered his labourers back aboard the Swaraj Major and drove away. The rest of us dispersed slowly and with some reluctance. As my two friends and I lingered to peer at the hole we heard the sounds of a klaxon and bells and saw a small battered boat heading in towards the landing. The ferry had got off its mudbank earlier than anticipated.

It bumped heavily against a protective dockside skirting of sunken, sawn-off palm trunks and, led by Miss Sweet Thunder, we half dozen waiting passengers went aboard. So did my friends; they conducted a bantering conversation with the ticket collector, a perspiring, earnest-looking man who seemed to have much on his mind. As sacks of copra, cardamom and ginger were piled into the aft cabin the nut merchant said, 'This fellow will keep an eye on you. He is Syrian Christian also. If you want anything, just ask.' They went ashore and, as we cast off, stood with their hands raised in salute.

Waving back, I reflected that India was a giant web of interlocking personal networks which, once infiltrated, would keep passing you along indefinitely. Heading off into the backwaters the ferry made good speed, passing a fine lakeside house with a speedboat moored at its private dock. 'Spice millionaire,' remarked the ticket collector. 'Not rupee. Dollar!'

We veered over to the other side, running along a low, intimate coast indented with creek mouths and tiny palm-fringed inlets. The coconut groves were so dense it was like peering into a succession of quiet, intimate, dimly lit rooms. Shadows and the smell of woodsmoke indicated the presence of people, an occasional sunbeam penetrating the trees to illuminate the corner of a house, shirts drying on a line, a woman sweeping a courtyard, naked children gazing out towards the racket of our ancient diesels. We halted at a tiny palm-sheltered wharf and a boy jumped off, vanishing into the grove as abruptly as though passing through his own front door.

Then we set out across a broad lagoon scattered with Chinese fishing nets and floating human heads. When the heads, wagging agitatedly, began drifting out of our way I realized they belonged to men walking across the shallow lake bottom; a few gave us glittering smiles as we chugged by, most took no notice. The TC said they were fishermen trawling by hand; each year several were killed by the country boats which, proceeding silently under sail through dim, murky light, delivered them a mortal blow to the back of the skull. A country boat went surging past now, dragon prow as intricately carved as a medieval altar piece, its cargo two tethered goats and a silver-handled coffin.

The TC said the bottom walkers were poor men who aspired, above all else, to the wealth and status of a Chinese 'fish machine'. These, suspended a few feet above the water like huge, surreal butterflies, spoke of better, easier, more spacious lives. Men had been known to kill for possession of one, though marriage into a net-owning family was the usual way for those craving advancement. I nodded, seeing the advantages of having such a device. Set on a wooden platform, lowered and raised by an archaic Archimedean cantilever weighted with rocks, you simply lit a lamp to lure the shoals, dropped your net into the night tide and cranked it up again in the morning, full of money.

We turned into a narrow, winding canal and made a chai stop, piling ashore to buy tea and samosas at a palm-thatched stall in a small clearing. Miss Sweet Thunder complained that the stall-keeper was over-charging. A very cool, composed lady, she told me she was a teacher returning to her primary school after visiting friends in Varkala. I asked what the monsoon was like in these backwaters and she shrugged. 'Air and water become indistinguishable. Chalk is so damp it will not write on blackboard. The children suffer from bad respiratory problems and TB is quite common.'

When I told her of my journey she gave me a quizzical look. 'Where is your umbrella?'

'Actually,' I said, startled, 'I haven't got one.'

She laughed, shook her head and went back on board. I followed, nonplussed, determined to purchase an umbrella first thing next morning. We passed tiny spits of land on which entire families lived, some sharing an area no larger than a country boat with several animals and a lone coconut tree. In the groves and gardens women paused in their work to watch us go by, their bright garments and absolute stillness reminding me of figures rendered in stained glass. The engineer complained of 'serious leakage' and, from time to time, baled out the bilges with a tin can.

Where was the monsoon now? There were hopeful signs. High gauzy stratus veils evident earlier had thickened, darkening the air and dulling the lustrous lacquered shine of the palms. Then I noted that people on the banks were carrying umbrellas. Soon afterwards, as we continued sailing through fairish weather, the TC began bustling about lowering heavy sailcloth screens.

'Rain?' I asked.

'Yes. In five minutes. Very heavy. Monsoon rain.'

It came hissing across the water, not as heavy as the burst at

Kovalam but still carrying enough weight to give the canal a light topping of froth. Could this be the vanguard of the Cochin burst? The TC said no; that wasn't expected in town till after dark. Crossing a small lagoon we encountered more bottom walkers, all miserably lifting dripping hands from the water to wipe the rain from their eyes. At a small clearing containing a stand of flowering trees Miss Sweet Thunder disembarked. Two women awaited her and, after brief greetings, they hurried away beneath their umbrellas.

The light grew dim and the rain clattered against the canvas. There was an angry altercation between our skipper and two scrawny boatmen poling a wallam laden with coir doormats. We had scraped its lovely scrollworked bow and they stood railing in the wet at this act of artistic vandalism. Later we slowed to negotiate a canal choked with purple hyacinths, the blossoms peeling thickly away from our sides and forming a deep green furrow behind. I got Samuel Purchas out of my bag and started reading about Cochin in 1567. 'Cochin is next unto Goa, the chiefest place that the Portugals have in the Indies, and there is great trade of Spices, Drugges, and all other sorts of Merchandize for the Kingdome of Portugall, and there within the land is the Kingdome of Pepper, which Pepper the Portugals lade in their shippes by bulke, and not in Sackes.'

I imagined the Portugals loading their unbagged pepper, eyes streaming, rocked by sneezes, cursing as they worked. A peanut vendor came aboard offering nuts still warm from the frying pan. They were the best I had ever eaten and, as he prepared to jump off again, I hastily bought more. 'Cochin is two Cities, one of the Portugals, and another of the King of Cochin: that of the Portugals is situate neerest unto the Sea, and that of the King of Cochin is a mile and a halfe up higher in the land.' Both were set on the banks of a broad, deep river flowing out of the mountains of the King of Pepper – whose subjects included many Christians of St Thomas's Order. St Thomas, poor Doubting Thomas, had travelled extensively in South India and, in AD 78, been martyred on a hill near the present site of Madras Airport.

We reached Aleppey, a town built on canals, in the early evening. On the bus into Cochin a chatty young man told me I should visit Aleppey for the snake-boat races at the end of the monsoon. 'We compete for the Nehru Cup. Each boat has a hundred rowers and many thousands come to watch.'

'What sort of boats are they?'

'Dug-out boats sir, richly carved and decorated like wedding cakes!'

A huge glittering surf boomed on the beach. I peered at the south-west horizon seeking some sign of the burst, but the young man told me it would not appear tonight. 'On the radio they said all signs are propitious for sunrise tomorrow. The air is moist, dew point is rising and we are assailed by butterflies.'

'I saw butterflies at Quilon,' I said. 'Blue ones.'

He smiled. 'They are a *most* propitious sign.'

My hotel stood on Willingdon Island, a piece of flat reclaimed land at the end of a causeway. I ordered a lamb curry for dinner. The waiter, who had a smirking, taunting manner, asked how hot I wanted it. Irritated, I told him I wanted it as hot as they could make it. The dish he placed silently before me caused palpitations of the heart, pounding in the temples, heavy perspiring and much general discomfort. The waiter loitered, grinning. Two cooks slipped out of the kitchen to watch. Reminding myself that I was in the ancient demesne of the King of Pepper I struggled on, finally wiping my plate clean and the smiles off their faces.

Afterwards, in the bar, I joined two middle-aged teetotallers who were disputing a local Malayalam newspaper report regarding the last time the monsoon had reached Kerala on 2 June. I bought them lime sodas and they translated for me. The paper said 1932, but they maintained it had occurred much more recently. 'It was year my youngest daughter, Dimple, was born,' said one. 'She is five so it must have been '82.'

'Dimple is six,' said his friend.

'Oh! Well, yes, but six only just.'

I left them arguing companionably and read a bit of Y. P. Rao before bed. A meteorologist named Narayanan had observed radar line echoes of rain squalls approaching Trivandrum, each roughly the size of Jamaica and visible on his screen while still 100 kilometres out to sea. On crossing the city the echoes broke into individual 100-kilometre-long cells which, travelling in convoy 15 kilometres apart, headed up the coast at an average speed of 40 kilometres an hour.

Among the papers listed by Rao for further reading was one called 'Radar Observations of Rain at Poona'.

In the next room an American woman was trying to make herself heard on the phone, shouting about silver ingots, though whether she was calling someone in Cochin or California I could not tell. Outside, the wind began to rise.

4 JUNE

I awoke to blue skies and birdsong. Shadowed by a smart little pilot boat a rusty Greek tanker steamed past my window, making for the open sea. Slim, rakish ferries were dashing around like frigates, linking the harbour islands – Willingdon and Bolgatty – with Fort Cochin and Mattancherry on the southern peninsula, and Ernakulam on the mainland. Ark-shaped wooden rice barges moved ponderously by, sails working fitfully in the light morning wind. The skipper of one, sitting on deck reading a newspaper, gravely lifted a hand to me. I drank some strong South Indian coffee and, though disconcerted by the continuing non-appearance of the monsoon, felt my spirits lifted by the proximity of this bright waterside city.

Vasco da Gama, installed as Portuguese Viceroy of the Indies, died here in 1524 and, until they shipped his remains home to Lisbon fourteen years later, lay buried in Fort Cochin's St Francis Church. It must have been a dangerous little town then. Da Gama had to keep the peace between his Portuguese merchants and the King of Cochin, a restless, footloose, often rebellious character with a personal bodyguard of homicidal aristocrats called *nairi* who, like Islamic fundamentalists, regarded it as glorious to die for the cause. Naked from the waist up, they wore their long hair in teetering, gravity-defying cockscombs and held all wives to be common property. (A sword propped by a wife's door indicated that its owner was exercising his rights inside.) Both sexes affected 'monstrous great' holes in their ear lobes. A visiting traveller named Caesar Frederick, measuring the circumference of one, put his arm through right 'up to the shoulder'. Their appetite for combat was notorious.

They harassed the Portuguese on land and, putting to sea in pirate fleets, all along the Malabar Coast.

Only the arrival of the monsoon could force a truce. Then the *nairi* went home, hung up their weapons and accompanied their women (or someone's women) on picnics to the countryside. While slaves pared their nails, rubbed their feet and scratched their heads, they gorged themselves on mangoes and, lolling by flooded ponds and streams, 'delighted to swimme and to bathe themselves'.

One of da Gama's preoccupations would have been the safety of his fleet during the burst and when, strolling around Willingdon Island, I came across the Port Authority building, it occurred to me that the present harbour master was, in one sense, the old conquistador's direct heir and successor.

I went in and, while waiting to catch the eye of the clerk in the reception booth, examined a large varnished board hanging in a cloister. It was headed 'Visual Storm Warning Section' and its brief paragraphs had been intricately painted by a signwriter in English and Malayalam.

I   There is a region of squally weather in which a storm
    may be forming.
II A storm has formed.
III The Port is threatened by stormy weather.
VII Port will experience severe weather from a cyclone
    expected to move over or close to the Port.

I asked the clerk for the harbour master's name.

'Captain Verghese Kuruvilla,' he said.

'Can I see him?'

'Not without previous appointment.' He picked up his pen. 'You are ship's master?'

'No. I'm writing a book.'

'What about?'

'The monsoon.'

He had wispy grey hair and a pendulous lower lip. He gave me a long, searching look. 'I think you must be quite eccentric,' he said finally and, for some reason, the notion seemed to please him. 'Give me your card. I will take you to harbour master.'

Moments later I found myself being ushered into a sunny office. Captain Kuruvilla seemed unsurprised by the intrusion. A keen-eyed, affable man in navy whites with four gold bars on either shoulder, he waved me to a chair and continued signing papers as I explained myself. Then he picked up a phone and said, 'Please ask Captain George and Captain Matthew to come in.' He replaced the phone. 'They are my senior pilots,' he said. 'They know Cochin Harbour as well as I do.' He retrieved his pen and went on signing. Chalked on a board were the names of the harbour vessels at his disposal that day; one, a hopper barge named *Gertrude Grigg*, perhaps immortalized some long-departed memsahib.

'When is the monsoon arriving?' I asked.

'This afternoon,' he said, without looking up. 'About four o'clock.'

The senior pilots entered moments later, two neat, smiling men who told me they boarded the inbound ships about five miles out, jumping from the deck of the Port Authority cutter to the Jacob's ladder slung down the vessel's side. During the monsoon squalls you got a six-foot swell running, so the jump required judgement. One colleague who recently mistimed his leap fell and broke his back.

'He wants to know about monsoon,' the harbour master informed them. He looked up. 'Today we will hoist signal No. III,' he said. 'Small craft warning. Black triangle with apex inverted. It will be raised by Director Ports (Minor) who has authority invested under the Act to do so.'

'It is a cautionary signal,' said Captain George. 'And it means that any small boats going out are not covered by insurance.'

'Is the harbour safe during the monsoon?' I asked.

Captain Kuruvilla bridled slightly. 'This is one of world's finest ports for weather. If you keep everything absolutely pukka it can stay open 365 days a year. We usually get squalls for first three days of monsoon and sometimes, out beyond the harbour, lofty waterspouts. After that it is just plain rain.'

Captain George said, 'Monsoon also causes a remarkable safety phenomenon. One that defies explanation.'

'Mystery mudbanks!' said Captain Matthew.

'When the monsoon bursts,' said Captain George, 'these mud-banks – lateritic soil lying on the seabed about five miles out – are stirred into a state of viscous suspension. Some unique quality in the mud calms the sea and makes the area over the mudbank a natural harbour. However violent the weather round about, the mudbank water will be smooth.'

'The rougher the seas outside,' said Captain Matthew, 'the calmer they are inside. You must see it to believe it.'

'The mudbanks are still as forest pools,' said Captain George. 'The ancient traders knew this and it was their reason for coming to Cochin. With the seas raging all around they could lie contendedly far off the coast to load their cargo, take on fresh water, fruit, vegetables and so on.'

'There are shrimps also,' said Captain Matthew.

'Certainly. The mudbank water is seething with them. You can almost scoop them up by hand. The phenomenon is called Chakara and lasts a few days only but, during that time, you can take 40,000 rupees of shrimp in a single catch. Kerala's Marxist government has decreed that only the small traditional fishermen in wallams may have access to this gold rush. The mechanized fellows in their little trawlers are not supposed to take part but, of course, they do, and the most terrific battles break out. By law the small men may defend their rights with swords. They use their swords with great vigour, fighting off the trawlermen like pirates. Then, suddenly, the shrimps are gone and, after the monsoon withdraws, the mudbanks too.'

'My aunty told me,' said Captain Matthew, 'that a health officer believed calming effect was due to bacteria from millions of floating coconut husks.'

Captain Kuruvilla looked up, plainly astonished. '*Coconut husks?*' he said.

'Yes, sir. According to my aunty.'

The harbour master's face was invaded by doubt. Then, sighing, he said, 'Well, anyway, this island we are on, Willingdon, 128 square kilometres, is also monsoon mud. It was reclaimed in two years, using a single dredger which later, by chance, sank. We had to alter the shipping channel by one degree to take cognizance of the wreck after blowing the top off with dynamite. The engineer responsible for this reclamation project was an Englishman named Sir Robert Bristow – a remarkable man shunned by the other

British because he married a nun. If you wish to know more about the harbour an excellent book has been written by chairman of Port Trust, Dr Babu Paul, who is only administrator in India with Ph.D in Theology.'

I asked Captain Kuruvilla where I might see some spice shops. 'Oh, Jew Town is where you will find the big traders and the Pepper Exchange,' he said. 'It's only ten minutes by taxi.' I thanked the captains for their time and set off, too embarrassed to tell them my main reason for visiting Jew Town was to buy an umbrella.

It lay across the causeway at Mattancherry, a tiny community living around the oldest synagogue in the Commonwealth. The origins of this surprising settlement go back to the arrival in Cochin of St Thomas in AD 52. It became a centre of the spice trade then and remains so today, a warren of narrow, swept streets, tumbledown buildings and dark little shops smelling of pepper, cloves, ginger, turmeric, cardamom and cumin. The synagogue standing in their midst was light, airy and spotless, the morning light gleaming on polished metal, precious stones and a floor paved with lustrous blue willow-pattern tiles.

'Every one of them different,' remarked the lean, pale-skinned old man who emerged suddenly from a doorway opposite and urged me to enter. 'They were brought from Canton in 1762.' He considered me with his head cocked to one side. 'Are you Jewish?'

'No. I've come to buy an umbrella.'

He nodded. 'Go to the place round the corner beyond Ganesh Trading. A Mr Chakravatty. Tell him Jacky Cohen sent you. And don't accept his first price.'

'Is he Jewish?'

'Chakravatty? No. There are no Jewish umbrella sellers left. Most of our people have gone away. There are only thirty-one of us here now – seven families. And next month one of the young men is emigrating to Israel. Marriage is now a big problem. We haven't had a local wedding for seventeen years – though a few months ago a couple from Manchester called here to get married on their way to Australia. His name was Kagan.'

I wandered around the resplendent little place, reading the inscribed brass plates. 'This mosaic flooring was done with the generous donation of Mr Luis Lindau of Mexico. In revered memory of his father, Mr Max Lindau.' Another read: 'In loving memory of Sabattai Koder, Warden of this Synagogue for over 40 years.' The atmosphere was calm and reverent, the air faintly scented with spices. Mr Cohen told me that the Cochin Jews, though a beleaguered minority, remained pillars of the local community. 'One is a retired colonel of the Indian Army, one a lieutenant-commander in the Navy. There are three lawyers, two doctors and an income tax consultant.'

'But no rabbi?'

He smiled. 'The elders are qualified to hold marriages and religious services. In fact yesterday we conducted the festival of Shabuoth, held on 3 June, the date of the monsoon's arrival.'

'You were a day early.'

'It happens,' he said. 'God and the weather men do not always see eye to eye.'

I walked down Jew Cemetery Lane to Mr Chakravatty's little shop, but he had sold out of umbrellas. 'Panic buying,' he said crisply, peering through thick spectacles. 'Burst coming this afternoon. Umbrellas, galoshes, general rainwear – everything gone.' He hesitated and then, with some reluctance, added, 'You may find a few items remaining over at Ernakulam. Near railway station. But they will be inferior and you will have to get move on. When the monsoon arrives many shops will close while people promenade in streets.'

Nearby, in the low, dim, thick-walled rooms of Rainbow Enterprises, a friendly young man offered me a washed kernel of black pepper. 'Garden Farm variety,' he said eagerly, urging me to take a bite. I did, and it went off in my head like a firecracker. 'This luxury pepper, sir, much loved in the Soviet Union. I buy direct from hill farmers at Sultan Battery.' He called it Sooltan Batteree.

Outside, the sky remained blue, the breeze fitful, the sea calm. I bought oranges at a small shop advertising 'Bread, Bun and Fruity' and, back at the hotel, read the *Indian Express* over an iced Kingfisher beer. 'Monsoon Advances' announced the confident front page headline. 'The south-west monsoon that set in over South Kerala yesterday has advanced towards the north, bringing heavy rain over Malabar and North Lakshadweep. Fishermen have been warned not to venture out to sea, as strong westerly winds reaching a speed of 50–60 k.p.h. are likely along the North Kerala coast.'

Copious amounts of rain had been registered at twenty-one centres to the south and, at Kottayam, the first monsoon fatalities recorded. Four members of a picnic party drowned while bathing 'in the flood waters of a stream at the Teekov Estates. While two bodies were recovered by the other members of the party who had swum ashore, the bodies of the other two were located by a searching party of fire brigade this morning.'

Leafing through the paper I noted that the political correspondents were using seasonal similes. 'In the dark clouds gathering thick on the external as well as internal horizons of India, a silver lining is provided by the unanimous approach taken by important Opposition parties . . .'

I called David McCririch, described by Babu Varghese as the last of Cochin's resident British traders. He sounded a little wary but suggested a meeting the following evening. 'You may as well come around to the house for a drink,' he said. 'We might even go on to the club. I'll pick you up at 4.30.'

'I'll be waiting.'

'There's a little jetty at the bottom of the garden behind your hotel. Wait on that. I go home in the company launch.'

It began to cloud over early in the afternoon – long, high cirriform streamers which thickened and darkened and turned into heavy bubbles of cumulus. I watched an Indian Airlines 737 descend into Cochin, tunnelling through the cloud, leaving a dissipation trail of clear air behind it. The wind came soon afterwards and, on the harbour, the lumbering rice barges began to pitch and toss. Spray broke over the bows of a crowded ferry tearing by to Ernakulam and I could see the standing passengers swaying about. On a patch of waste ground near Bristow Road a man stood flying a kite. He had a beaky nose and thick, tangled silvery hair. The kite soared so high it was barely visible.

'How long is the string?' I asked.

'I don't know. A hundred metres, perhaps. Actually, it isn't mine. I am holding it for a friend.' He tugged at the latticed wooden spindle but the kite, cavorting like a bird, did not respond. 'In China they are calling this Climbing the Heights,' he said. 'They put primitive flutes in the kites which make moaning noises in the wind.'

'Where's your friend?'

'He had to visit his mother.'

We watched the kite. 'According to the ancient Vedic classics,' I said, 'this south-west wind is supposed to have healing qualities. Isn't it good for the eyesight?'

He grunted. 'I am not inclined to believe that stuff – and I speak as a teacher of Indian history, ancient and modern. Anyway, winds also have harmful properties. East wind provokes phlegm and gives you ulcers; north dissipates phlegm but gives you TB. The south and west are the sweetest winds, specially this one, the west, which is very lemony and light.'

I said the west wind was forecast to blow at between 50 and 60 k.p.h. today.

'I am meaning light in the sense of innate qualities.' He frowned. 'As in light hearts, light music, light verse.' Then he glanced at me. 'Might I ask a favour? Would you be kind enough to take the kite for a few moments? I must dash off quickly.'

Seeing the doubt invade my face he added, 'I have to answer a call of nature.'

'Very well. But you promise to return?'

'My friend will probably be back even before me,' he said, handing me the spindle and hurrying away.

The last time I had taken charge of one of these flimsy tissue-paper-and-bamboo tetrahedrons had been as a boy in the Fiji Islands. My Indian school friends taught me the trick of first passing the twine through a compound of flour paste and crushed light bulbs so that, in flight, it had the cutting edge of a scalpel; drifting your kite downwind on to an opponent's you severed his line and kept his kite as a trophy of war. Now, standing on that Cochin wasteland, I felt the old skills returning. I was able to manage the kite instinctively, holding it balanced in the eye of the wind, enjoying this privileged contact with the monsoon. Sometimes the wind swirled, coming simultaneously from all directions and making the kite spin, but mostly it blew with growing strength and certitude.

A car slowed with two men in it. They laughed and shouted something derisory. Then, just as I was wondering how long I must stay here, a small boy rode up on an old Raleigh bike, dismounted and walked across.

'Is this your kite?' I asked.

He nodded, wordlessly.

I handed it over and continued on my way.

I put through a random call to External Affairs in Delhi and, to my astonishment, someone picked up the phone. I asked to speak to Prasad Rao and a faint, crackling voice said he was on long leave.

The voice heard my anguished groan. 'What is wrong? Who is this?' it said sharply.

I introduced myself.

'Ah, yes. You are monsoon man, correct? I am P. D. Gupta and I have taken over your case. All relevant applications have been made and I am hoping news will be good. Please call back early next week.'

At 1 p.m. the serious cloud build-up started. Two hours fifty minutes later racing cumulus extinguished the sun and left everything washed in an inky violet light. At 4.50, announced by deafening ground-level thunderclaps, the monsoon finally rode into Cochin. The cloud-base blew through the trees like smoke; rain foamed on the hotel's harbourside lawn and produced a bank of hanging mist opaque as hill fog. In the coffee shop the waiters rushed to the windows, clapping and yelling, their customers forgotten. One, emerging from the kitchen bearing a teapot destined for the conference room (where, it was rumoured, executives of the Indian Spices Board sat in closed session), glimpsed the magniloquent spectacle outside, banged the teapot down on my table and ran to join them crying, 'Ho! Ho! Ho!'

Heaving a door open I stepped outside. Soaked to the skin within seconds I felt a wonderful sense of flooding warmth and invigoration; it was, indubitably, a little bit like being born again. Raindrops rang like coins on the flagstoned path and the air was filled with fusillades of crimson flowers from the flamboyant trees; they went arcing by like tracer and, raked by an especially mean burst, I can testify that flamboyant blossoms hitting you in the eye at 60 k.p.h. cause pain and temporary loss of vision. At Fort Cochin they were ringing the bells in St Francis Church. In the

dark harbour small boats ran for home. Waves bursting over the
scalloped sea wall were suffused, curiously, with pink light. The
jetty, set under a small wooden gazebo, vanished beneath heavy
surf. Orange tiles cladding the gazebo's steeply pitched roof began
to tremble until, like clay pigeons being sprung, they went whirling
off into the murk one by one.

Then, from the corner of an eye still watering from the flower
strike, I witnessed an astonishing scene. Two straining waiters held
the coffee shop door open while a party of men and women filed
into the storm. The men wore button-down shirts and smart
business suits, the women best-quality silk saris and high-heeled
shoes; as they emerged, they opened their arms and lifted their
faces to the rain.

The Spices Board had come out to greet the monsoon.

They made for the jetty, strolling, laughing out loud, calling,
revolving slowly in a kind of dreamlike gavotte. In the gazebo they
stood knee-deep in seething water while the wind blew spiralling
flumes of rain up over the peak of the disintegrating roof; the
flumes united there in a fountainhead which, along with the tiles,
kept getting snatched away. Buffeted by the gusts, unbalanced by
the waves, the Spices Board executives clung to each other with
water in their eyes and looks of sublime happiness on their faces. A
young woman in a soaked and flapping gold-coloured sari laughed
at me and clapped her hands. 'Paradise will be like this!' she
shouted.

Back in the coffee shop, though, an emergency had been declared.
A young food and beverages manager stood bawling at his waiters,
ordering them to bring mops, buckets, plastic sheeting and old
bedspreads. From the surrounds of each door and window rain
came seeping in like the sea invading a leaking ship. Indeed, it
wasn't hard to imagine that the coffee shop had been floated off by
the flood tide and now drifted perilously across Cochin Harbour.
Some trick of the light gave the intruding freshets the lambency of
flame. Once on the floor, though, it became plain water, starting to
lie about in very significant quantities; as it lapped at my shoes the
young manager thrust a mop at me. 'Sir, please lend a hand!'

Everyone was in an excellent humour. Guests and waiters worked cheerily together and, after we had sealed off major problem areas like percolating door frames and made the coffee shop reasonably – though by no. means totally – secure, there were drinks on the house. We all stood around, toasting the monsoon in country liquor distilled from cashew flowers.

When the Spices Board finally trailed in calling for hot tea and towels, making new puddles and undoing much of our good work, we greeted them with pursed lips and the darkest of looks.

The morning after next I planned to catch a bus to Calicut, two hours to the north, then another bus – perhaps one of the new Super De Luxe Colour Video Coaches – on to Goa. The monsoon would be in Calicut tonight and that was fine; I wanted, this time, to arrive behind it. Goa, though, was a different matter. Anxious not to miss the monsoon party of my friends, the Baptistas, and unable to raise them on the phone, I needed to get there comfortably ahead of the burst.

A brusque man at the Cochin Meteorological Office estimated it would reach Goa in four days, on 8 June. Well, that would give me a clear forty-eight hours on the road. Now my travelling companion roared and trumpeted away out there in the dark garden, the waves clumping against the sea wall, blown leaves and twigs pattering against my window, more water pouring in through the frame. I listened contentedly. At least it was here, where I could keep an eye on it, and giving Cochin a vintage performance.

There was a faint sound at my door and a piece of paper came sliding underneath. I opened it quickly and saw the lady in the gold-coloured sari padding up the corridor, slipping papers under every door, leaving damp footprints on the carpet. Turning, she spotted me and smiled. The sari still clung to her body, which was full and very fine, and her smile had that same brilliance I had seen in the garden. Wanting to talk to her I asked whether the monsoon's arrival had been noted in the minutes of the Spices Board meeting.

She said, 'We are only affiliates of Spices Board. But we are spices *people*.'

Then she moved on and I picked up her paper. It carried a printed message reading:

ARE YOU HOOKED TO SMOKING? UNHOOK YOURSELF! Every
time you itch for a cigarette reach into your pocket and pop
in a cardamom. A few days of this and you are a free man. A
new man!
    Cardamom achieves two things in one stroke: It breaks a
killer-habit and builds a healthy one. Cardamom adds fragrance to your breath, aids digestion, improves appetite,
eliminates giddiness and prevents or cures several disorders.

This second exposure to the burst had no effect on the speed of my
watch or the state of my neck. But that night I dreamed that, out
walking on the upper declivities of the Western Ghats, I got struck
by lightning and found myself able to speak nineteen languages.

5 JUNE

The initial thrust of the monsoon had moved on by morning,
leaving a few random squalls behind. A big green container ship,
Genoa-registered and sitting deep enough to cover the Tropical Sea
Water loading line on her Plimsoll mark, went heading out through
the rain. Watching it, I reflected that the presence of Italian
freighters in Cochin was merely the continuation of a practice
begun when the Romans first 'discovered' the monsoon. Once they
realized its winds would blow their galleys out and then blow them
home again, and that the remarkable monsoon mudbanks guaranteed them safe anchorages, they became regular visitors. The
quantities of Roman coins found on this part of the Malabar Coast
testify to the Roman craze for Indian luxury goods. Ancient records
note shipments of pepper, pearls, ivory, fine silks, betel, diamonds,
jacinths, tortoiseshell, rice, ghee, honey, cotton, muslins, 'sashes',
cinnamon-leaf, ginger grass, bactrian and indigo.
    It was Nero who put Cochin on the Roman map. He wore
Indian silks and bathed in Indian spikenard. His bedchamber was
decked in Indian pearls, his palace in Indian gems and tortoiseshell.
He installed a plumbing system of gold and silver pipes which ran
with distilled Indian fragrances. The rich competed with each
other in an orgy of excess. They were mad for the products of India

and the Roman Senate began to look like a convention of maharajas. Though Seneca complained about the ostentation – 'precious woods bought at huge prices, crystal and agate vessels lavishly displayed' – he himself owned five hundred tables with legs of Indian ivory. Petronius reported acidly that Roman courtesans were demanding payment in Indian jewels and essences (poorer women, unable to afford the real thing, had to make do with paste imitations of Indian originals).

The Roman Empire perished but Cochin, shrewdly exploiting its monsoon winds and mudbank sanctuaries, continued trading. Da Gama, aware of the *monção* and accompanied by a knowledgeable Gujarati pilot, sailed in on the crest of the 1498 burst and, at Calicut a few miles up the coast, loaded up with spices. Back in Lisbon these earned him a 600-per-cent profit. The Portuguese hurriedly established a colony in Cochin, buying pepper ('The shrub is like unto our Ivie tree'), ginger ('It groweth like unto our Garlicke'), cloves ('Their Tree is like to our Bay tree'), sandalwood ('The white Sandoll is wood very sweet'), camphor ('a precious thing among the Indians, and sold dearer than gold'), musk (taken from 'a litle beast like unto a yong Roe . . . they beat him to death . . . cut out the bones, and beat the flesh with the blood very small, and fill the skin with it'), benjamin, amber and a host of precious stones.

Wondering what kind of stuff the Italian ship might have been taking home now I arranged to call on Manju Menon at Ocean Containers. Mr Menon, a dapper man with the language and manners of an Oxford High Table, shrugged and said, 'My dear chap, little changes. We still trade in tea, coffee, black pepper, cashews, ginger, chilli and spices. There have been a few new developments since the Portuguese were here, of course. We now export seafood and knitwear – mostly handloom stuff from Cannanore. We used to send frogs' legs to France but, much to the dismay of the local farmers who made extra rupees by catching the frogs, our conservationists have had a ban imposed; you need a thriving frog population to keep the mosquitoes down.'

A servant brought tea and English biscuits. We settled back in our chairs. Rain beat on the windows and the wind moaned in from the sea. It was very cosy.

'But you are interested in the monsoon? Well, it slows us up. You can't load containers on to the ships because they start spinning in the wind. I do not share the romantic view held by many of my countrymen. A good Hindu is supposed to remember the monsoon in his prayers and, back in the days when he also prayed for his king, would even refer to him as the "rain-maker". For me, though, there's nothing metaphysical or symbolic about it. It's merely a period when the phones go down and the lights fail. Old people, feeling the chill, take out their socks and shawls. The problems of keeping clothes and shoes dry are formidable; you must place naked light bulbs in every cupboard and, always assuming the electricity is working, keep them burning day and night. And it's the time mildew grows on books; when your *Complete Works of Shakespeare* starts turning pea green a certain melancholy, inevitably, sets in.'

I bought a paper on the way home and was instantly transfixed by a headline on the front page. 'Heavy Rain Lashes Goa,' it said. 'Monsoon Due Today.' *Today*? It wasn't supposed to reach Goa for another three days. In a state of bewilderment bordering on panic I hurried to Cox and Kings, the travel agency, and asked about flights.

The clerk, a thin, fastidious man with a heavy moustache, said, 'The next is tomorrow morning. But it may not be able to land. They are having flooded runways, bad visibility and so on.'

'Is there a seat?'

'On this flight that may not land?'

'The same,' I said.

'No.'

'Can you put me on stand-by?'

He gave me the look of someone who'd just had a gun pulled on him, sucked hard at his moustache and yanked the telephone towards him. The telephone wasn't working and he announced this with a triumphant light in his eye. But other people in the office were yelling down phones and I begged him to try again. When he finally got through he made it sound like a bad line to Yokohama. Gloomily, he told me to report to the airport on Willingdon at 8 a.m. and, as I left, delivered his parting shot. 'There are already nine other standy-bys. And Goa weather forecast for tomorrow is very, very bad.' He beamed at me. 'Have a nice day!'

I wondered about the nature of this monsoon. The personality emerging was like that of a troublesome relative about whom responsible family members were constantly worrying – he's disappeared again, he's turned up on so-and-so's doorstep, he's in trouble with the police, he got drunk on the train and finished up in Minneapolis. I would have to keep a very, very close eye on it.

David McCririch's company launch was a venerable straight-stemmed wooden pinnace with an enclosed aft cabin where three executives sat in safari suits. The sea around the hotel jetty had abated and become a heavy, oily swell. It made the launch pitch and roll and the coxswain, nosing in cautiously, clearly liked it as little as I did. 'Jump, sir!' he cried. He threw his engine full astern while I was still in the air. I came heavily down on a deck which was sharply rising and also going backwards.

In the cabin Mr McCririch, a trim, bearded, quietly spoken man in his forties, introduced me to his two Indian colleagues. Their company, Harrison Malayalam, owned tea and coffee plantations. They had all worked in the field, managing plantations themselves and now, elevated to high office, daily rode back and forth in their fine old admiral's barge. 'It is a perk,' one of them said.

At Port Cochin, reached a few minutes later, chauffeur-driven Hindustan Ambassador saloons awaited them. Mr McCririch sent his driver home and took the wheel himself. 'These cars are built to last forty years,' he said. 'It's an awesome idea. Forty years on Indian roads! Forty monsoons! The price you pay, though, is minimal acceleration. It can take several days to go from nought to sixty.'

We set off through cramped streets lined with thick-walled buildings erected a couple of centuries earlier by the Dutch. Bales of tea, nuts, coir and spices were being manhandled on and off trucks, causing small, resigned traffic jams. We passed a random arrangement of ancient stones named Vasco da Gama Square for the tourists, then stopped off at St Francis Church to see the empty tomb which once held the remains of the Admiral of India. Built by the Portuguese midway through the sixteenth century, St Francis has echoed with the languages and ecclesiastical preoccupations of the European powers who moved in and out of Cochin. In the seventeenth century it became Dutch Protestant, in the eighteenth Anglican. Now it is used by the Church of South India; but, having absorbed all these faiths, the church reflects none. It is just an old warehouse with a bell on top and, as we walked out, Mr McCririch directed a cautious glance at the belfry.

'The last time I brought someone here,' he said, 'the bell fell down. It's a huge thing, cast in bronze, and it came crashing to earth seconds after I'd passed. There was an almighty thud and later I kept wondering whether, from an insurance point of view, being killed by the bloody thing would have been regarded as an act of God.'

The McCririch residence, a two-storeyed villa standing behind a high wall, lay in the leafiest, most exclusive part of Cochin. He nodded at other villas visible through the trees. 'There were fifty British families here when we first came,' he said. 'It was like Tunbridge Wells in the tropics. My wife, Anne-Marie, is Norwegian so I seem to be the last. And next year we're going too.'

Anne-Marie, a good-looking woman in a green cotton frock, came out to meet the car. She had blonde hair, tired eyes and the quick, uncertain smile of someone unaccustomed to entertaining strangers. There were fallen flowers all over the lawn, and the pale evening sky yielded light, fitful showers.

'Is anything the matter?' asked David.

'It's the power.'

'Oh, goodness,' he said, resignedly. 'The monsoon really has started.'

'All afternoon it's been on-off,' she said. 'Now it's more off than on.'

'Freezer okay?'

'So far, yes.' She hesitated. 'Please can we go to the club? You can show Alex.' To me she said, 'We always go when David gets back from the office. I'm cooped up in the house all day long and I have to get out.'

The Cochin Club, a sprawling, tile-roofed bungalow, still contains a magnificent curved bar cut like a pulpit from solid rosewood. But there was nobody there. It sported neither barman nor bottles, the only tenuous sign of life an elephant's head mounted on the wall behind. The pallid light seemed as stale as the air and I reckoned the room's sad circumstances effectively precluded the presence of ghosts. The shades of the gin-swilling curry-guzzlers who had once made these rafters ring wouldn't be seen dead, so to speak, in such a place.

'We stopped doing drinks some time ago,' said David. 'The government suddenly upped the liquor permit for clubs to 50,000 rupees. We couldn't possibly afford that.'

He waved away an elderly bearer who darted at me from the shadows clutching a visitors' book, and led us to the library, another dim, musty room lined with glass-fronted cases of paperbacks. At a small desk a white-uniformed clerk sat before an ink pad and a date stamp. He was drowsing when we entered but now sat up straight with an expression of great alertness.

'I buy the books,' said David. 'My budget allows for seven a month. I choose them from the review pages of the *Daily Telegraph*.'

'People will turn up later,' said Anne-Marie. 'These days they are all Indians, of course, but they are a very decent crowd. They are our friends.'

We drove back through the cool shadows of the monsoon dusk. A kingfisher flared past the McCririchs' gate. Their living room was enormous, high-ceilinged and sparsely furnished in the tropical manner. It was dark. 'We'd love to ask you to dinner,' said David, 'but I'm afraid it's cook's night off.'

He had cold beer, though, and fetched it from the kitchen, which was lit. A 40-foot-long electrical cable consisting of several short cables randomly connected led from the kitchen to a glass tank containing a few lethargic tropical fish. A blower was discharging bubbles into the tank. Anne-Marie said she had spent half the morning constructing this life-support system.

'We have three separate electrical circuits in the house – there's no particular reason for that; it's just the way it was built – so when the rains come and one circuit fails I can connect the fish up to another. In this climate you have to stay ahead of the game.'

'What if they all fail?' I asked.

'Well, it happens,' she said, quietly.

The living-room lights suddenly came on and we all smiled at each other. David poured more beer and talked of his tea plantations in the hills. Anne-Marie brought a dish of walnuts. She said she missed her daughters. Both were in England, one at school, the other completing a secretarial course before going off to Italy. Rain pattered on the leaves outside. A car came sloshing through the gloom and stopped at the house next door.

The blower serving the fish tank suddenly went quiet. Circuit two was down. This signified the loss of the air-conditioning and the lights in the upstairs bedrooms and, as Anne-Marie sat staring fixedly at her silent tank, circuit one went also, darkening the living room. Seconds later the failure of the kitchen light indicated that all three circuits were inoperative.

'The freezer,' said Anne-Marie. 'It's absolutely full of food.' She sounded close to tears.

'Why don't you call the electricity people?' I asked.

'That is a hollow joke,' said Anne-Marie.

'They've knocked off,' said David. 'Anyway, their engineers wouldn't go out in this weather, not in the dark. A line's down somewhere – probably hit by a falling tree. They won't start looking till morning.'

Sitting there in the silent, unpowered house, we spoke of the monsoon. Anne-Marie said the worst thing was snakes. 'The rains bring them out. Once we had a cobra in our woodshed. We never saw it but the cook said it was there. He had never seen it either but, in the Indian way, he knew. And he started to get very agitated.'

'We called in the snake charmer,' said David.

'He just walked into the woodshed and said, "Yes, you have a cobra here." Then he fumbled around in all that firewood and yanked it out with his bare hands.' I sensed her shudder. 'It was so . . . thick.'

Each year, after the rains began, David routinely summoned the snake charmer, who would stand in the garden, playing his pipe. 'They'd come out from all over, dozens of them, and crawl right up to him. He had a shallow basket and he just popped them in, like groceries. Then he sold them to some medical institute where they milked them for the venom.'

'Do you remember the time his basket was absolutely filled with snakes and, suddenly, he tipped it over?'

The lights came on. The fish tank blower began to hiss and, from the kitchen, came the reassuring hum of the freezer. But, even as Anne-Marie laughed and clapped her hands, all three circuits died again. In the living room the silence and tension grew. David cleared his throat and told the snake basket story.

'The charmer had got so many he suddenly demanded a surcharge. Two rupees per snake, I think. I told him it wasn't on, so he just kicked the basket over and let them all loose again.'

'It was a very shocking moment,' said Anne Marie. 'One of the girls was just a baby then. I had her in my arms and I ran away.'

It was pretty depressing, sitting there in the gloom, so I suggested we go to my hotel for a drink. David agreed with alacrity but, as we stood, all the circuits came back on. Anne Marie, blinking at the fish tank, said she would stay. Then, as they went off again, she decided to come. As we drove out through the gate the whole house suddenly lit up and flashed mockingly at us, radiance pouring from every window. David braked sharply and Anne-Marie, gazing back, said, 'Oh, Lord. I think ... perhaps we ... No! The hell with it! Let's go and have some vodka!'

Later I chatted to a Canadian who told me he had just come from a monsoon party at the house of an Anglo-Indian business acquaintance. 'We spent the whole God-damn evening dancing Swiss reels,' he reported incredulously.

Y. P. Rao wrote: 'George and Datta report that a monsoon depression of September 1963 was formed out of the remnants of a typhoon from the Pacific.' These remnants were steered to India by an anticyclone and, on arrival, turned into a rain-laden 'warm tongue'.

I knew that western Pacific sea temperatures and hurricane activity were among the many global factors considered by Indians trying to predict the monsoon. (They must also take into account the barometric pressures in Buenos Aires, Jakarta, Darwin and the Seychelles, rainfall in Java, Zimbabwe and Zanzibar, winter snowfalls in the Himalayas, even the depth of the Antarctic ice cap.) But this was the first time I had seen it suggested that cloud-borne water from the South Seas might sail halfway round the world to join the Indian rains.

The idea of our patch of ocean being a tributory, however minor, of the great summer monsoon would have pleased my father. It would have demonstrated that we were more useful than many supposed. Such was people's ignorance of our islands that, whenever he managed to get a few weeks' leave in Australia, and charging neither fees nor expenses, my father gave lectures. He became a kind of unofficial spokesman for the New Hebrides, frank about the depopulation and public health problems but also offering lyrical descriptions of the group's tranquil beauty and friendly natives, even its investment, real estate and vacation possibilities.

There was a curious aftermath to these church-hall activities. When, a few weeks after the German surrender, wild rumours began circulating that Hitler had arrived in a U-boat crammed with stolen Rembrandts and Nazi gold (a story still given credence twenty years later) I became convinced that the substance of my father's lectures had been confidentially circulated in Berlin. He modestly discounted the idea but also wondered how, if the story were true, Hitler had ever got to hear of us.

My father felt Hitler should not be hanged but placed in charge of promotions and publicity for the whole of Western Melanesia. He might be a lunatic but he would certainly put us on the map.

I packed and worried about seat availability on the morning flight to Goa. I tried to call the Baptistas in Bombay but the line yielded only a series of harp-like strumming noises. Something was happening out on the dark harbour. Two pilot cutters and a police launch went racing by in the rain, reminding me of an earlier Cochin Harbour emergency reported in Purchas. An anonymous Portuguese seaman, helping to hang a new rudder on a ship preparing to depart for Lisbon in 1583, was attacked by a shark. It took one leg clean off at the middle of his thigh and then, as the sailor put down an arm to feel his wound, took the arm too 'and also a peece of his buttocke'.

The lights went off and, groping like a blind man, I made my way to bed.

Chapter Five

❀

I shared a taxi to the airport with a heavy-set, pipe-smoking bookseller on the Madras stand-by list. He told me that the Indian Airlines national computer network was down. 'That is not unusual,' he said. 'It's a frail, sickly creature with only a tenuous hold on life.'

A scrum of people surged and heaved around the stand-by counter. It was manned by a single clerk who kept muttering to someone seated behind a faded pink curtain. The bookseller, shoving with me, using his briefcase with casual ruthlessness, thought this concealed clerk might be operating the emergency seat-allocation system. 'He will be using a crystal ball,' he said. 'Perhaps even dice or tea-leaves.'

When, reaching the counter, we finally caught the clerk's eye, he told me there was plenty of room on the Goa plane but big problems at Goa. 'They got two inches yesterday,' he said. 'You know they have monsoon now?'

'Yes.'

'There is waterlogging on aerodrome. And bad weather, min. vis., impossible conditions for landing. Yesterday Bombay Airbus made two attempts but captain call it off and go home. He will try again today.'

'And we shall try also?' I asked.

'Yes, we shall try.' He handed us our boarding passes. 'Madras is clear, but for Goa there will be some delay. Phones are down and we are still awaiting latest weather update.'

The bookseller said, 'Any excuse. The last time I flew Bombay–

Karachi with you people there was a nine-hour wait because the Airbus had been struck by a pigeon.'

The clerk laughed. 'That's a good one!'

We passed through security. 'Remove all key and coinage from pockets!' cried the officer. In the departure lounge the bookseller said, 'It is *quality* of their excuses that sets IA apart from every other airline in the world. The computer goes dead, the plane don't show up, there is chronic overbooking, but from the Excuses Commissariat you always get work of the very highest standard.' He stuffed clove-scented tobacco into his pipe. 'A tiger ate the pilot.' Tamping it down he said, 'That is the kind of premise they like to start with. You can do some very interesting things with an idea like that, exploring it, building on it, changing the facts to suit the gullibility of your audience – but never losing the element of shock and surprise.'

I laughed and asked him what he had been selling in Cochin.

'Not selling,' he said. 'Buying. Yesterday at Ernakulam I managed to acquire a first edition of the *Glossary of the Madras Presidency*, a late-nineteenth-century volume – mine's slightly foxed but otherwise in excellent condition – for which a customer at home will pay a small fortune. During Britain's imperial days India was divided into four such Presidencies, and the *Glossary* covers every conceivable aspect of their rule.'

He lit his pipe.

'Including the weather?'

I saw an eyebrow raised through the smoke. 'Certainly the weather. We Indians are obsessed by the subject and so were the British. Madras, remember, had Asia's first observatory, built in 1792.'

'But you don't get the monsoon.'

'Not this monsoon. We get the winter monsoon, running roughly from October to Christmas. It's a fairly minor affair compared to the summer one, but it's featured in another rare and wonderful book – almost two thousand peasants' proverbs collected and published by British officials of the Presidency. Perhaps a quarter of them are monsoon proverbs.'

'Do you know any?'

A voice on the Tannoy announced that the Madras flight was now ready for boarding.

'Oh, God,' he said. 'I used to. My father did. He was a land-owner. There's one about a rainbow in the east promising enough rain to make your tank overflow. And if you saw shooting stars on certain nights you weren't supposed to plant in the valleys; torrential rain would wash away your crops. A lunar eclipse also meant heavy rain. So did Venus setting south of the moon. A new moon on a Tuesday, however, promised drought and starvation.'

He knocked out his pipe and stood. 'Sons were equated with rainfall, in the sense that a successful farmer needed plenty of both; many proverbs made that point. But the one that best sums it up is, "If the sky fails, the earth will surely fail too".'

He raised a hand and hurried away.

The Goa flight was called moments later. Aboard the half-empty 737 a tall, friendly stewardess offered me liquorice-flavoured fennel seeds, cotton wool for my ears and three newspapers. These confirmed that the monsoon was abroad in Goa, all right, and displaying the hooligan side of its nature. Many shops in low-lying areas had been flooded. Traffic on National Highway 17 was diverted when 'the temporary kutcha bund across a rivulet at Verna was washed away'. The failure of the makeshift arrangement (bypassing a culvert 'damaged during the language agitation in December') led to jams, hot tempers, even a spate of minor accidents, and people on the spot had been quick to voice their indignation. 'It was the unanimous view of all travellers that the concerned authorities should have hurried with the work in view of the oncoming monsoon.'

When the stewardess brought coffee I showed her the report and asked what was meant by 'language agitation'.

She said, 'It is a long-standing problem. Goans want Konkani, their traditional language, to be made the official language of Goa. Delhi said no, so in Goa there were riots.'

I sipped my coffee. The 737 reached its cruising altitude and throttled back. Through a scattering of cirrus far below I could see that we were following the coast, flying up the lofty green battlements of the Western Ghats, 600 miles long and up to 5,000 feet high. Monsoon winds deflected around the mountains formed offshore vortices, powerful enough to snap an aircraft in two, which were discharging heavy, sustained rain into the sea.

We passed over the red roofs of Calicut, where Vasco da Gama made his first Indian landfall. Along here, in 1789, Tipu Sultan had engaged the British in a famous campaign that demonstrated how mobile, fast-moving guerrilla forces will always outflank a static army commanded by dull, conservative generals. Tipu, operating from a series of fortified hilltop *droogs*, ran rings around the British as they ponderously mounted the Ghats with their armaments – each cannon pushed by an elephant while scores of men and oxen hauled on drag-ropes – and a stupefying amount of personal baggage. A typical captain went into battle with a large bed, several chairs, a folding table, two pairs of candle shades, twenty-four linen suits, several dozen bottles of wine, brandy and gin, tea, sugar and biscuits, a hamper of live poultry, a milch goat, seven trunks containing cooking utensils, cutlery, crystal and table linen, and a palanquin. The palanquin coolies were followed by a head boy, a lesser boy, a cook, an ostler, a grass-cutter and two bullock drivers for the four baggage bullocks.

We passed over Mangalore, the world's busiest cashew nut port.

In the *Goa Herald* they were advertising rainwear. 'Don't Let the Monsoon Be an Impediment in Your Daily Routine!' A cartoon showed a crowd of drenched Goans preparing to disembark from a D-Day-style landing craft. The ad, inserted by Malsons, the House of Quality Rainwear, was for a range of products called Duckback.

A baby had arrived in Goa with the burst. 'Leonora & Gromiko praise the Lord and joyfully announce the birth of their first born bonny boy on 5th June at Dr Rebello Hospital, Margao.'

The *Times of India* reported 'traces of rain' in Bombay. The monsoon wasn't due there for another four days; so, despite a forecast that included gusty winds and one or two showers, I wasn't unduly worried. It was normal enough for the time of year. I made a mental note, though, to keep an eye on developments in Bombay.

Twenty minutes out of Goa, in clear air, the captain switched on the seat-belt sign, flashing it twice for emphasis. Glancing out of the window, I saw why. Several miles ahead the horizon was walled off. The wall seemed to run laterally for 180 degrees and vertically from the sea to the sun. No path could be discerned around it and, as far as I could judge, none through. This huge black structure was slab-sided all the way up, giving off the faint shine of dressed stone and possessing, evidently, a mass and density to match. In its shadow small eddies and undertows caused the 737 to flex its wings. When it flew into the wall it staggered and fell, the violence of the drop suggesting a sudden conflict of forces, gravity matching engine thrust perhaps; then it bottomed out with a juddering bang and, for the first time, I found myself inside the core of the monsoon.

We were enclosed in a misty cell, faintly marbeloid and giving off a soft, mysterious brightness. Some trick of diffracted light produced a glowing pink corona. This flashed on and off with metronomic regularity and, even as I exalted at witnessing some evidence of the monsoon's pulse, I realized it must be the 737's rooftop beacon. The cloud chamber enclosing us seemed to lead off into others. There were hints of corridors and hallways, domed ante-rooms and courtyards going on for miles. That beguiling radiance permeated everywhere. I observed all this with something close to elation. Indian Airlines had brought me right into the monsoon's lair.

But, by God, it was rough in there. The atmosphere, despite appearances, was curdled and lumpy, and we were making very heavy weather of it. Monsoon cumulus is subject to a phenomenon called Conditional Instability of the Second Kind, caused by the eccentric passage of heat through its various layers and, banging through all that grumous air, I thought we might be getting some of it now.

During the violent early turbulence the tall stewardess, checking people's belts, had half-fallen into an empty seat across the aisle. She fastened her own belt very tightly, then sat with fingers pressed to her temples and eyes closed. Now she opened them and glanced over.

'I am hating this,' she said. 'I have just finished training, you know. This is my first monsoon in the profession.'

'We'll be landing soon.'

'The sky becomes a wild place. Sometimes you wonder how plane can survive. It becomes a tiny frail thing – a moth.'

She bent her head and closed her eyes again.

The 737 went banging and lurching on, subtle tonal changes coming from its whining turbines. It started its descent, sometimes making lateral slewing motions, sometimes leaping and diving. All along the cabin's length the heads of passengers nodded, shook and swayed in unison. Everyone was clinging on. Then, with a final wild flourish, it broke through the murk and Goa lay below.

It was a land of mirrors. Miles of flooded paddies and puddled roads reflected the pewtery light in a shining mosaic that rippled right along the horizon. It looked serenely beautiful, a glass kingdom set in a water garden.

We touched down beside two women washing pots in a runway storm drain. A security officer manning a non-operational crossing barrier waved us by with one hand while, with the other, he held back an impatient press of lorries, cyclists and pedestrians. Another 737, taking off, vanished into its own spray. It became a whirling white cloud that went howling down the runway like a tiny tropical storm.

In the terminal a young man said, 'Welcome!' and handed me a pamphlet. It said:

ASK A GOAN – HAND ON HIS HEART – WHEN HE LOVES GOA BEST. 'WHEN IT RAINS . . .' In Goa during the rains the earth reaches out to wind and water. Emerald discovers the land. The soil is scented with life, green, flowering, newly risen. Turn where you will, the images of a rich, fresh land celebrate the eye.

It is a time for good company, a lively bottle, song, great food, the fellowship of friends. Visitors vow they will return with the next rains. And even honeymooners have been known to rise, go forth and make happy new discoveries.

I went to the hotel information desk. A beaming, thin-faced girl in a T-shirt saying 'Get Wet in Goa!' told me the Fort Aguada Beach had rooms to spare.

'You'll like it,' she promised. 'It is big resort hotel, full of nice people, just the place to stay now.'

'I'm not very keen on resort hotels.'

She laughed out loud. 'Sir, this is party time!'

Out in the car park I found a rusting yellow bus bound for the Fort Aguada. It was already full of vacationing families just in from Bombay but room was made for me by a sleek, well-fed man who was told, sharply, by his wife to move up. I shared the bench seat with him and his twin sons. They wore exact scaled-down versions of the clothes their father wore – bow ties, long flannel trousers, brown tweed hacking jackets and maroon waistcoats. The boys yawned fretfully and sucked their thumbs. Their father said they were five.

The driver had an assistant who would lay duckboards if the road became slippery. A friendly, gregarious young man, he told us about a new public staircase being built beside the river at Bendwado. He said that for some months a rump of opposition councillors had complained that the contractor was using substandard materials. Instead of filling the staircase depression with river rubble he filled it with mud; instead of using cement for the staircase proper, he used river rubble. The opposition councillors warned that it wouldn't survive a single day of the monsoon and, of course, they were right.

'It fell yesterday,' said the assistant, 'with first gush of rains. It was just wash away like sand.'

My neighbour, the Bombay man, laughed and the driver suddenly spoke up. 'It cost 40,000 rupees,' he said peevishly.

We began to take note of the scenery. Glassy inlets were skirted by flooded, canal-like roads so that, everywhere we looked, water was incorporated into the landscape with an almost Venetian nonchalance. By the same token, of course, each glimpse of water had some aspect of Goa reflected in it – coconut groves, small villages, white churches, men on bicycles. Sometimes, running several inches deep, the bus left a long wake behind; the road was firm, though, and the duckboards were not required. Everywhere we saw canoes, boats and barges beached for the duration of the monsoon. Goa's sea-going community had come ashore. The assistant said they would mend their nets, work in the paddies, go to church and make babies. That got an immoderate laugh from the Bombay contingent.

The rain began sluicing down as we arrived at the Fort Aguada Beach Resort and everyone dashed indoors. The reception desk overlooked a huge, echoing public area, open to the elements on one side, filled with running, shouting children and adults playing cards. The clerk who checked me in said whist and canasta were

very big this season. Did I play? No? Well, he was sure I would
find other things to do.

I stood in my room and watched the rain dismantle the drowned
garden outside. It crashed through the shrubbery, knocking down
flowers and leaves. A small detachment of storm troopers fought to
contain the damage. In full monsoon gear, the top of the Duckback
range, they looked ready for service on the Russian Front: high
black boots, smart long-skirted grey coats with high collars, Bala-
clava helmets covering everything but the eyes, nose and mouth.
Two wore swimming goggles. Crouching in the puddles like a line
of sappers checking for mines, they placed the fallen vegetation in
gunny sacks, then turned and painstakingly worked their way
back.

There was no directory by the phone When I told the operator
I wanted the local number of a Mr Baptista, initial A, she laughed.
'There are many Baptistas in Goa. Several will be initial A. Have
you no address?'

'None.'

Then I remembered Mrs Baptista saying the monsoon parties
were thrown by her parents. Not knowing their name I opted,
instead, for the Baptistas' Bombay number. The operator tried it
twice. 'It is the rains,' she said. 'They have soaked the cables and
we are having problems making Bombay connections.'

Long concrete passageways, open on one side, gave access to the
rooms at the Fort Aguada Beach Resort. Water cascaded off the
tiled roof in an unbroken sheet and flame-coloured bouganvillaea
blossoms, dislodged by the deluge, were strewn along the passageways. I saw a young couple, probably honeymooners, pause to look
at them. The girl said, 'This orange species is called "Miss
Manilla".'

Her companion scooped up a glowing, dripping handful and
offered it to her. She pressed his hand to her face and immersed
herself in the wet flowers. Some stuck to her and, murmuring
contentedly, he pulled them off.

'I am plucking you,' he said.

She gave a throaty laugh.

*

In the open public area a second uniformed assault squad, directed by a bossy supervisor sporting an umbrella and pith helmet, were erecting storm shutters. Blown rain had forced the card players back a dozen yards and now they sat looking fondly upon the well-dressed children who were making noisy sorties into the unshuttered areas and getting themselves soaking wet. A little girl, barely coherent with excitement, yelled, 'Daddy, I am shivering!'

A traveller in Purchas wrote, 'Goa is the most principall Citie which the Portugals have in India, wherein the Vice-roy remaineth with his Court. It is a fine Citie, and for an Indian Towne very fair.' It contained orchards, gardens and palm groves; the monsoon, though, was a puzzling phenomenon. At an inland settlement two days' march from Goa, he found, 'There is no passing in the streets but with Horses, the waters bee so high.'

It came on a western wind, and began with thunder and lightning. Then steady, continuous rain set in. The Portuguese called it winter and, before the burst, made extensive preparations. They laid up food and provisions, brought their ships into the river, unfurnished the tacklings, covered everything with mats. Shoals and sandbanks stopped up the rivermouth. The sea made such 'a roaring and noise that men can neither heare nor see'.

The atmosphere was heavy and melancholic. The Portuguese sat around in shirts and linen breeches, played cards with their neighbours, whiled away the time and puzzled constantly over the acute pleasure the monsoon seemed to bring to the Indians. They, exposing themselves adoringly to the rains, rode on flower-decked swings suspended from trees, plunged into flooded tanks and called to each other like children.

The sea certainly made a great roaring and noise now. Fifty yards out from the beach a kind of Martello tower, fashioned from local red laterite, part of the ancient Portuguese fortifications, was being clubbed by giant waves. Every few seconds it just sank, leaving a lofty waterspout to buoy the wreck. The waves crashing on the beach were real mid-ocean rollers, smooth and pewtery in the late afternoon light, a series of lofty grey eminences that seemed to come sliding out of the sky. A notice proclaiming 'Bathing Swimming Dangerous during Monsoon' seemed almost humorously self-evident.

At the head of the beach, men in palm-leaf shacks were selling 'Tibetan' trinkets and Yummy ice-cream. The articulate young ice-cream vendor told me he was one of Goa's many unemployed doctors. 'If you ever need emergency treatment go to the labour exchange,' he advised. When I mentioned the purpose of my journey he said, 'You should have been around last week. Further up the beach here there is a particular spot where, for a few days before the monsoon's burst, the sea produces certain substances that help people with rheumatism. Hundreds come from all over the state, even further, just to stand in the water.'

I stared at him. 'And it works?'

He shrugged. 'It seems to. But don't ask me why. In India cause and effect are not always obviously related.'

Half a mile behind the beach, in a small village set in a palm grove, I found a country liquor shop selling coconut fenny distilled from the crown of the palm, the drink of the monsoon. A single tiny room with a barred window, it contained three men who told me the strength of fenny was such that it could only be comfortably taken in cool weather. I tried some. It was very strong with a kind of curious cheesy aftertaste. The proprietor said his stocks had to be ready before the rains came. 'Moss grows on the trunks of the coconut trees. They are always wet and so slippery they cannot be climbed.'

I had another, this time with lime juice. Fishing around in a cupboard he produced a booklet called *Goan Fenny Cocktails*. 'You can mix it with anything,' he said earnestly. I glanced through the recipes. For a Flying Hornet you mixed fenny with vodka and fruit juices, for a Vizmit with crème de menthe and gin, for a Soprano with coconut water, for an Illusion with port wine, brandy and thick cream.

The cover blurb proclaimed, 'Author has done a through [sic] study of the Fenny blending with different other drinks and have concockted [sic] the recipes which are presented in this book and have personally tried out all the Cocktail and have served to the galaxy of prominent people of the world.'

*

In the hotel's crowded, boisterous foyer a man pulled up a chair, uninvited, to my table. He was middle aged, with soft, puffy features and big yellow teeth.

'Are you here alone?' he asked.

'Yes.'

'Would you like some female company?' He had a fluting voice and a faint lisp.

'No, thanks.'

'Sir, I represent interests of a group of beautiful girls who have come down from Bombay for the season. We call them the Water Nymphs and they are Bombay's best, sir, young, gorgeous, charming and intelligent. They have university degrees and public diplomas. One is a radiographer, one a qualified court reporter, one an astronomer, one speaks four —'

'An astronomer!'

'Yes.' He gazed at me hopefully. 'You are interested in the stars? She knows them all. You could just talk to her. If you give me room number I will arrange for her to call in for a chat.'

I told him my social calendar was full up and, with a sigh, he got up and walked away.

The Shells Restaurant, at dinner, was so crowded with exuberant families I had to share a table. My companions, a jolly Dutch couple in their late fifties, said they had flown down from Delhi for the weekend. 'We have come for the rains,' she said. 'It is sheer heaven. Yesterday the temperature in Delhi was 43 degrees Celsius.'

'In the shade,' said her husband.

He ran an engineering consultancy in Delhi. She had been born in Indonesia and imprisoned by the Japanese during the war. A Dutch friend of mine, also born and raised in Indonesia, suffered the same fate. My dinner companion knew of her family, and we talked comfortably together. When I said I belonged to the generation, now middle aged, which had missed the war by the skin of its teeth and – in my case – regretted it, the Dutchman grew suddenly exasperated.

'Alex, that is a foolish thing to say. I was in it. So was Mo. It was no fun. We still have the scars, physical and mental.'

He insisted on paying for the wine and, as he did so, Mo said to me, 'What are your plans for this evening?'

I said I had no plans.

To her husband she said, 'Couldn't he come to the party?'

Counting his change he said, 'I don't see why not.' He glanced over. 'Being alone on a Saturday night in Goa just now wouldn't be much fun.'

'It's a monsoon do,' she said, 'given by a Delhi chap we know. He's in textiles, filthy rich and ultra social. With him it's always a case of the more the merrier.'

We took a taxi. The house was not far away, a large beachside property lit up like a liner, and humming with raised voices and old Beach Boys tapes. The host, introduced to me as Bunny, told me I was welcome. He was a burly man with crinkly grey hair, gold-rimmed glasses and a cool, self-possessed look. He held a glass of whisky and said, 'I have only one question. Are you a practising Muslim?'

'Absolutely not.'

'Excellent! I have orange juice but, really, it is against my religion. The scotch is Black Label; there is French champagne; the wines are vintage; it is all good stuff. Go to it!'

Servants patrolled the rooms with trays of drinks but many guests seemed to be helping themselves from a large, bottle-strewn table in the lounge. This was being supervised by Ronnie, who had a flushed, drinking man's face and clearly knew a thing or two about wine. He was selecting the bottles, bidding a servant open them, yakking away like a fairground barker. A handsome woman asked for something red and French.

'Margaux!' he cried, pointing at a bottle. 'The '84!'

The sweating servant attacked it with his corkscrew.

'Voilà!' cried Ronnie as the cork popped out.

'Ronnie, shouldn't you let it breathe a little?' the woman asked.

He rolled his eyes at her. 'For you, darling, I will even give it the kiss of life.'

She giggled and took her wine. I spotted a nice Pouilly Fuisse of which Ronnie approved.

'Good choice!' The servant plunged in the corkscrew but it broke. 'By God, metal fatigue! Fetch another.'

What Ronnie meant was another bottle. I was handed this,

safely opened, and a glass. 'First rule of army on the march – always carry essential supplies with you.'

I took my supplies and wandered away. A lady doctor told me that her sari, a gauzy mauve with gold threads, was so finely woven it could be pulled through a wedding ring. A middle-aged man showed her the palm of his hand. 'Look at this, Iris, there's a little lump there. What could it be?'

'It's a ganglion,' said the doctor. 'Nothing to worry about. The recommended treatment is to bash it with the family bible.'

There was dancing in a large, shadowy room overlooking the sea. The rain had stopped and, though I saw no moon, the sea gave off a strange subtle radiance that seemed to permeate everywhere. I joined a gnarled old man with a white beard who sat watching the dancers, chin in hand. 'Have you come across these Water Nymphs?' he asked me.

'No.' I told him, though, I had been cornered by their pimp.

He nodded. 'Narayan. I know him. He used to be in advertising. One of the girls is a real dreamboat. Primula. A real 24-carat dreamboat.'

'Is she the astronomer?'

He frowned. 'Astronomer? What has Narayan been telling you? Those girls are just typists.'

On the veranda, describing my monsoon quest to a rather tipsy couple, I said I planned to arrive in Bombay the day before the burst – due, of course, on 10 June.

Another man, overhearing, intervened. 'The myth of the tenth!' he cried. 'People have it fixed in their minds like some basic law of science. But truth is it never gets there on tenth. On eighth, ninth, eleventh, fifteenth, yes, but never on this famous appointed day.'

'Oh,' I said.

'This year they are saying the ninth, even the eighth. I flew down from Bombay this afternoon, and conditions were certainly favourable for onset: moderate showers, dark skies, strong breeze. There is great feeling of anticipation in the city. People know it is coming.'

The young woman said, 'We call this a monsoon party but really it's just . . . Fellini. It could be anywhere. For the real celebrations you must visit the peasants. You must go to the remote villages.'

'Rajasthan!' proclaimed her husband.

I had put my bottle down somewhere and wandered off to find it, wondering if I could possibly get an airline seat to Bombay on the eighth – just two days away. Or a bus. Or even hitch a lift. In Cochin, though, I had been warned that wild animals made the Goa-to-Bombay road dangerous after dark. There was a steamer service but it had been suspended for the duration of the monsoon.

I found my bottle and stood listening to a large, perspiring man delivering a monologue on the problems of obtaining spare parts in India for Daimlers. He seemed to be addressing a girl who stood some distance away and sideways on, and was conspicuously not paying any attention. She was pretty, and clearly bored, and I thought I might ask her to dance.

Then, in the corner of a room containing an empty, brightly lit billiards table, I saw Aloysius Baptista. He was with a group, talking animatedly, making his listeners laugh. I walked across and touched his arm; he turned with a faint frown and no sign of recognition.

'Mr Baptista, I'm Alex Frater. We met in London three months ago, at the National Hospital.'

The frown deepened. Then he suddenly shouted, 'Nervous Diseases! You were the chap at Nervous Diseases!'

This made the people in our immediate vicinity look pretty nervous themselves. I said, 'I was there with a neck problem; you had migraine. We talked in the out-patients waiting room.'

'About the monsoon!' he cried. 'You were going to follow . . . My God, is that what you are doing here?'

'Absolutely!'

He stared at me. 'Rita!' he yelled. 'Where is Rita?'

'She is dancing,' someone said.

'Ask her to come.' He laughed and shook my hand. 'Andrew. Is that right?'

'Alex.'

'We spoke of you afterwards. We wondered if you would do it. Actually, we thought you probably wouldn't.'

'I tried to call you.'

'Ah, we have been rushing about all over the place!'

The lady who had gone to fetch Rita returned looking discomforted. She avoided Aloysius's eye and said something to her husband. He cleared his throat and stared at the floor.

'Otherwise engaged, is she?' said Aloysius.

She said, 'Ally, I don't know where she is.'

'Well! She will join us in due course.' He beamed at me.

Silence ran through our little group like a contagion. Then one of the men said, 'Frater. Is that right? As in the Latin for brother? Oddly enough not long ago I read a book by someone of that name. It was about mission work in the New Hebrides and contained some excellent stuff on volcanoes.'

I stared at him. He was tall and fine-featured, with thinning hair and lively, interested eyes.

Aloysius said, 'Shashi here is a vulcanologist. He is forever rushing off to toast his muffins beside some new lava flow. Aren't you, Shashi?'

'My grandfather wrote that book,' I said. 'It was called *Midst Volcanic Fires* and published, I think, in 1921. His name was Maurice.'

The vulcanologist smiled and raised a forefinger. 'The Reverend Maurice.'

'That's him.'

Aloysius, impatient, said, 'Andrew, I am trying to compose a limerick about quarks. An old friend, who is editor of a learned scientific journal, wants me to provide his readers with a little light relief. Perhaps you can help me. What rhymes with quark? Really, it is quite an easy word. Clerk. Dark. Lark. Fark.'

'Fark?' said the lady who had gone to look for his wife. 'What is that, Ally?'

'A London cockney term for sexual intercourse,' said Aloysius. 'It is what the pearly kings and queens say. Fark you, sunshine. Don't they, Andrew? It is almost a term of endearment.'

Another silence fell, more strained than the last. People started to drift away. Aloysius stood there grinning at me. Whisky stained the front of his frilly pink shirt.

'I can usually do limericks off the top of my head,' he said. 'It's a gift.'

Then he sat heavily on a sofa and I sat with him.

'How are the headaches?' I asked.

'Oh, actually, I am in a non-headache phase just now.'

'Have you been gliding?'

'Gliding?' He gave me a slow, re-focussing blink. 'No. Rita's young brother died two months ago. A climbing accident in the Andes. He fell into a glacier; the body was never found. He and Rita were very close.' He sat up and tapped my chest. 'Here's a funny thing! His body will reappear, in a certain place on a certain day, in twenty-five years' time. We have the date written somewhere. The authorities can measure precisely the rate at which the glacier moves. Then the ice will yield him up, perfectly preserved, looking just as he did the day he died. I shall go to meet him, of course. Rita, I think won't.' He smiled. 'I will be fifty-eight, imagine! And he will be just . . . a youngster.'

When Rita walked in I barely recognized her. She wore a sari, plum-coloured, with a red caste mark on her forehead. She looked special and different; she even moved differently. I remembered her saying the rains made her feel very Indian.

'There you are,' she said to her husband.

'You remember Andrew?' he said, sadly. 'Our friend from Nervous Diseases in London? You met in the waiting room while I was seeing that man about my headaches.'

'Oh, yes.' She seemed uncertain.

'You told me about the monsoon,' I said. 'And the name's Alex.'

Aloysius said, 'We asked you to our party!'

'Well, you must come, of course,' said his wife. 'It's on Thursday. But it won't be like this. It will be more of a family affair.'

'I'll be in Bombay,' I said. 'Chasing the burst.'

She gave me that peering, green-eyed look, then smiled. 'I do remember you!'

She laughed and gave my hand a squeeze. 'How is the neck?'

'Bearing up.'

'He is following the monsoon,' Aloysius told her. 'We talked about it in the hospital.'

'Actually, you two gave me the idea. It's as much yours as mine.'

It was the wrong thing to say. I was making them a party to my enterprise, imposing some kind of obligation and commitment; they suddenly saw me as a potential house guest, a borrower of money, a claimant on their time and attention. Aloysius just chuckled and said, 'Nonsense, we've never had a decent idea in our lives', but, when another couple wandered in and called to them, I sensed their relief. 'Before you leave you must come to lunch,' she said, but in a vague, non-specific way. I left them with their friends and slipped off in search of a drink, something stronger this time.

The evening, seen mostly through the bottom of a whisky glass, soon began slipping out of focus. All over the house they were dancing cha-chas to thundering Edmundo Ross tapes. I glimpsed the Baptistas a couple of more times, though not together. Once Aloysius shouted to me, 'Alan! Alan! Come here! I must show you this trick!' but I lost him in the crush. I saw Rita dancing with Ronnie, the wine buff, and thought of cutting in, but decided against it. There were shadowy figures out on the beach. 'Are they skinny dipping?' a man enquired. 'It would be dangerous in this undertow.'

I overhead someone say Water Nymphs had been sighted in the games room.

A lugubrious, well-fleshed woman in a Parisian dress sighed and shook her head. 'There will be tears before bedtime,' she announced. 'Mark my words.'

I asked Iris, the doctor, to prove to me her sari could be pulled through a wedding ring. She gave a deep laugh. 'Now look here, we haven't even been formally introduced!' She told me the Baptistas quarrelled a lot. They were going through a sticky patch. Rita was seeing other men. The death of her brother had something to do with it. 'The girl's on tranks,' she said. 'And Ally drinks like a fish.'

Here at the party people were on other things. There was ganja, Kashmiri resin, a whole menu of available substances. I stuck to the Black Label.

Mo, my Dutch friend, said, 'Are you glad you came?'

'You bet! It's a great party.'

She looked flushed and happy. 'Bunny just called the Observatory. In the past twenty-four hours they have registered five inches!'

They would be registering even more now. For several minutes it came down so torrentially that the drumming on the roof drowned out the Edmundo Ross tapes. Everyone cheered but continued jigging about. 'We are doing a rain dance!' they cried.

7 JUNE

One of Britain's best legacies to India is the tradition of good Sunday newspapers. Waking late, with a terrible head, I fetched some and took them back to bed. Bombay awaiting the burst made all the front pages. There had already been sharp showers and enough wind to uproot a few trees. Bombay's Meteorologist-in-Charge, Mr K. K. Chakravarty, reckoned it would arrive in forty-eight hours. The *Indian Express* reported that 'Crowds in the evening walked merrily, enjoying the drizzles. Children ran along suburban streets singing a welcome to the rain. Pot holes on the city roads turned into muddy poodles [*sic*] dirtying pedestrians as motor traffic rolled on.'

The *Times of India* confirmed that things were looking good for the monsoon's 'advancement into the city'.

Elsewhere, though, the subcontinent remained drought-stricken. Two-fifths of rural India and a hundred of her largest cities suffered an acute scarcity of water. An estimated 100 million people were receiving inadequate rations. I read with astonishment that Shillong, the old Meghalaya hill station from where, with luck, I would embark on my final leg to Cherrapunji, was suffering too. 'Situated in a record rainfall zone,' said the *Times*, 'and less than 50 km away from Cherrapunjee, the world's wettest place, Shillong's taps, wells and reservoirs have run dry for the best part of last month.'

The situation in Madras was so desperate that giant supertankers were being converted to ship water in from Orissa, a voyage of 1,600 km. In some places the taps flowed for only twenty minutes every three days. The 'garden city' of Bangalore was withering and dying. Even Delhi, favoured because of the personal requirements of the politicians residing there, seemed unable to cope. In all affected urban areas, however, it was the poor who suffered. The rich, somehow, always got their water. The *Times* said, 'Water – unfiltered, full of microbes and at times visibly filthy – can cost up to Rs 8 for a bucket of three gallons in scores of Indian towns. The poorer you are, the more you pay for it.' There was a disturbing, and growing, trend of violence by officials distributing water in the bustees, or neighbourhoods, of the poor.

In Uttar Pradesh fourteen people had died in a heat wave.

The heat also frayed tempers. An altercation broke out between two men dining at separate tables in an Andheri restaurant. One lost his temper with the other for 'looking daggers at him. They left the restaurant and on the street they started abusing each other. Finally Sudhakar fired a round of his revolver at Azam, who was however unhurt.' A head constable disarmed Sudhakar, and charged him with attempted murder.

In the local *Panjim Herald* a Dr Amonkar advertised treatments for kidney stones, warts, stammering and night blindness.

The same paper contained a long, jolly piece by Val & Tino called 'Come to Goa when It Drizzles'. They wrote lyrically of the greening of the countryside, of sunless beaches, rainbows and cloud-bound hills. 'Get high on the humid smell of the mucky mud. The croaking of the frogs at midnight, the buzz of the fire-flies criss-crossing the sky, the millipedes crawling on the cow-dung floor nearby and the sight of a thousand things is too beautiful to put into words. Que bonita este Goa!'

I took a shower and went to visit Old Goa, the ancient Portuguese capital.

A large tree had fallen, blocking part of the road. I left the bus and joined a lively crowd of spectators. Two fire engines were parked nearby and firemen with axes scurried in and out of the foliage like squirrels, making the leaves tremble with the force of their blows. I chatted to a young man who had seen it happen and was excitedly describing the event to anyone who would listen. 'I was beside it, relieving my bladder, when it started to tremble and there were loud noises under my feet. I ran. It fell slowly, creaking, creaking, the leaves all shivering, and hit ground like thunderclap. Sir, I am damn lucky to be alive.'

I noted that the spare wheel of his motor scooter bore a cover embroidered with the words 'O Mary Bless us'.

The number of people killed each monsoon by tree falls has not been established, though a surveyor I met in Delhi reckoned on one fatality for every 200 square miles of forest. Ironically, the decline of India's forest cover is therefore saving lives.

*

In 1510 the Portuguese began building a city here which was intended to rival Lisbon itself. In the course of the next three centuries, mostly using lime plaster laid over laterite, they put up cathedrals, churches, convents, palaces and triumphal arches. Wandering around behind several awed Bombay families in their Sunday best, I was reminded of a great estate frittered away by idle, decadent aristocrats. In its heyday this had been the capital of Portugal's eastern empire, its viceroys administering possessions as far afield as the Chinese opium port of Macau and the sandalwood island of Timor. Here, in the boulevards of their city, the Portuguese proceeded with soft, slow steps, pausing constantly to exchange courtesies with friends, the men extending a leg, stooping and sweeping the ground with their heavily plumed hats. Slaves carried their rapiers and the velvet cushions on which they would kneel to hear mass. In the rainy season other slaves bore veils for their heads and scarlet cloaks which, during cloudbursts, would swathe them from head to foot in improvised storm-proof tepees.

They seem to have been a querulous, prickly lot, quick to take offence, constantly on the look-out for slights, real or imagined. The slighted gathered a dozen friends and beat their victims senseless with sandbags and bamboo staves.

Promiscuous wives were a common cause of trouble. A Dutch merchant named Van Linschoten, visiting in 1583, wrote primly of their 'unsatiable lusts which grind a man to powder and sweepe him away like dust'. Most women, he claimed, took lovers, the married ones first stupefying their husband by spiking their wine with *duetroa* herbs. For up to twenty-four hours the husband lay there 'like a dead man ... while in his presence (the wives) may doe what they will, and take their pleasure'. Afterwards, revived by slaves washing his feet in cold water, the husband awoke refreshed, remembering nothing.

When a Portuguese ship was due on the night tide, brahmin merchants lit fires and blew trumpets to guide its pilot.

The town was thronged with Indians who had done well out of the Portuguese. They sold them silks, satins, damasks and Chinese porcelain. One side of a certain road was given over to jewellers and goldsmiths, the other to makers of bedsteads and stools. There were coppersmiths and carpenters, dealers in timber, grain and rare Indian artefacts. Indians managed the viceroy's rents and revenues, dominated the money-lending and brokerage businesses.

Most notably, they also cornered the medical profession. Goa's celebrated 'heathen physicians' were the only non-Portuguese – ambassadors apart – permitted to wear the plumed hats and do those deep obeisances in the street. They dealt routinely with cases of the pox, piles, the bloody flux, tropical ulcers and, of course, the burning agues and fevers prevalent during the monsoon. Portuguese physicians bled patients. The Indians, instead, prescribed their traditional Ayurvedic infusions of herbs, oils and unguents and, very often, got results.

The most remarkable building in the old capital, the Basilica of Bom Jesus, contains the osseous remains of St Francis Xavier in a glass coffin. A Spanish-born graduate of the University of Paris, he came to Goa with his breviary and crucifix in 1542. After preaching up and down the Coromandel and Malabar coasts he paid a proselytizing visit to the King of Yamaguchi in Japan but, on his way home, aged forty-six, fell ill and died. Local sentiment demanded the body be returned to Goa. Though incomplete – two toes were bitten off by a frenzied Portuguese female in 1554 ('Typical!' one imagines Van Linschoten sniffing) and a hand severed and shipped to Rome for a relic-collecting Pope – it remains so well preserved that, to this day, it is brought out every ten years and displayed to the faithful.

On the way back to the hotel I thought of my grandfather. Certain comparisons with St Francis Xavier were in order. Maurice belonged to that generation of Scotsmen who, inspired by Dr David Livingstone, wanted to evangelize the whole world. After graduating in theology at Glasgow University he was ordained and then accepted by the Church of Scotland for mission work abroad. Some thought he was wasting his gifts. Maurice possessed a beautiful voice, rugged good looks, ice-blue eyes, a quick intelligence and terrific, spontaneous charm. Had he opted for a smart Edinburgh ministry and thrown himself into Synodal politics he may well, eventually, have worn the silver-buckled shoes and lace-fronted shirt of the Moderator. But Maurice wasn't interested in that kind of malarkey.

The New Hebrides, to which he and his new wife, Janey, were posted in 1900, had also been settled by the Portuguese. In 1606 Pedro Fernandez Quiros, the last of the conquistadors, landed on one of the northern islands and, thinking he had discovered Australia, named it La Austrialia del Espiritu Santu. It was a lush, bountiful place teeming with 'herons and duck likes those of Castile, wild pigeons, rushes and reed mace', and he determined to found a capital which would be as great as Goa itself. He befriended the natives with gifts of silk trousers and falcon bells, then formed his officers into a town council and ordered them to start building the city of New Jerusalem. But they hadn't the stomach for it. Discontent grew into mutiny; malaria weakened them; the natives – who, never discovering their true purpose, wore the silk trousers as bonnets – turned on the Portuguese; and, finally accepting the inevitable, Quiros sailed away.

His island, now called Santo, lies less than a hundred miles from Paama, the island allocated to Maurice and Janey. As they approached it across the bluest sea they had ever seen they noted the presence of numerous attendant islands, mostly mountainous, with veils of pale smoke drifting from their summits. Some consisted of a single Fuji-like eminence, others of a cordillera linked by a hog's back arrangement of saddles and spurs thickly clad in glistening rain forest. The enriched volcanic soil produced displays that were almost operatic. Trees shot up to prodigious heights, their flowers so lambent they could be spotted, like beacons, from passing ships. Only the drifting hilltop smoke indicated that, at any moment, this castaway's dream could erupt in a holocaust of fire.

Maurice joked with the chiefs and befriended the children (he did conjuring tricks), cleared land, planted a garden and an orchard of Chinese Swatow oranges, put up a house and learned the language. Then he got down to work.

On Paama, a mere six miles long, he built twenty-one churches. A couple of miles across the water a live volcano, Lopevi, reared 5,000 feet from the sea and there, beneath the nut trees at its base, he built three more. He built churches in the shadow of another volcano on Ambrym, and more on the island of Epi. Any atoll sustaining human life got a church and, tirelessly, Maurice preached in all of them. He was an advocate of economic self-sufficiency, and the Paamese grew accustomed to hearing sermons on crop rotation, animal husbandry and the making of charcoal. In his spare time, to keep his mind sharp, he translated the Acts of the Apostles into Paamese.

He became, in his fashion, a conquistador too. As Paama's absolute ruler he unified its warring tribes, even put a stop to cannibalism. My father, who spent much of his childhood on the island, believed he did it through sheer force of personality. The practice disgusted Maurice, and his furious confrontations with the sullen offenders – Maurice shaking with rage, eyes blazing, that Shakespearian actor's voice pitched so loud it could be heard half a mile away – seem to have frightened them. The practice became covert and then gradually died away altogether.

Paama lay thirty-six hours by launch from our island and, when my father could find the time, we would visit. While he held clinics Maurice would walk me around his domain and, if I was lucky, take me into the rain forest. Nothing remotely like it grew on our island. I learned to identify teak, koko, lignum vitae, satinwood, wild nutmeg, rambutan, breadfruit, soursop, kauri, Tahitian chestnut, Indian almond, African tulip, flamboyant and jacaranda. My favourites were the great cloistered banyan, the kind of tree under which a closed order of serious-minded people – Dinky Toys collectors, or swappers of Players cigarette cards of Famous Meteorological Phenomena – could meet in all weathers, and the prodigious rain tree itself. I knew this place had been made by a happy accident of rich volcanic soil and Niagara-like precipitation; the result gave rain a new dimension. Rain had helped build the superstructure of the forest, become part of its fabric and texture. Here it was the stuff of alchemy. An army of gardeners labouring for a hundred years could never have achieved anything so beautiful.

Maurice said it had first taken root during the Great Flood. 'You talk of heavy precipitation, Sandy,' he said, using the Scottish diminutive of my name, 'and you're right to do so, but what I have in mind is the kind of rain the likes of you and me couldn't even imagine.'

Well, I could, actually. The Cherrapunji picture provided a clue but Maurice, though also an admirer of the work, insisted it bore no relation to what had happened here. 'A wee shower by com-

parison, rain for the roses, God in benevolent mood. What I have
in mind is God setting the black handkerchief on his head and
handing down Rain as Punishment,'

This notion was sometimes explored by Maurice and my father
sitting out on the veranda in the evenings, Maurice puffing at his
Passing Cloud after-dinner cigarette (a tin of fifty lasted him fifty
days) and keeping an eye on his volcanoes.

He had got the Great Flood story from the natives. It was part of
their ancestral memory, a kind of database passed down through
the generations with such accuracy that the tales retained the
freshness and impact of good journalism; the arrival of Quiros and
the Portuguese in Santo, for example, was recounted as though it
had happened yesterday, with full descriptions of the ships, the
falcon bells, the lozenge-shaped bronze bullets used by the soldiers.
Maurice claimed the same sources had told him of the Flood – rain
that extinguished the volcanoes, turned the mountaintops into
islands and the natives into tribes of nomadic canoe people. He
said the world's rain forests emerged from the silt left after the
waters receded.

My father discounted the story. He said the Paamese had almost
certainly pinched the idea from the Old Testament and amended it
to suit local audiences. Maurice, though, believed it implicitly.

My mother thought he was going native.

There was some evidence to support this. The islanders believed
their own gods lived inside the volcanoes and, when an eruption
threatened, threw coconuts in to appease them. And though Maurice jokily named the volcano gods for female movie stars – 'I see
Garbo's sleeping it off' of 'Betty Grable was breaking wind this
morning' – he admitted, on occasion, to throwing coconuts too.

He got advance warning of volcanic activity through the soles of
his feet. If the signals were proving elusive he discarded his shoes.
On one famous occasion, taking tea barefoot with a French planter
on Ambrym, he announced that a volcano would soon burst out in
the middle of his garden. A few minutes later it did – rhyolite lava
emerging in a 'glowing cloud' eruption – scaring the wits out of the
planter but adding to Maurice's growing reputation as a seer.

But he wasn't infallible. One afternoon during our last visit to
Paama I heard him yelling, 'Carmen Miranda has gone raving

mad!' before rushing off with my father to organize a fleet of rescue craft. It was the big solo volcano on Lopevi this time, and we watched a glowing lava rivulet ooze down its flanks while dense brown smoke rolled low over the sea and a column of compressed steam shot thousands of feet into the sky; it generated enough electricity to make lightning ripple through the clouds. Cinders pattered on our roof like hailstones. The air was full of Pele's Hair, a glassy volcanic discharge with a gossamer-like density, lighter than snowflakes. Then black rain began falling, staining our clothes like ink. I knew Lopevi was supposed to be docile because a picnic there had been proposed and when, looking like chimney-sweeps, Maurice and my father returned I asked why it had gone up so suddenly.

'God knows,' said Maurice.

But which God? Carmen Miranda or the one who dwelt on high with the angels?

The bus taking me back to the Fort Aguada halted at a section of flooded road. Duckboards placed beneath the wheels proved ineffective so we all piled out to collect stones and small rocks from the verges. The Bombay families enjoyed this. Their menfolk issued loud, contradictory orders as the scampering kids gleefully got their feet wet and the womenfolk, still aboard, watched resignedly. Each time the bus inched forward there were cheers. This was a genuine monsoon experience, real frontier stuff.

Flooded paddies, silvery in the soft, mellow light of late afternoon, flanked the road. Bunded or walled to retain their water, they were full of women planting rice seedlings. Bent double, working furiously, they dotted the landscape like groups of famished feeding birds, undisturbed by the men ploughing around them with buffalo. I was reminded that, by 2050, India anticipates a population of 1,235 million and an annual food grain requirement of 280 million tons. It will be produced, in all probability, by methods very similar to those I was witnessing today – small farmers and their families hock-deep in mud, blessing each seedling before placing it in the earth, blessing the rains and praying for their continuation.

At the hotel I listened to a brisk woman giving advice on the radio about personal hygiene during the summer monsoon. Excessive perspiration would be the thing to watch out for. Sweat mixing with surface bacteria produced body odour and stained clothing. Listeners were advised to take three baths a day and vigorously scrub the neck, armpits and genital region. Armpits must be kept hair-free. Cotton underwear and loose cotton clothing – with sweat-absorbing cotton shields under the arms – should be worn at all times and changed twice daily. Feet required powdering each morning and, in the evenings, a soaking in cold water to which a measure of salt had been added. Office workers were told to keep deodorant or talc in their desks, together with generous supplies of light, lemony cologne. Even better, she said, was a good skin tonic, preferably rose-based, which should be poured into a bowl and placed in the fridge. Cotton-wool pads left to soak in the fluid would, properly chilled, provide refreshing skin and neck wipes.

I turned her off and went down to the bar.

It was full of kids. They sat at tables and gave peremptory orders to the waiters. 'Bring lime juice! Bring soda!' One little girl in a lacy white frock imperiously demanded extra ice for her lemonade and, ignored by the waiter, yelled 'Daddy! Daddy!' to a man drinking beer with a friend in the corner. He sighed, crossed the room and told the waiter to fetch the ice.

At a table near me a studious-looking boy of nine was reading aloud to his two small, fidgeting sisters from the *Times of India*. The story, which I first took to be true, concerned a village where no rain had fallen for ten years. This was due to the elopement of a seventy-year-old grocer with the barber's teenage daughter. One villager said human wickedness had obviously kept the rains away; another said more sinister agencies might be to blame and spoke of a drought-stricken kingdom in the west where, one day, clouds suddenly appeared. The king ordered his pundits to chant the magic hymns that would cause the clouds to discharge their rain. The boy read, 'As the spells were recited the clouds grew bigger and darker and seemed as though they were ready to burst. Everybody in the kingdom cried for joy. Then there was a terrible flash of lightning and the clouds vanished.'

The two small sisters stopped fidgeting and listened intently.

'Vanished?' said one.

'Yes,' said her brother.

'That is awful.'

The boy continued, 'The king consulted his astrologers. They said, "Your majesty, there's a thief in the heavens. He has stolen the rains. He has filled his bags with the clouds and disappeared to sell the precious clouds to the ruler of a neighbouring kingdom".'

The other girl said, 'If I could steal the rains I would not sell them. I would keep them all for myself.'

Her sister said, 'Would you give me some?'

'No.'

Their brother said, 'Shut up, you two, I haven't finished.'

'Not just one teeny cloud?'

'No.'

'You are a selfish bitch,' said the little girl to her sister.

The boy sighed and closed the paper. Their father, a big, pot-bellied man in a Hawaiian shirt, appeared with a glass of beer in his hand. 'Upstairs,' he said. 'Time to change for dinner. Mummy is waiting.'

Two Bombay men, talking about the drought, complained that the government was being lazy about water harvesting. The country needed more check dams and percolation dams, more *nala*-bundings, *gulli*-bundings and underground rubble trenches. Most of the monsoon rain still ran back into the sea. Here a retention rate of only 10 per cent would supply Goa with water sufficient for all its needs.

A couple of well-to-do Chinese Singaporeans spoke of the eastern or Bay of Bengal arm of the summer monsoon, which brushes the Lion City durings its passage up to Calcutta and the Gangetic Plain. Sitting at the bar drinking Manhattans they told me they had been to Bombay, and were spending the weekend in Goa before heading for Madras to catch their flight home. 'We wanted a taste of the Arabian Sea monsoon,' said the man, 'so that we could tell our son about it. He works for the Singapore Met Office.'

'He is a forecaster,' said the woman proudly. 'Only honours graduates can become forecasters in Singapore. Candidates with ordinary degrees just become plotters and observers.'

They showed me a photograph of a thin, bespectacled young man standing on a green hilltop surrounded by his instruments.

'This was taken in the Cameron Highlands, Malaysia, where he was posted for a six-month tour of duty,' said his father. 'We went to visit him there.'

'We ate strawberries!' said the woman.

Her husband identified the instruments. 'That is a cup counter anemometer made by Negretti and Zambra of London. This small circular tank is the evaporation pan. And this crystal ball is the sunshine recorder. It burns a line into a piece of green paper, the sunshine card, containing the relevant compass bearings – 6 to 18 degrees.'

'Who made that?' I asked.

'J. J. Hicks of Hatton Garden.'

His wife smiled. 'My husband takes a great interest in the careers of our children.'

'What's the Singapore monsoon like?' I asked.

'Not quite as operatic as it is here,' he said. 'What our summer monsoons are famous for are Sumatras. These are line squalls – dense walls of cumulonimbus cloud over 200 miles long which suddenly appear from nowhere.'

'They appear, actually, from the direction of Sumatra,' said his wife.

'The temperature can drop 20 degrees in a few seconds,' he continued, in a slightly sharper voice. 'There are severe thunderstorms, winds up to 50 knots and torrential rain. Sumatras rarely last for more than thirty minutes and are an early morning phenomenon. They occur most frequently between 3 a.m. and 9 a.m.'

'Our son hopes to become a Sumatra specialist,' said the woman.

Her husband nodded. 'In Singapore weather, that is definitely the way to the top.'

There was entertainment during dinner in the Shells Restaurant. The theme was folkloric. Our breezy MC said, 'Well, folks, I trust you've all been having a ball in the rain. Isn't Goa great?'

Some of the scores of children dining with their parents yelled, 'Yes!' Others yelled, 'No!' and blew raspberries.

The MC, frowning, leant into his microphone and blew one thunderously back. It was an act of aggression that astonished the children, reducing them to silence.

'Right! Well, as some of you folks know, when the monsoon is late here our young Christian farmers carry loads of rocks up mountainsides as an act of penance. But not this year! The rains came right on the button so those young farmers are pretty happy. Instead of lugging rocks, they've come here to entertain us. Ladies and gentlemen, boys and girls, please will you welcome Goan farmers dancing to celebrate the arrival of the monsoon!'

To the sounds of generous applause and a few subversive raspberries three effeminate young men came skipping in with their hands on their hips. They wore crimson loincloths and headbands and were accompanied by three ravishingly pretty girls. The appearance of the 'farmers' amused the vacationing Bombay businessmen who made jokes about the Goan economy; was its agriculture really secure in the hands of wimps such as these? Soon the artistes were replaced by others. All the routines celebrated rain, crops, bounty, relief, exhilaration. In the best a youth worked energetically around a circular plywood prop with a bucket suspended over the top. A kindly woman at the next table explained, 'He is jumping into a well,' she said. 'It is famous local custom.'

After the show many of the children went to sleep with their heads on the tables. The band played cha-chas and their parents got up to dance. Twenty minutes later, midway through a Latin Americanized rendering of 'She Wore an Itsy Witzy Teeny Weeny Yellow Polka Dot Bikini', the power failed. The band's electric amplifier groaned into silence and, in the pitch darkness, waiters with torches invaded the room. They distributed candles and matches. The children were woken, unsurprised by the blackness, and in good humour we all dispersed, candles twinkling, marching off like lines of pilgrims.

Outside, the rain fell, torrentially and comfortingly.

8 JUNE

The *Times of India* said the monsoon had reached Ratnagiri, in south Konkan. Favourable conditions continued to prevail in

Bombay, where it was due tomorrow. (In Delhi, though, they had registered 45 degree Celsius, the highest temperature of the season; indeed, the whole of northern India 'continued to reel under blistering heat with the mercury soaring to an alarming 46 degrees Celsius at Hissar'.) I rang Indian Airlines and, in the time it took to get through, ate some breakfast, wrote a letter to my wife and chatted to a chambermaid whose brainy nephew, that evening in Bombay, would receive an award from the hand of the Postmaster General for his work in the promotion of postal life insurance.

The man who finally answered seemed astonished by my request for a seat next morning. He was not rude, just incredulous, perhaps even a little bewildered. 'Bombay?' he said. 'Tomorrow?'

'Yes.'

'This flights are book solid for two weeks.'

'It's very urgent.'

'They are chock-a-block.'

'Can you put me on stand-by?'

He said he could. I would be No. 36 in the stand-by queue. He took down details, including my age – routinely required by Indian Airlines – and told me to report, at an ungodly hour, to the stand-by desk at the airport.

Then I put a call through to External Affairs in Delhi. While waiting I read an angry letter in the *Navhind Times*, a Goan paper, entitled 'Electric Pole'. It said:

In Malbhat Electric Pole No. MSN B/9 on Saudade Road is at present a little bended and with a big crack. Some 20 days ago one loaded truck dashed against this pole but till now as rainy season has already started no action is taken by Electricity Department.

This letter is just to inform the authorities to exchange this pole as early as possible and keep Malbhat residents safe from future calamity.

In Delhi a voice said, 'Ugh?'

'Can I speak to Mr P. D. Gupta, please?'

'Gupta is not in his seat.'

'Is he in the room?'

'Gupta is not being in his seat or his room.'

'Where is he?' I asked.

'Gupta has gone away.'

'Is Mr Prasad Rao still on long leave?'

'Yes, yes, Rao is on leave also.'

I started explaining about the Cherrapunji permission but he cut me off. 'I know nothing of such matters. You must talk to Gupta or Rao. They have the files.'

'But they're not there.'

He said, 'No', and hung up the phone.

I crossed the Mandovi River in a landing craft and disembarked at Panjim, the capital. With its narrow, winding streets and red tiled roofs it still had a very Portuguese look. I found a small, shadowy shop selling school stationery equipment. A sign outside said 'Herald'. It was supervised by a balding man, bespectacled in frames of heavy tortoiseshell, seated behind an enormous Victorian cash register. Each time he struck the keys there was a peal of bells and numbered ivory tablets spun in the display window. I queued up behind a youth buying an atlas and three little girls buying what seemed' to be the latest craze in Goan schools – small pink pig-shaped erasers with blue eyes, retailing at a rupee each.

When I arrived at the cash register I told the shopkeeper I had come to see Mr Narayan.

He frowned at me. 'Who?'

'The editor, Mr Rajan Narayan. The boss.'

'He is not boss!' said the man, his voice loud and combative. 'Narayan work for me. I am owning *Herald*.'

'I called him earlier. He said he could see me.'

'What about?'

'We are fellow-journalists. This is just a courtesy visit.'

'Well, for a few minutes only. Narayan has many urgent duties to perform.'

A rickety staircase took me past a room containing an ancient printing press to a cubicle where two men sat gossiping with their feet propped on a heaped, untidy desk. They were casually dressed and held stained coffee mugs. The older said he was Rajan Narayan, the younger Norman Dantas, the assistant editor. Both were keen, bright and welcoming. Rajan ordered fresh coffee and, without much prompting, talked about the reality of Goa in the rains. 'In terms of domestic tourism the monsoon promotion is a clever move,' he said. 'Indians are incredibly romantic about rain and, as you have seen, they're coming in huge numbers. Next, I think, they'll start promoting in the Middle East. The idea should prove even more appealing to the Arabs.'

'They have no plans for promotions in England!' said Norman.

'I think Goa can stand up to the tourist invasion. The sense of local identity here is very strong. Before the Portuguese left in 1961 Goa had been separated from India for four and a half centuries. We have insisted on our right to continue speaking Konkani but we are loyal Indians nevertheless. And with good reason. Since independence we have more schools, more doctors – and a free press!'

Norman said more Goans lived in the UK and Canada than in Goa itself. The English Goans supported 102 Goan associations, numerous Goan churches and five football pitches in Kent. All, however, felt uniquely Goan and recently, under temperate English skies, had been holding public meetings to express their outrage over the mass destruction of Goa's trees. Its forest cover was down to 6 per cent and its rainfall to 60 inches, half the norm; rain helps make forests and forests help make rain, but if both continued deteriorating – the classic Indian conundrum – each would eventually cancel out the other.

Rajan, blowing on his coffee, said, 'If you see someone embracing a tree as the axemen approach don't be surprised. We are all doing it, people of every age and class. Finally the message has got through to central government in Delhi and, with some reluctance, they are putting money into forestry.'

'But not much is actually getting to the forest,' said Norman. 'Corruption is widespread. Politicians have business links with the timber contractors so that, for example, a contractor will get a licence to fell one acre but then fells three. His politician partner steps in to protect him and "fix" it with the authorities. They split the proceeds and both get rich. It's happening locally and nationally. Timber is fetching high prices these days.'

'Do you know who these men are?'

'Lists of names are being compiled. Not only here. All over the country.'

'Will they be prosecuted?'

He laughed. 'It depends how much they are prepared to spend on their defence.'

Sufficient rain still fell on Goa, however, for the monsoon's arrival to be celebrated in traditional style on 20 June, the Feast of St John, when all the wells had filled up.

'St John jumped twice in his mother's womb,' said Norman, 'so young men wearing laurel crowns go around jumping twice into people's wells. Each well-owner gives them a bottle of coconut fenny and, as the day wears on, the jumpers get progressively more tanked up. By the afternoon they are doing really wild jumps.'

'Silly jumps,' said Rajan.

'I have seen young foreigners jumping also. Perhaps they think it is a new thing to do, like running with the bulls at Pamplona.' The telephone rang faintly, then stopped again. 'If the rains have not come by 13 June, the Feast of St Anthony, the propitious thing to do with your well is to lower a statue of St Anthony into it. This is virtually guaranteed to induce the monsoon.'

Rajan said, 'Many Konkani folk songs have to do with the monsoon's different stages. Our local culture is entirely dependent upon it, of course – no monsoon, no full wells; no full wells, no food; no food, no culture. There is always a great sigh of relief when it sets in. Even the municipal council is forgiven for not fixing the roads or unblocking the drains.'

He asked about my plans. I said I had a tenuous stand-by booking for Bombay in the morning. He picked up the phone. 'Let me talk to my friend Fernandez at Indian Airlines,' he said.

In the course of a brief conversation he outlined my problem and invited Fernandez on a duck hunt. Then he scribbled a brief note and handed it to me. It read, 'My dear Fernandez. This is further to our telephonic confab. Please help Mr Alexander Frater to get on flight tomorrow. R. Narayan.'

When I thanked him he smiled faintly and said, 'Oh, don't worry. We are a small community.'

Indian Airlines occupied premises in the Dempo Building, facing the river. Fernandez sat behind a polished desk with both hands pressed to a hugely swollen jaw. It ballooned out from under his spectacles and, unceasingly, he popped cloves into his mouth and chewed them vigorously; the smell in his office reminded me of the clove distillery at Zanzibar. He was so miserable he could barely speak but he stood, left the room and, after a quarter of an hour, returned bearing a 'top priority' chitty from the computer. It was numbered and coded and bore a list of names, mine among them, together with his signature and personal rubber stamp.

'That will get you on,' he mumbled.

I tried to thank this kind man but he waved me away and returned to his desk, wishing to be alone with his pain.

One day the previous summer Panjim's fine new road bridge had fallen into the Mandovi River, killing four people. It was the usual story – inferior materials, too much sand and rubble, not enough concrete. Standing at the stern of the veteran landing craft operating the ferry service, I was approached by a merry, twinkling-eyed old man who asked for alms. I put my hand in my pocket and realized I only had 100-rupee notes, each worth £5. To give him so much would be ostentatious, worse even than giving him nothing. But worse for who? A hundred roops would sustain him for a month. People watched curiously. I thought of Fernandez, who had displayed charity towards me. The old man's smile was gentle and quizzical.

'No,' I said.

He turned away. Three neat little girls sitting with their mother gave me bleak looks, took out their purses and handed him coins. The mother, a fat woman with large gold studs in her Roman nose, glanced at me contemptuously and gave him a one-rupee note. I stared miserably down at the creamy brown water brimming, broth-like, with chunks of floating vegetation. As we docked by the bus station on the other side I went in search of the old man but he had vanished. In India the indecisive don't get second chances.

Certain phenomena relating to the monsoon are named for the men who discovered them. Thus we have the Coriolis force and two kinds of atmospheric wave, the Rossby and Kelvin. There is Reynolds stress, Walker circulation, the Sverdrup transport, the Troup index (Sandy Troup was a noted Australian climatologist) and the Ekman spiral. The latter is an ascending corkscrew wind that breeds low-level monsoon clouds and heavy precipitation. It works by friction and, away from land, even imposes itself on the ocean, duplicating in the sea what is going on in the sky. Upwellings of cold water from the deep trace the same spiral patterns as the wind, and fish are subjected to the same surging forces as birds.

That evening, at a small thatched bar by the beach, I bumped into Shashi, the vulcanologist, talking animatedly to a middle-aged hippy with a thin, lined face and bare arms. They were speckled with inflamed mosquito bites which he kept scratching. His faded blue eyes jumped about in a disjointed way and a rubber band held his greying pony-tail in place. A small, beetle-shaped cicatrice was tattooed on his shoulder.

Shashi waved me over, offered me a drink and introduced his companion.

'This is Ekman,' he said in a jokey, long-suffering way.

'Hi,' said Ekman.

Shashi said, 'Ekman is an anthropologist. He and I were at Cambridge together. He got a First. And look at him now.'

Ekman grinned. 'I've been on the road,' he said. He had a strong trace of English north country in his voice.

'Alex's grandfather was out in the New Hebrides,' said Shashi. 'A missionary. He wrote some good stuff about volcanoes.'

Ekman's eyes ceased their wandering. 'Which island?' he said.

'Paama.'

'Is that near Malekula?'

'It's next door.'

Ekman spoke to Shashi. 'That's where Bernard Deacon was. I must have talked to you about him. He did anthropology at Cambridge back in the 1920s, then went out to Malekula to study custom.'

'You talked about lots of people,' said Shashi.

'Well, he was special. Brilliant! But the poor sod got blackwater fever and died at twenty-four because, according to the Malekulans, he broke a taboo. He went to some immensely sacred place up in the hills and saw what they were keeping there.' Ekman lit a cigarette and frowned into the middle distance.

'Well?' said Shashi.

'He says it was Noah's Ark.'

Shashi smiled, but I didn't.

'And was it?' I asked.

He shrugged. 'To the people of the Malekulan long-headed culture, yes, absolutely. If you're saying was it a big boat built from Middle Eastern oak, then no. What Deacon saw was a home-made replica. But that was just as remarkable.'

'They probably got the idea from the missionaries,' said Shashi.

I had listened to a conversation like this more than forty years earlier, on Paama, and now heard with absolute clarity the voices of Maurice and my father sitting out on the veranda after dinner. I saw the shadowy Swatow orange trees beyond the well, even smelt fragrant Passing Cloud smoke and the scent of the moon lilies planted below.

'My grandfather thought the Great Flood came to the islands,' I said. 'He would have believed in the Ark.'

'I think I kind of believe it too,' said Ekman.

Shashi ordered more beers and we talked of other things. I asked Ekman if he was related to a climatologist well known in monsoon circles. He wasn't, but listened closely to a summary of his names-ake's spiral.

I was content. Either literally or metaphysically Maurice's rain forest seemed to be a product of the Flood after all – the distinction barely mattered. Outside the bar a sparrow-like woman with a tiny child on her hip asked for money. I gave her 100 rupees and walked back to the hotel through a warm, heavy deluge overlaid with peals of thunder.

At the Fort Aguada I chatted to a Bombay agronomist who said it was a shame I had to leave tomorrow. I would miss the fireflies, due in a week or two. They filled the dark garden with their soft, surprising radiance, limning the trees, even drifting through the rooms. 'The kids collect them in jars,' he said. 'Each year they come here and lend splendour to the monsoon nights.'

Chapter Six

❖

9 JUNE

The captain of the Airbus, speaking at 31,000 feet in a cloudless morning sky, announced Bombay in fourteen minutes. A flanking turn to join the inbound traffic revealed that the city was enclosed in a massive slate-coloured marquee of rain. From up here its roof had a smooth, well-worked appearance – though, sinking closer, I saw that it was actually a sea of roiling waves, billows and breakers. They threw up chimerical spouts of black foam which kept getting vaporized by hurricane-force winds. When the Airbus dropped in it bounced out again. Our ride to the ground was a wild, plunging one, Bombay finally glimpsed through streaming windows as a dim, misty abstraction offering hints of a city but little hard evidence.

Silver roads wound through dark hills enveloped in even darker cloud, their bases lapped by huge interlocking puddles. The distant downtown skyscrapers were vague and dissembled as pillars of smoke.

We landed, taxied up to the stand and parked beside another Airbus preparing for push-back. Rain sheeted off its wings as men in dripping waterproof capes closed the cargo doors. The Santa Cruz domestic arrivals hall stood seventy yards away with a car-wash arrangement of gushing waterspouts ranged across its entrance. Passing through meant total immersion and, inside, blood-curdling curses and blasphemies were being uttered by the soaking, gasping passengers.

Waiting for my bag I watched a big white Mercedes draw up alongside a Hawker Siddley 124 executive jet that had just arrived.

The aircraft door opened and a man, two veiled women and four children disembarked but, instead of scampering to the car, they stood wonderingly with faces raised and hands outstretched. I was joined by a uniformed security man rolling a cigarette.

'Arabs,' he said. 'Now they will start coming – Saudis, Kuwaitis and so on visiting Bombay just to see water falling out of the sky. Those people are from Dubai. They will go to the Oberoi, sit in the rain for a week, then fly home.'

'When did the monsoon get here?' I asked.

'Last night,' he said.

'It was early.'

He shrugged. 'Not early enough for us.'

The luggage carousel began to turn, its dripping load making it look like a brimming rectangular viaduct. I watched a waterlogged cardboard box slowly disintegrate to reveal a tangle of sodden, brightly coloured women's garments. As the carousel began distributing them remorselessly around the baggage hall a teenage girl jumped on to it and ran agitatedly up and down, snatching at the clothes. She descended tearfully, arms filled with wet washing, crying, 'Oh, God, what shall I do with them?'

The taxi I hailed outside had come through so many monsoons there was a tide mark of corrosion running around the bottom of the doors. Like a Plimsoll line, it seemed to indicate the depth of water over which the driver was not licensed to operate. Braving the rain he sprang out, seized my bag, ushered me in, threw the bag in after me, then rushed round to board himself.

These courtesies, as rare in Bombay as they are in London, were surprising, but not so surprising as the cab's interior. It had been transformed into a tiny world of order and tranquillity. A gaudy statuette of the Virgin Mary stood on the dashboard with postcards of snowy Himalayan landscapes glued beneath, each illuminated by a coloured Christmas-tree light. Garlands of jasmine filled the car with fragrance. Behind my seat more lights flanked a miniature gilded cage containing a toy nightingale. There was thick crimson carpeting on the floor and, pasted to the rear of the driver's seat, pictures of girls, temples, tigers, cumulus clouds in a dark monsoon sky. A sign fixed to the dashboard said 'Bless Us!', another, 'This vehicle was purchased with funds from the Union Bank'.

The driver, young, dark-skinned, intense, took a small bottle from his glove box and beckoned me forward. He placed a dab of sandalwood perfume on my wrists and then plunged his hands into the jumble of wires that hung from the dashboard. These, touched together in sequence, got the engine going. The noise it made was unusual, like steam whistles accompanied by deep percussive bangs. He activated the single wiper, which fitfully stirred the torrent coursing down the windscreen, then turned and smiled at me.

'Are you comfortable?'

'Yes, thank you.'

Cautiously he joined the traffic hurtling into town, the vehicles all semi-obscured by spray and travelling like speed boats. Racing to beat the lights we hit our first billabong of standing water. It thundered into the wheel wells and gushed up past the windows, causing the car to slew wildly; a lorry overtaking on the wrong side missed us by the width of a raindrop. Horns blared. The driver, his thin shoulders hunched, jaw muscles working, gripped the wheel like the reins of a runaway horse.

Plumed wakes warned there was more ahead.

'Puddle,' muttered the driver, slowing.

Puddle? It was a small inland sea, its further coast barely visible to the naked eye, but our crossing was accomplished without difficulty since this one had a benign puddle god. The driver's confidence grew. We entered the next at a fair speed but, midway over, there was a sudden lurch and a muffled, shocking thud; we spun slowly, sheeting water, to face the way we had come. The car lay at an odd angle and all the Christmas-tree lights had gone out. For a few seconds we sat in stunned silence and then the driver threw open the door. What he saw caused him to clutch his head in anguish.

The front offside wheel had come off. It still occupied the wheel well, but was no longer attached to the axle. We stared at it while water enclosed us. We stood in it up to our ankles; it fell on us out of the sky and came at us laterally as surf from passing vehicles. I had never felt so wet or exposed. And we were marooned amid speeding traffic in conditions of minimum visibility.

It was the driver who acted. Moaning softly, half-blinded by rain, he heaved my bag out and ran with it to the side of the road before dodging back and locking his doors. Then he went sprinting off in the direction of Bombay and, within seconds, was lost in the downpour.

He had left me outside a colony of squatters' shacks, small ephemeral dwellings made from scavenged materials. This was garbage-dump architecture, its constituent parts abandoned by the affluent world outside but put to good use here. I noted packing-crate timber, rusting corrugated iron, bits of polystyrene insulating materials, lengths of piping and plastic sheeting.

The inhabitants clustered in their hovels watching expressionlessly. Then a small, bony, unshaven man stepped forward, picked up my bag and beckoned to me. I entered his home through a doorway made from an iron bed frame. The interior was dry, ordered and cosy. He placed the bag on a leeped floor fashioned from cowdung and mud, beaten flat and raised above the flood outside. A woman sat on it with a baby girl in her lap. In a corner, on an embroidered cloth, two polished brass bowls glowed like Chinese lanterns. Mud bricks nearby contained the ashes of a fire. Kindling lay stacked alongside, together with several iron pots, tin plates and cups, a bottle of ghee and a bucket of water.

The dappled light had the soft iridescence of a rainbow's interior. It came from a wall made entirely from plastic shopping bags, blue, red, green and yellow, which also laid a ghostly mosaic across the floor. Some bore commercial logos; one said Thai Royal Orchid Service, others Rajaram Quality Wines and Peter Stuyvesant.

The man indicated that I should sit.

I apologized for making his house wet and he replied affably in a language I did not understand. The woman and the child eyed me in silence as I watched the rain coursing down the plastic wall. It made small furrows and gullies, like sinews moving under skin. A wind gust caused the wall to billow and spring a small leak. The man lit a candle and carefully ran the tip of the flame along the edges of the sundered bags, bonding them securely. After checking for other areas of weakness he blew out the candle and smiled at me.

Neighbours peered in, then went away again. Seated there in that tiny house of lights it occurred to me that I was being sheltered by the homeless of Bombay, some of the million scavengers who must live on the streets and arrange what shelter they can. I felt no sense of threat or menace. Most, I guessed, were country people, driven into town by famine, flood or failed harvest – and thus victims of the monsoon's excesses – and now they were displaying the inflexible rules of country hospitality.

I was evicted, eventually, by the baby. Without warning, her eyes fixed unblinkingly on mine, she let out a wail and then a series of screams that drowned the noise of the rain and traffic and brought neighbours running to the door. The mother remained impassive; the father shook his head and smiled. 'Don't worry about it,' he seemed to be saying. But that infant needed food; so did its parents. I gave the father some money and, clumsily, pointed at the baby and then at my mouth. I saw a flicker of anger in his face and felt a kind of mortified confusion. What was wrong? Did he think I wanted the baby for lunch? I went to the roadside and, a moment later, flagged down a cab. Only then did I understand why he was upset. I had, God help me, been urging the hungry to eat.

The clerk at the Taj Mahal Hotel on Apollo Bunder assured me the monsoon was due tomorrow. What I had just come through, according to the weather bureau, was mere heavy showers.

'This is deeply confusing,' I said.

He said, 'Sir, it is deeply confusing time of year.'

Glacing through the *Times of India* property pages I thought of the family who had sheltered me. Bombay's 2,000 slum districts – one has the dubious distinction of being the largest in Asia – contain half its population. Six million people live in squalid one-room tenements, a million more on the streets. What had caught my eye was a discreet, elegant display ad which read, 'Luxurious flats at Walkeshwar, 2,500 sq ft and above with terrace, full marble, panoramic sea view, natural scenic surroundings, ample car parking, garden and aristocratic society.' The price wasn't mentioned. Interested parties were simply given a box number to write to.

I went to see Pritish Nandy, a poet who, after writing forty acclaimed books of verse, accepted the editorship of a popular radical magazine, the *Illustrated Weekly of India*, because he wanted to fight on the side of the people. A clever, fast-talking man fizzing with energy, he sat in a glass-walled office at the end of a busy editorial floor, passing page proofs, answering the phone and advising staff who kept putting their heads through the door.

'During the four years I've been doing this job I haven't written a single poem,' he said, cheerfully. 'And I probably never will again. As a journalist I often feel I'm whoring with words but, in the work I'm doing now, there is no place for the innocence, vulnerability and tentativeness with which a poet handles language. I live in a country where every year millions are pulled down below the breadline, where the corrupt and degenerate often win. As a poet I couldn't do anything about that. A poet can't force a government to take action in a drought area where people are living off worms and the roots of trees.' He grinned. 'But a determined editor can. We're tough, we fight, we get into scraps and we get things done. We also administer a kick up the backside of our rulers if they become too complacent. On Independence Day, for example, when everyone was supposed to be feeling very patriotic, we ran a special famine issue. The government didn't like that at all, but if the monsoon had failed this year 100 million people would have gone hungry.'

A young man in shirt-sleeves rushed in with a page proof headlined 'Heat and Lust'.

Pritish Nandy perused it for a few seconds, his head cocked to one side. He roared, 'Good! Good!' and the young man rushed out again.

'So you were not the only person who gave a big sigh of relief when it showed up. You're only getting a book out of it; yours is actually the least important requirement of anyone in the country. But to most, as you must have discovered by now, it represents life itself. To Rajiv Gandhi it meant nothing less than political survival. It saved his skin. If the monsoon hadn't appeared on cue last week his government would have fallen. That's a fact, and I assure you no one in India followed those famous Trivandrum weather forecasts more anxiously than he did.'

I asked Mr Nandy how he had regarded the monsoon as a child.

He said, 'I know it's the most beautiful and evocative of our seasons but I'd wake up in the afternoons when it rained and feel totally lost. I still remember looking out through the iron grille at our waterlogged street and being gnawed by a sense of deep foreboding, an inexplicable metaphysical fear. It was the dominant metaphor in my poetry – though that's all behind me now, of course.'

'You see no romance in the monsoon?'

'Not in the big cities. Go to the window! Where's the romance in mud, slush, rats and floods? Or in the anguish of watching those who live in the streets trying to cope? Sometimes, watching the shack-dwellers, the whores and the homeless struggling to save their possessions, trying to find somewhere to sleep, I think they must perish. But they don't, and often I wonder if I would have the courage to survive down there. I'm one of the lucky ones, you see. I have a roof, a bed, a car; I can take the monsoon on my own terms. But for many of my fellow-citizens it is a period of misery and hardship.'

I asked Mr Nandy if there was anything about the monsoon of which he approved.

'Well, after the torrid heat and constant whiplash of the summer sun, those first rains are delicious, a revelation.' He hesitated. 'I suppose what I like especially about the monsoon is the way it restores the colours of India. Lambent green plains verging on emerald, lavender hills, grey skies, that wonderful soft light. And also the way it restores your peace of mind. It allows you to drift into a comfortable physical state and a very, very restful mental state.'

His voice had grown dreamy. But suddenly Pritish Nandy jumped up. 'It has been jolly nice meeting you. On your way out will you please tell that man at the third desk, the one in the red pullover and spectacles, that I want to see him at once!'

The clerk at reception had been right. Officially the monsoon was not due for another two days. The *Times of India* reported that, at the moment, it was dallying in the town of Akola, uprooting trees, damaging rooftops, even bringing down overhead wires near the district library. At Raigad it had 'rained incessantly' all night.

But a lot of Bombay people seemed to think it was here already. The doorman at the Taj certainly did. I got to know him as I left the building late in the afternoon to investigate gunfire in the street outside. 'Glasses!' he shouted as I came rushing through the swing door.

I went blind but, before I crashed sightlessly down the steps, he grabbed my arms. I whipped off my spectacles and instantly my sight was restored in full. The lenses were completely fogged over, coated with an impenetrable layer of condensation. He said, 'It happens when you walk from air-conditioned lobby into moist monsoon atmosphere. For the Japanese it is a big problem. Often they are coming out in groups, walking very fast, and I can catch only one or two. The others go bouncy bouncy and enter car on hands and knees!'

I thanked him and put the glasses away.

'What's the shooting?' I said.

'It's a wedding.'

'They're quarrelling already?'

'No, no. It is crackers only.'

He was a Sikh, turbaned and bearded, with steady eyes. Outside, the rain had stopped. I said, 'When will the monsoon come?'

'Monsoon is here,' he said.

'The Met Office say tomorrow or the next day.'

The doorman said, 'I say today.'

I descended, cautiously, to the street to view these monsoon nuptials. The procession was led by a brass band wearing gold-tasselled crimson shakos and gold-frogged crimson jackets. The trumpeters blew loudly and discordantly; the drummers ferociously attacked their instruments; and apprentice bandsmen ran around lighting and throwing Bengal bangers with the earnestness of men engaged in very serious work.

The wedding party came behind, some marching, some dancing, some just ambling along shouting companionably to each other. That this was a high-class affair was demonstrated by the size and splendour of the band and the affluent, well-tailored look of the guests. Several dozen child beggars scampered along beside them, watched closely by the bandsmen. Indeed, as they approached a side entrance of the hotel, the drummers began shouting threateningly at the beggars and even some of the trumpeters lowered their instruments and joined in, their voices angry and hectoring.

The bride, a pretty, bright-eyed girl in a creamy silk sari, went through the door with the guests jostling behind. Her father lingered, hands deep in his jacket pockets. All at once the beggars charged towards him, and the band, breaking ranks, did the same. He laughed and began throwing rupee notes. Clouds of them fluttered through the heavy air, and beggars and bandsmen fought grimly and silently in the street to possess them. The beggars – smaller, tougher and more adroit, working like miners deep in the maul – did best. Then their benefactor, his pockets emptied, gave a brief wave and vanished inside.

In the coffee shop a waitress said, 'Of course I will bring beer if you insist, but I think you should try the mangoes.' She looked like a beauty queen and her expression was earnest and quizzical.

'I actually wanted a drink,' I said.

'We put them in blender and you half-sip, half-eat with a spoon.'

I ordered the mangoes. At the next table an elderly man sat with his son, who was well dressed in a sharp, flashy sort of way. The older man seemed very distressed. 'You are being reckless, *reckless*!' he cried.

'He will be a good business partner.' The other spoke sullenly with eyes averted.

'He will *not*! His father was a fool and so is he.'

The waitress returned and set a tall glass before me. 'There we are, the classic fruit of the monsoon,' she said, then stood back with folded arms, watching. The contents of the glass were a warm, glowing orange; faint hints of fire indicated that perhaps crystals from the sun had been dropped like sugar lumps into the blender too. It smelled of flowers and, mixed in with the wonderful mango tastes, the fruit gave off hints of cinnamon and rare spices. I finished every last drop.

'They were absolutely the best I've ever had,' I said.

She smiled and touched my hand. 'That will please my father,' she said. 'Early this morning I picked them in his garden.'

10 JUNE

In the *Indian Post* a report dated 9 June said, 'The South-West monsoon has advanced towards Greater Bombay, according to a city weather bureau report this evening, which means rains are here to stay for the next three months.' Cloudy skies and heavy showers were predicted for today. So, denied by some, acknowledged by others, confusing many, it had indeed sneaked in yesterday under the cloak of its own advance downpours and now, if the authorities had got it right, was in position over the city. Recalling the emphatic nature of its arrival at Trivandrum and Cochin I wondered about this curiously covert Bombay burst and, for my own peace of mind, took a taxi out to the Meteorological Centre at Colaba.

Localized flooding sent us on a roundabout route. It was a pleasant run, affording glimpses of the sea and a beach on which a fleet of fishing boats stood high and dry, hauled up for the monsoon and now being turned into dwellings. Intrigued, I stopped the taxi and went to look. The hulls, resting on stones, had been raised a couple of feet off the sand. Above, bamboo joists ran from central ridgepoles over which the fishermen were now placing thatched roofs; extensive overhanging eaves would provide additional shelter for anyone standing beneath. Iron pots and brick fireplaces indicated that the kitchens were located under the sterns. More thatch walled in the superstructures forward and aft, creating snug, weatherproof living areas accessible by ladder.

A lanky young man in a breechclout invited me to scale his rickety ladder. I did so and found his family there – a woman and three young children busy arranging bed-rolls, cushions, mats, even brass ornaments and a vase containing freshly picked flowers. A mirror stood propped against a partly dismantled diesel engine. Though it reeked of fish and fuel oil, the interior was starting to take on a homely look.

The flowers were mauve and white, very like the crinum lilies which traditionally come into bloom a week before the burst and, like the pied-crested cuckoo, are regarded as one of its precursors. Back in the taxi I questioned the driver about them but he said lilies had little relevance to the monsoon. For him it was a time of flooded roads, endless jams and breakdowns, starting and ignition problems, rust and corrosion, seats made constantly wet by damp passengers, permanent puddles on the floor from their venting umbrellas. During the course of the next three months his windscreen wiper motor would burn out at least once, probably twice.

'No, this is not good time in Bombay,' he said. 'And always the monsoon bring death. The first was this morning. A big boulder displaced by rain fell into a *chowk* near Afghan Church. It killed a woman.'

As we drew up at the Met Office the air was moist and dim, with a curious blue opacity. The building stood in a tree-filled compound which gave off the smells of a garden after rain. Inside I passed a wall plaque which said INDIAN OCEAN FLOOR. I asked the man at the reception desk if we were supposed to be on the seabed and he pointed wordlessly to a second sign, 'Meteorology in the Service of Mariners'. Then he listened as I begged for a few moments with someone in authority.

'How far up you wish to go?' he asked.

'As far as possible.'

'Assistant Director V. P. Bannerji?'

'Well, yes! If he would see me.'

'I will find out.'

He picked up the phone and I took stock of my surroundings. I heard one shirt-sleeved man say to another, 'Oh, Ronnie, have you seen my current atlas? I must check some upwellings', and found myself thinking of the Royal Society in London which, more than three hundred years earlier, had taken the first steps to ensure the safety of mariners in monsoon waters. The Society's classic *Directions for Sea-Men, Bound for Far Voyages*, published in 1666, paved the way for other life-saving volumes – Captain Joseph Huddart's *Oriental Navigator* of 1735 and Captain James Capper's *Observations on the Winds and Monsoon* of 1801 – but the men of the Royal Society hadn't stopped there.

This Indian phenomenon became one of their great preoccupations. The Secretary, Edmond Halley, discoverer of the comet bearing his name, friend of Newton and author of the original monsoon flow chart, tried to explain it in terms of the physical sciences. Halley found himself profoundly interested in 'the Action of the Sun Beams upon the Air and Water' and his findings inspired another Fellow of the Society, George Hadley, to present a dazzling five-page paper which anticipated the Coriolis force by introducing the earth's rotation into the monsoon equation.

Other men began fitting pieces into the puzzle. In 1817 Alexander von Humboldt raised the matter of global heat distribution. Heinrich Dove, founder of the Prussian Meteorological Institute in 1848, investigated the role of the summer trades blowing up from the Southern hemisphere. And Captain Matthew Fontaine Maury, head of the US Navy Depot of Charts and Instruments, painstakingly collected data from 11,697 mariners in the Bay of Bengal, then concluded, quite wrongly, that the south-west monsoon started in the north and worked its way south at between fifteen and twenty miles a day. The shades of these men, I reflected, would have drifted peacefully around the 'Indian Ocean Floor'.

The man at reception said V. P. Bannerji would see me.

But the meteorologist, small and bespectacled with a balding, squarish head, watched resignedly as I produced my notebook. He thought I merely wished to pay my respects and shake his hand. He hadn't realized I wanted an interview, and sighed loudly at my first question: when had the burst actually arrived over Bombay?

'June the eighth,' he said.

'But yesterday, on the ninth, you were reported as saying it would come today or tomorrow, the tenth or eleventh.'

'You have misinterpreted the data,' he said. 'It was a quiet onset, but perfectly clear. Usually, of course, it comes with a bang, squalls and what not, but this year it was just heavy rain.'

'Was it on time last year?'

'No. Then it was very late. A rogue cyclonic system hijacked it across the Arabian Sea to Oman. Cyclonic systems are usually dependable carriers and very fast; in 1971 one brought the monsoon up from Trivandrum in two days only. Low pressure is also a good carrier. It is slower, but gives widespread and prolonged rains.'

'Will this be a good monsoon?'

'The prediction for June–September issued by the Additional Director General, Meteorological Office, Poona, is that rainfall will be normal.'

I asked about Bombay's service for mariners.

'We issue warnings to fishermen – though, at this time, only the larger craft are allowed out. We have eleven different storm signals which are posted in all ports likely to be affected and, of course, we call the fishermen's co-operative societies and tell them. Daily, at four fixed times, we broadcast these warnings and, even when they are far out at sea, the fishermen tune in their radios. If there is no warning we say so. No warning today. And we do it every day of the year so they form the habit of listening. But, of course, the monsoon period is the busiest time. That is when you have the greatest likelihood of tropical cyclones or deep depressions. These we can predict up to three or four days ahead. Further than that you cannot see.'

The wooden observatory tower stood outside his window. It was a pretty rustic structure, yellow with decorative green balconies. A dove sat preening itself on the wind direction indicator.

'How do you warn the city if a tropical cyclone is coming?'

'A Cyclone Alert is issued forty-eight hours in advance of a blow, a Cyclone Warning twenty-four hours in advance. We also issue Heavy Rain Alert when we expect falls of between 71 and 130 mm over a 24-hour period. When we anticipate more than 130 mm we issue a Very Heavy Rain Alert.'

Mr Bannerji yawned and gazed wistfully at his watch.

But when I wondered whether recent monsoons were displaying any particular trend he suddenly looked interested. 'You mean, do better monsoon times lie ahead? Well, there is evidence that the monsoon follows a 76-year cycle, the good phase coming when the sun's diameter is larger than average. Greater solar radiation produces a high temperature gradient that makes the atmosphere more conducive to rain over tropical regions. Since 1965 we seem to be passing through a deficient phase of the sun which, we think, will last till 1990. Then more bountiful rains should return. Meanwhile, though rainfall is down, flooding is up. This is because in Bombay we have tarred or cemented all our streets and compounds, blocking natural seepage into the earth.'

The observatory dove cooed and fixed its gaze expectantly on Mr Bannerji. 'I think that bird wants to be fed,' I said.

He frowned. 'Now you are asking me to feed the birds? Look, many people work under me here and I must do their salary, supervision, promotions, everything.' But the oblique, reassuring glance he directed at the dove seemed to say, yes, yes, be patient, when this fellow goes I have crumbs for you.

Heading down to the 'Indian Ocean Floor' I passed a room in

which half a dozen earnest young meteorologists were having a
tutorial. Their teacher, a lean ascetic-looking man in sandals, spoke
of the effect of monsoon winds on the currents, of picking up
monsoon signals at depth, of oceanic meanders, streamers, eddies
and whorls. For twenty minutes I lingered out of sight as he
inducted these neophytes into the lore of wind and water. There
were references to planetary advection, vortex stretching, vertical
friction, wind stress curl and resting oceans. Though I understood
little of it, I felt a curious sense of elation as, finally, I left them and
made quietly for the stairs.

An ambiguous onset seemed to be a hallmark of the Bombay
monsoon. In 1940 Nehru wrote:

> I have been to Bombay so many times, but I have never seen
> the coming of the monsoon there. I had been told and I had
> read that this coming of the first rains was an event in
> Bombay; they came with pomp and circumstance and over-
> whelmed the city with their lavish gift.
>
> So I looked forward to the coming of the monsoon and
> became a watcher of the skies, waiting to spot the heralds that
> preceded the attack. A few showers came. Oh, that was
> nothing, I was told; the monsoon has yet to come. Heavier
> rains followed, but I ignored them and waited for some
> extraordinary happening. While I waited I learned from
> various people that the monsoon had definitely come and
> established itself. Where was the pomp and circumstance and
> glory of the attack, and the combat between cloud and land,
> and the surging and lashing sea? Like a thief in the night the
> monsoon had come to Bombay . . . Another illusion gone.

Warden Road possesses a natural concavity which, each year,
floods to a depth of two or three feet. Midway over, there is a
submerged plinth built from bricks by the neighbourhood kids.
Periodically a small boy will stand on the plinth, its height ensuring
that the water comes only to his ankles. Approaching motorists use
this nonchalant figure as a visual depth reference and, more often
than not, drive straight in. As their engines stall and water pours

through the doors the other kids appear and begin negotiations. Their charge for pushing a car out is 10 rupees. Year after year the children work this scam and, year after year, Bombay's cursing motorists fall for it.

The afternoon was dry and surprisingly bright, but so humid that match-heads assumed the consistency of crayon and refused to strike. I strolled around the Gateway of India, the basalt triumphal arch erected by the British in 1924, feeling the feathery touch of child beggars on my arms. I gave coins to one, who dashed off and handed them to a haggard, lank-haired crone squatting on the pavement nearby, suckling a baby. Her breast, though, was round and full and I realized she must still be in her twenties. Everything is relative, though in India relativity is geared to medieval expectations. The average Bombay woman dies at fifty-four.

Beside the Gateway curious little wooden cruise boats were berthing at a set of worn, seaweed-slippery stone steps battered by breaking waves. The craft, built like miniature ocean liners, were high, multi-decked and top heavy, with gaudily painted false funnels set behind capacious bridge houses. Here, yelling instructions, wearing braided admirals' caps and spinning their huge tea-clipper wheels, stood the captains. One after the other the boats came in, spray bursting over their bows as they plunged and wallowed in the wild monsoon swell.

Then, as two men held on to the bucking craft with ropes, the passengers jumped. I joined the crowd of spectators and watched with my heart in my mouth. Each leap was an act of heroism. People of all ages were doing it, even stout old ladies clasping umbrellas and handbags; patiently they awaited their turn, then, judging the moment, springing across the boiling water to safety. And they climbed back up to the Gateway smiling. It had been a bit of a lark, a fitting end to a nice afternoon excursion.

Shipping moved in and out of the harbour. I watched a sleek French guided-missile cruiser drop anchor as two big container vessels made for the Arabian Sea. Back in my room I got out a facsimile copy of the *East-India Pilot*, published in London in 1778, and looked up the section called 'Directions for Sailing from Bombay in the Time of the SW Monsoon'. It said:

At this season of the year, as soon as you are without the
harbour of Bombay, there runs a prodigious sea which, with a
strong ebb tide, occasions it to break as if you were in shoal
water. Make your utmost endeavours to get an offing, taking
advantage of all the shifts of wind, always observing to stand
on that tack you can make most westing of; the wind will shift
2, 3 and sometimes 4 points at a time in the squalls, which are
frequent with almost incessant rain; but by no means be
prevailed on to come to an anchor. The best lat. to get an
offing is 18 deg. 30 min.'

I wondered if the navigators of those outward-bound container
ships had been in touch with anyone on the 'Indian Ocean Floor'.
Their vessels might be ten storeys high and as long as city blocks
but they too needed up-to-the-minute information on the shifting
winds and prodigious seas that were the hallmark of the south-west
monsoon.

At 6 p.m. a deep shadow slid across Bombay which caused people
to glance up instinctively. But whatever had darkened the city,
imposing extra degrees of blackness over the normal onset of
evening, had darkened the sky as well. There was nothing to be
seen. This ecliptic shadow seemed to be coming from far beyond
the atmosphere and it induced a curious sense of stillness; even the
traffic grew hushed, as though the motorists were too awed to
sound their horns. I had been watching men aboard the French
cruiser attempting to load a grey, torpedo-shaped object which,
hanging from a derrick, kept spinning in the wind. Now, all at
once, the wind ceased and they lowered and stowed the object
without further ado. The sea looked leaden and oily.

The monsoon was about to stage a show for Bombay and,
anxious to obtain a grandstand view, I took a lift to the Apollo Bar
on the twentieth floor of the Taj. The wind seemed to have been
funnelled indoors; it roared up the elevator shaft and made the cage
bucket skywards through heavy turbulence. In the Apollo I found
a dozen officers from the French ship drinking exotic cocktails. The
wardroom atmosphere was full of badinage and raised, bantering
voices. Several pretty girls sat nearby, watching expectantly.

Then the sailors saw what was going on outside. They fell silent and hurried to the windows. Giant black screens were being pulled across the harbour, obliterating the anchored vessels like chalk ships being erased from a blackboard. More screens were drawn over the city, extinguishing acres of lights, whole suburbs and business districts. We were alone, marooned twenty storeys up in the darkness, wondering about the nature of this black-out. No wind blew and not a drop of rain fell. The French, subdued, returned to their drinks and spoke in hushed voices. One, wearing a surgeon's crimson flashes, caught my eye. 'I think maybe it is the end of the world,' he said, not entirely joking.

Then the phone rang and everyone jumped. The barman picked it up. 'Is there a Mr Frater here?' he said.

'Yes.'

'Reception would like a word with you.'

The lady in reception told me that a Mr Ghosh wished to see me. He had been very persistent and made her call all around the hotel. I said I knew no one of that name. What did he want? I heard the murmur of voices and then she came back on the line with a small bubbling laugh.

'He is a rain-maker,' she said.

'Oh.'

She tried to contain her laughter. 'Shall I put him on?'

'Please.'

The voice that addressed me next was so loud even the French could hear it. They looked around as Mr Ghosh said he wished to show me a device he had just invented. It would revolutionize the world's weather yet was so compact it could be carried in a briefcase; what he desired was publicity, a write-up in my London newspaper and a mention in my book. If I had nothing better to do he would be grateful if I would come down to the lobby for a talk.

'Are you going to demonstrate it?' I asked.

Mr Ghosh, apparently yelling up the lift shaft, said, 'Sir, police will not allow because of flooding risk. They are treating my device with respect bordering on panic, and I have given undertaking not to activate it in built-up areas without first notifying them. Frogmen and rubber boats may be required.'

'I'll be right down,' I said. 'But the lobby's very crowded. How will I know you?'

He said, 'Sir, you will know me', and hung up.

As I left the Apollo the French, who had caught every word of this, were laughing. 'Il se peut qu'il aille faire une danse des pluies,' I heard one of them say.

Mr Ghosh stood in the lobby with a raised umbrella over his head. He wore silver waterproofed boots, a shiny grey waterproof cape and a rain bonnet, and was being watched in an amused way by most of the people there. As I hurried over, Mr Ghosh snapped the umbrella shut and shook hands.

'H. N. Ghosh,' he said, speaking in a normal voice. He led me to a vacant sofa and threw himself down. The rain bonnet came off, revealing a few strands of grey hair laid precisely across his gleaming scalp. He was small and broad-shouldered, with a large nose and pale, deep-set eyes that peered out of their sockets like mice, each independently swivelling and quartering the lobby; as one gazed speculatively at me the other attended to a briefcase which Mr Ghosh was now opening.

From it he produced three black metal cylinders which, wordlessly, he began screwing together. The assembled device looked like a small bazooka, about two feet long and fitted with a stock containing a row of red buttons.

'You can hold,' he said.

I took it and peered down the barrel. I saw silvery tulip-shaped valves protruding from a jumble of coloured wires. There were two adjoining tin lids set obliquely over the valves, one inscribed with the words 'Cow & Gate', the other 'Natural Breadcrumbs'. Carefully I handed it back to Mr Ghosh.

The eyes swung together and gave me a warm, beaming look. 'I call this the Precipitator and it works on the principle of cloud modification. That is, changing their buoyancy or the size of their particles.'

'Seeding them,' I said.

'Yes, in a sense. But that is usually done by scattering dry ice, sodium chloride and so forth. For this you need aeroplanes, rockets or, like the Russians, artillery shells. All are costly and complicated. My device works on acoustical techniques. It is same basic principle as a dog whistle, inaudible to the human ear, and is transmitted electronically like a radio beam on a tropospheric forward scatter pattern.' He frowned. 'You understand?'

'Well, more or less.'

'Up to now acoustical precipitation has worked only in a laboratory cloud chamber where standing sound waves can be set up. Working alone, however, and with no resources, I have achieved breakthrough scientists have been seeking for years. And it took me three months only! My sound waves fill clouds with sonic resonance. Like a sustained musical note cracking crystal it destabilizes the condensation nuclei which form the droplets. They cling together, grow plump, then fall like apples from the bough.'

He gave me a broad, happy smile.

'Does it work?'

'Of course it works. Last week I am taking it every day up to Hanging Gardens on Malabar Hill. And the result you can see all around. It was I who caused monsoon to come early.'

He sat there making soft little popping noises with his mouth, one eye inspecting his Precipitator, the other trained unblinkingly on a pretty girl in a mini-skirt walking past with a poodle.

Then a quiet voice behind us said, 'Father, there you are. It is time to come home.'

A tall young man stood there, hands in the pockets of a plastic mac, his expression wavering between exasperation and concern.

'I am talking to this journalist,' said Mr Ghosh shortly. 'He is from London.'

The young man sat down too. 'Mother is anxious,' he said. 'And your dinner is ready.' To me he said, 'I hope he has not been a nuisance.'

'Not at all,' I said. 'It's been really interesting.'

'I'm afraid it was I who sent him here,' he continued apologetically. 'I had heard from a friend at the *Illustrated Weekly* that you were talking to Pritish Nandy. He mentioned your name and said you were staying at the Taj. Father was having one of his depressions today so I told him about this writer who was following the monsoon in the hope that it would amuse him. Two minutes later he'd grabbed his Precipitator and shot out of the house.'

'Well, I'm very glad he did,' I said.

'He's a mathematician, you know. Or was before his illness, which is of a psychological nature. Now he designs kitchen equipment.' He smiled. 'With occasional diversions into other areas.'

Mr Ghosh had paid no attention to any of this. Fussily he cleared his throat. 'One thing I have not discussed is the legal aspect of my work. We may assume a man has property rights in the clouds above his land, but does he own the water that falls from them on to his gardens and pastures? And if I have caused that water to fall, does any part of it belong to me? If not, should I be paid a fixed fee or a royalty sum? That is something courts must soon decide.'

'We must go now,' said Mr Ghosh's son. He carefully dismantled the Precipitator and put it back in the briefcase. Then he took his father's hand and, without a backward glance, they stood and walked out into that eerie black dusk.

Perhaps the best known of India's rain-makers is Mr Thomas Jacob of Kerala. A darling of the media, he also uses a device that sends 'coded' electronic impulses into the atmosphere. On 6 April he told newsmen in drought-stricken Trivandrum that he would break the drought within fourteen days. On 17 April there was such heavy, sustained rain in Trivandrum that power supplies and traffic were disrupted. Mr Jacob, who sends his impulses into the atmosphere for between five and ten minutes every three hours, claims he has reached his present level of expertise and self-assurance after practising assiduously for fifteen years.

He could not be found when I asked to meet him.

Efforts to make cumulus clouds deliquescent have even been attempted with powerful sprays directed from the ground, though meteorological orthodoxy prefers more traditional methods. Here the *Times of India* reports on one:

From the middle of July a Dakota aircraft hired from a Bombay firm has been taking off from Ahmedabad airport to chase the rain-bearing clouds and 'seed' them to induce precipitation. Captain Bhalla, pilot of the aircraft, has been on such missions before and can recognize the dark rain-bearing clouds among the dry sterile ones and the dangerous thunder clouds.

The Dakota took off on every 'seedable' day carrying a ton of seeding material (a dust-fine mixture of common salt and soapstone). As the aircraft arrives at the target area Captain Bhalla gives the signal to begin 'seeding'. A couple of workers rush to empty the gunny bags into the special gadget in the belly and the seeding material whizzes past, leaving a white trail behind. After being repeatedly seeded the clouds grow darker and show evidence of precipitation. Raindrops begin to lash at the windscreen and the crew members beam with a sense of fulfilment.

The purest way of invoking rain is by song. The ancient rain-making ragas, sung by masters, could even move the gods – especially Indra who, riding a white elephant with four tusks, is charged with dispensing or withholding the rains.

Two powerful ragas are still cited today. The first, *Deepak*, generated such heat that it burned the throat of the singer and caused every candle in his vicinity spontaneously to burst into flame. The second, *Malhar*, cooled the singer's throat and brought rain copious enough to extinguish the candles and water the crops.

T. V. A. Seshan, for twenty years Professor of Economics at Madras University and later a journalist of great distinction, can also sing a raga which makes rain. But the last time he did it the consequences left him so shaken he vowed never to try again.

A small man with expressive hands and a mind in which ideas tumble and converge like watercourses, he now acts as a temple consultant to Hindu communities in North America and Australia. Perched on a chair at the Taj he told me that temples were his passion and obsession.

'I visit the sites of new ones abroad and advise on everything from the placing of the sanctum sanctorum to the primary and secondary idols. Male idols must be carved from masculine granite which gives off a deep, bell-like tone when tapped with a knuckle, female ones from feminine granite that produces the tinkle of anklets. It is physically impossible to carve a female statue from

masculine granite – the breasts will crack open – and vice versa.
Few people know that. Did you?'

'No,' I said.

'The quality of the congregation, though, is something I cannot
control. You are interested in rain and you probably wish to know if
a devout, temple-going congregation is more likely to invoke heavy
showers than a lazy, shiftless one. The answer is yes. Take Kerala, for
example, where the people are exceptionally devout and, as a
consequence, very, very good at rain. They achieve it through
patient chanting and the lighting of cloud-seeding fires; you will see
them in villages all over the place. At Kanniyakumari they can even
do mantras that reverse floods! By contrast the citizens of Madras
town, who are not so devout, haven't seen a drop for five years.'

I asked him to describe his own experience.

He paused, lips pursed. 'I sang *Raining Nectar*, a famous precipitation raga that normally needs a competent singer with a trained
voice; the syllables, the texture, are most complicated. One day,
urged on by sceptical friends, I began beneath a perfectly clear
blue sky. After a while clouds appeared from nowhere and gathered
above our heads. I was quite astonished, of course, but managed to
sing on. Then, moments later, it happened.'

'You made rain?'

He shook his head, still rattled by the memory.

'I made a full-blooded thunderstorm.'

'Goodness!'

'And though, normally, I eschew all vanity I must admit I
walked around for the next few days feeling very proud of myself.
But then the realization of what I had done began to sink in. I
possessed powers that truly frightened me, and I resolved never to
use them again.'

'How would you describe these powers?' I asked.

'I cannot. In Madras there is a violinist who produces rain but,
when he plays the crucial chord that seeds the clouds, his fiddle
splits asunder, cracked from end to end. Why? We do not know,
but there is increasing evidence that the reasons may somehow be
rooted in science. For example, every village temple in my area
possesses a kind of clarinet which, if played daily, helps the crops
grow. A research team from one of our leading agricultural uni-

versities has studied the phenomenon and proved, beyond a shadow of a doubt, that it works. Now they are determined to find out how, and we await their conclusions with more than passing interest.'

The evening paper reported the presence of widespread thunder-showers in Meghalaya. This meant the monsoon must be nearing Cherrapunji and, though no rainfall figures were yet available, the Bay of Bengal arm seemed to be moving into India on schedule. I imagined it touching Singapore and activating the Sumatras, then heading north, soaking Thailand and turning Bangkok into a city so waterlogged it was in danger of sinking.

During my last visit to Bangkok I had called at the British Dispensary to discuss the Thai monsoon with Dr Patrick Dickson. The dispensary, a two-storeyed building with a chemist's shop on the ground floor, a surgery and waiting room upstairs, had sunk 102 centimetres in twenty years but Dr Dickson remained fatalistic; there was little he could do about it. A lean, handsome man of sixty-one in a brown silk Thai jacket, he had read medicine at Cambridge before coming to Bangkok and learning the language. Then he sat all his exams again in Thai so that he could start a local practice.

'The monsoon arrives here between the twelfth and nineteenth of May. It produces such humidity that the birds can leave vapour trails in the sky. Very soon the city floods and many boats appear in the streets; I've even seen people passing my surgery on wind-surfers. It looks like Venice and, without the traffic, has that peculiar Venetian quietness about it. One is aware of the silence.

'To avoid commuting I always go and live at my local hospital for several weeks. We're busy. Flu epidemics mark the change of every season; we have them when the rains come and when they go again. House calls, of course, are made by boat. I regularly visit a rich industrialist in a villa not far from the royal palace. I sail through his front door and tie up to the stairs, welcomed by a butler who makes me fast with a nautical knot. That house is sinking too. Each year the boats of visitors are tied further and further up the staircase. It's because people keep digging wells and interfering with the water table. Then the developers come along and put up whacking great heavy buildings. Add annual monsoon floods and you've got a recipe for disaster. But what the hell. I still couldn't imagine living anywhere else.'

I dined in a small, crowded Nepalese restaurant off the Colaba Causeway and, waiting for a table, chatted to a couple of middle-aged female science teachers dressed in a conservative Western style. We talked about the monsoon – one of the city's most popular topics just now – and I recounted V. P. Bannerji's theory that Bombay's rainfall had been erratic since 1965 due to a deficient phase of the sun. I was showing off a little, claiming credit for having met that day with the Assistant Director himself. The ladies, though, were unimpressed.

'It has nothing to do with the sun,' said one, emphatically. 'What happened in 1965 was that exhaust fumes discharged into the city's atmosphere finally began affecting the natural rhythms of the monsoon. Each year we put up 1,500 tons from traffic and 1,000 tons from industries like chemicals, fertilizers and textiles.'

'They form a layer just below the stratosphere,' said her friend, 'and something very odd takes place when monsoon clouds come in contact with it. They become light and drift away without dropping their rain. They are ghost clouds.'

'And now scientists are telling us,' said the other, 'that if this poisonous layer remains for any length of time it could breed a new form of micro-organism. The scientists are believing these micro-organisms could settle on Bombay during monsoon and spread the most harmful and strange diseases on earth.'

Dom Moraes, winner of the Newdigate Poetry Prize at Oxford and now a distinguished member of the Bombay literary set, told me the monsoon was dreaded by poor students. 'They're often driven from overcrowded homes to study in the streets. You see them sitting there, reading under lamp-posts. The rains, of course, drive them back indoors and their work suffers as a consequence; disappointing exam results are often attributed to the monsoon.'

I looked up clouds in Y. P. Rao, and discerned an intensity coming through the dry prose like salt. His associates, taken aloft by the Indian Air Force to study monsoon formations over the Arabian Sea, had found unsuspected high cloud streaming far above the loftiest cumulus tops, eight oktas of it at 45,000 feet. Rao mused that, though it resembled fractostratus in parts – possibly old cumulus crowns commandeered from the Western Ghats – there was some stuff at 37,000 feet which could have been anvil cirrus distorted by wind shear. Well! Matters were complicated further by the discovery of twenty-two rain bands running parallel to the wind and so dark inside that the pilots flew blind. Rao formed 'the impression of a chaotic sky'. The clouds were not in his cloud atlas. They didn't conform to the international cloud code categories. More work needed to be done.

Before going to bed I looked up at the sky also and observed a luminous circle which grew steadily in size and intensity until, suddenly, black clouds parted like curtains to reveal a full moon. I hadn't seen the moon since Trivandrum and now there was a white ring around it, set at 22 degrees, faintly and dangerously touched with red.

11 JUNE

I breakfasted off a glass of mangoes brought by the coffee-shop beauty queen. They were from commercial sources, she warned, not as succulent as her father's, and picked a day too early. In the paper I read a piece headed 'Grim Warning' which reported that India's tree cover had now been reduced to 10 per cent. The level of cover necessary for climatic and ecological stability was 33 per cent and, if the present rate of deforestation went unchecked, India would be a desert before the end of the century – at much the same time that its population was expected to pass the one billion mark.

Now the government was about to submerge 300,000 hectares of prime virgin forest for a couple of hydroelectric projects. Its own Department of the Environment had advised against it, 300,000 people would be displaced, but the zealots in Delhi were pressing on regardless. 'This relentless deforestation,' the paper said, 'leaves little scope for optimism about India's environmental future.'

I wondered if I was witnessing one of the last monsoons.

'What are your plans for today?' asked the beauty queen in that direct and intimate way so characteristic of Bombay.

'I'm going to buy a ticket to Delhi and have a look around.'

'The rains have made the city quite disgusting,' she said. 'There is slush everywhere and many roads are impassable. It is the usual story. The municipal corporation have been caught napping again.'

Before setting off I put a call through to P. D. Gupta in Delhi. He was at his desk and answered promptly.

'You've been away,' I said.

'A little local leave.' He sounded cautious.

'Any news?'

'Applications have gone to the state governments of Assam, Meghalaya and Nagaland. We can do nothing until they approve.'

'And will they?'

'Who can say?'

'Can't Delhi say?'

'Absolutely not! We give them large degree of autonomy.'

Perhaps that meant giving them enough rope to hang themselves; I thought of the Indian Army units on full alert in the three states.

'What's the weather like with you?' I asked.

'Hot! Scorching, in fact.'

'No rain yet?'

'Not a drop.'

'I'm flying up to Delhi tomorrow – Friday. Perhaps I could pop in and see you on Monday morning.'

There was a small pause. 'Yes.'

'First thing.'

Mr Gupta made a sound in the back of his throat. It was meant to sound sociable and welcoming but came out as a definite growl.

In the course of a wander around the town I saw plenty of standing water. In some places the smell of effluent predominated, in others of rank decay. Here raw sewage seeped through broken pavements; there children, dogs and horses scavenged on piles of rotting garbage. The rats were sleek and cocky.

At a bus stop behind the main station I watched a youngish man wading through water with his shoes and socks in one hand and a briefcase in the other. He wore a laundered white shirt and well-pressed trousers rolled up to the knees and, at the bus stop, carefully dried his feet with a towel taken from his briefcase. Then, rolling down his trousers and putting on his shoes and socks, he told me he had a clerical job at a jute factory and lived on the streets with his mother.

The hardest part was keeping up appearances for work; his boss didn't know he lived rough. He loathed the monsoon. It meant hardship, degradation, anxiety. 'It is only because of the courage of my mother that we manage. She is such a fighter, sir, you cannot imagine!'

I expressed surprise that clerical workers should be among the city's homeless. He gave me a mirthless smile and said he knew even of junior management chaps without a roof over their heads.

Waiting in a queue at the Indian Airlines office at Nariman Point a bluff, overweight Sikh complained about the state of the city. 'You are right to be getting out,' he said. 'The fun is only just starting. When we get the first real storms it will be much worse.'

Monsoon storms cause hundreds of incidents annually. Here are a few typical ones, plucked at random from the tally of recent years. They have sunk or grounded fishing boats in the harbour, flattened hutments at the Kurla Railway Colony and numerous shacks at John, damaged the lip of the concrete sea wall near the Marine Drive swimming pool, dashed the Port Trust steamer *Zephir* against the sea wall at Ballard Pier, blown away two giant cylindrical tanks at Sassoon Dock and almost killed eight rare panthers; a large uprooted tree missed their cage at Victoria Gardens Zoo by a whisker.

Each year in late June promenaders on Marine Drive are struck by rocks scooped from the ocean bed. These missiles, lobbed by the furious sea itself, even cause fatalities.

The clerk sold me a ticket to Delhi without argument or demurral. She even offered me a choice of flights.

My Sikh friend agreed this was highly unusual. 'There will be a reason,' he said. 'Perhaps she is gaining merit in case she is struck by lightning. In her next incarnation she does not wish to be a frog.'

I went for a stroll along Marine Drive. The sea state today was moderate, the wind promising rain within the hour; horse-drawn gharries parked along the front waited expectantly for it to set in. Then they would head for the Oberoi to pick up Arab families who liked to sally forth with the hood down. Drivers and horses often look miserable during these outings, but their high-spirited passengers smile broadly through every waterlogged minute.

A more traditional monsoon presence on Marine Drive is the corn-on-the-cob sellers. Camellia Panjabi, a glamorous Bombay hotel executive, said they come with the rains and, squatting under ragged umbrellas, prepare corn-on-the-cob over braziers of glowing coals. 'They sell it piping hot and you eat it walking with your friends in the rain. Everyone wears jasmine. It blooms in the burst and men weave it into ropes which, on Marine Drive, you always drape around your neck.'

At Chowpatty beach I watched a sculptor create a perfect woman's head from sand. Wetting it with sea water and moulding it with his fingers, he worked so skilfully that it began to assume a force and personality that soon attracted other spectators. But this wasn't the head of a beautiful young girl. His woman was middle aged, with a large, fleshy nose, heavy cheeks, a sagging chin and a bad-tempered demeanour. She glared across the beach, poised to bark a command at an errant grandchild.

Two unshaven men with tangled hair and thin, bony faces came and stood close to me. They gave off sour smells and their eyes were red and slickly greasy, as though swimming in pools of fat. I knew I had seen eyes like that before and then, all at once, I remembered the cannibals – half a dozen dissolute-looking, furtive-mannered men shackled outside the Vila court house years ago. My father had said, 'See their eyes? That's how you spot a cannibal, Sandy, and it's worth bearing in mind in case chaps like that ever ask you to lunch.'

I observed this pair warily. Muggings had been on the increase in Bombay due to the growing popularity of 'brown sugar' – unrefined heroin – and I wondered if it too showed in an addict's eyes. Human flesh could also be addictive, according to my father, especially the meat from the head and insides of the thighs. And he spoke with the authority of someone who had survived his first brush with cannibals at the age of five.

It was on Paama during the early days, when a raiding party had come for Maurice and Janey. Maurice, convinced the end was nigh, handed Janey his pistol and told her to shoot the boy before shooting herself. Then, as they ran from room to room looking for him, they became aware that the bellicose shouts of the cannibals had turned to laughter. My father had been taught to shake hands with every native visitor, and now he had gone into the garden to greet the cannibals. This apparent defiance from a small boy so charmed them that they shouldered their axes and, sportingly, went marching back to the hills.

What happened next on Chowpatty beach was so quick that now, months later, I am still not sure I have the sequence right. One of the men stepped in front of me. Though distracted, some instinct made me turn and face his collaborator. He produced a kind of truncheon and aimed it at my head. I yelled and executed a standing backward leap that took me right up off the ground. I found myself suspended above the beach, grateful for my escape; another split second and my corpse would have been hung from a tall wooden drum and, before dismemberment, beaten Paama-fashion with paddles to break the bones.

I became aware that my father was around here somewhere, trying to attract my attention. Hovering at a height of fifty feet or so, drifting among the bright paper kites, I conducted a systematic search for him but, puzzlingly, saw nothing. I wondered why I should be up here levitating and guessed it might be due to the monsoon and the huge forces at its command; I had become a mere speck, one of Mr Ghosh's cloud nuclei. I was dimly aware of a voice saying, 'Stand back! Give him air!' and then I perceived a face, thin and bespectacled, above mine, with other faces ranged behind it. Astonished, I realized I was lying on my back. The face spoke again. 'I saw whole incident. I think they only managed glancing blow but you must report it to police. These addicts are becoming real menace.'

I sat up and touched my head. There was a bump, tender to the touch, but it didn't hurt and, when I stood, embarrassment proved stronger than any shock or grogginess. I thanked the bespectacled man and assured him I would report the matter as soon as I saw a cop. Then, checking my money was still intact, I continued

cautiously on my way, carried along by a curious, burgeoning
sense of exhilaration.

At the head of the beach, among the hawkers of *bhelpuri* snacks and
kulfi ice cream, a stooped, white-haired man was painting under an
umbrella. He stood at a small wooden lectern, working with
intense concentration and ignoring the activity around him. Pausing to peer over his shoulder, I saw that he was finishing an Indian
miniature of the traditional school. It was a small, intricate, glowing
picture of two women under a mango tree, one kneeling before the
other. A stream flowed through the foreground. Pink lotuses
flowered in the stream and the tree was filled with vivid green birds
and unripe fruit. Noting my interest he said, without pausing in his
work, 'The barber's wife is applying henna to the feet of a noble
lady. The fruit and flowers are images of fecundity; she is about to
meet her lover.' He made a pair of dots with the point of his brush.
'Those are black bees. They represent erotic fulfilment.'

'It's beautiful,' I said.

He glanced at me. He had thick white eyebrows and a level
gaze. 'Rembrandt used to collect these things. Did you know?
Charles the First of England also. Foreigners think they are all
coming from Rajasthan but there were many schools – the Mughal,
Gujarat, Punjab Hills, Himalayan Hills and so forth.'

'Which school are you?' I asked.

He smiled. 'I am Bombay tourist school. I do same four paintings
only, copies of popular and famous classical pictures now in private
collections in America. I do this one, I do intoxicated ascetics –
monks taking marijuana in a temple garden – I do Krishna (who is
coloured blue) awaiting his lover, and I do lovers watching the
approaching rains. That is my best-seller.'

His completed pictures stood propped on a portable display
stand. The lovers watching the approaching rains were a celebration so animated that one could almost hear thunder, birdsong and
the voices of the women who thronged it. I suddenly longed to
possess the original.

He offered me his version for 150 rupees.

'I'll buy it if you tell me exactly what's going on,' I said.

He picked up his brush and began applying pale terracotta to the bodice of the barber's wife. 'The man is a prince. As the dark monsoon clouds gather over distant hills he stands on terrace of palace, embracing his lover. Lightning has startled the white cranes and they are flying wildly up into black sky. That peacock roosting beneath the terrace will soon go off and dance joyously in the forest; peacocks always dance at start of the monsoon, though, to be honest, I have never seen them do it. Maids carry the prince's fans and rose water pipe. The female musicians downstairs are serenading the rains and also our amorous couple. When the rain begins the couple will retire to the small pavilion and make love; as you see, a bed awaits them, the red counterpane signifying bliss. Down in the garden is a lotus pond and trees filled with birds. Parakeets are eating the ripening mangoes. In the valley, directly beneath the black cloud, stands a small town, part of the prince's estate. On the green hills all around cowherds are hurrying their animals to shelter.'

'But there's no rain.'

'Every single element in the picture is speaking of rain. The rain itself would be superfluous.'

I handed him the money and he slipped the picture into a cellophane envelope. I thanked him and turned to go. Then I turned back. 'How do you actually paint rain?'

'Rain is done with ropes of pearls,' he said.

Chapter Seven

❖

12 JUNE

'All of us green-eyed Delhi women,' said Mrs Reddy, pouring
jasmine tea, 'are descended from Alexander the Great.'

'She doesn't mean personally,' said Sanjay, her husband.

'Oh, yes I do. I have Alexander's nose, as shown on the coins.
The family resemblance is striking.'

She was a big-boned woman with pale skin and beautiful
features, and had just cooked us a dinner of curried lamb. Now,
driven from the house by a power cut that deprived us of air-
conditioning, we sat in the garden trying to get cool. They were
friends of one of my London neighbours and, when I phoned soon
after arriving in Delhi, insisted I dine with them that very evening.
Sanjay said he would pick me up at seven sharp. He didn't say he
would be riding a motor bike and I didn't think to ask. His
yammering Enfield Bullet went blasting through the traffic and
negotiated the roundabouts at gravity-defying angles. We had
races with a couple of Yamaha Rajdoots and, passing the Chanak-
yapuri Diplomatic Enclave, an old British Matchless ridden by
some speed-crazed attaché in a fighter pilot's helmet. Nearing his
house in the smart residential suburb of Defence Colony I told
Sanjay my chief reason for being in Delhi was to get clearance to
visit Cherrapunji.

'So you have come to see our bureaucrats!' he yelled over
his shoulder. 'I can promise you nothing but blood, sweat and
tears!'

Sanjay was in public relations and he knew everybody. His
friend and my London neighbour, Peter Able, worked in the same

line of business and, sitting there in the garden, we explored the possibilities inherent in their names. I said I had been at school with a boy called Amos Willink who, if offered a partnership, would enable them to have an agency named Reddy, Willink & Able.

Coming to the point, I asked whether he had any advice for me.

'I think the chances of you getting to Cherrapunji are pretty remote,' he said, slowly. 'You would have to go in through Shillong, the capital of Meghalaya, where the government always seems to be invoking its emergency powers. I don't know what's happening in Cherrapunji itself, but the whole area seems pretty unsettled.'

'Is this a wasted journey?' I asked.

'The instinctive response of our civil servants,' said Mrs Reddy, 'will be to withhold permission. They may tell you it's for your own protection but really it's because they are great defenders of entrenched positions. They like to dig in and hold the line. They also want a quiet life; you will be a problem, more paperwork, another file. It would be much easier for them if you just went away, and they will urge you to do this. They are timid men, scared of their bosses, scared of responsibility.' She smiled at me in the candlelight. 'You won't see many green-eyed descendants of Alexander in the upper echelons of our ministries.'

The thermometer registered 92 degrees Fahrenheit and the air had the perfect stillness of wine left to age in the cask. When Sanjay lit a cigarette and placed it in an ashtray the smoke ascended in a line so pure it was almost architectural. The eucalyptus he had planted for shade were motionless, a row of fossilized evergreens that filled the garden with their pungent medicinal smell. I looked for the moon in vain. It was masked by the heavy pall of heat and fine grey sand that, day and night, covered Delhi like a shroud. The sand, blown in from the Thar Desert, remained fixed in a mysterious state of suspension.

Mrs Reddy refilled my cup. 'You must keep drinking,' she said. 'In this climate you need, daily, at least one pint for every kilo of body weight. Otherwise dehydration sets in. After that, kidney stones.'

'You're kidding!'

'Indeed, I'm not. One is a direct consequence of the other. And dehydration can steal up on you without warning. One moment you think you're feeling fine, the next you are coming around in hospital with a drip in your arm.'

Sanjay said the monsoon was due on 29 June. The Meteorological Office reported that it was on schedule though he wasn't sure how they could tell.

'Seventeen days to go,' said his wife. 'And goodness, how they drag by. We are like children waiting for Christmas.'

'What are your plans for the weekend?' asked Sanjay.

'I haven't made any.'

'You should go to Deeg,' said Mrs Reddy, suddenly.

'Of course!' exclaimed Sanjay.

'What happens at Deeg?'

'It has the most beautiful monsoon pavilion in India,' she said, 'sitting beside a palace and a lesser pavilion also dedicated, in their way, to the rains. It is one of my favourite places – about five hours' drive from here, in Rajasthan. Sanjay,' she said, 'let us all go to Deeg tomorrow!'

'Tomorrow we have the Russians. They are coming for dinner. And on Sunday they expect us for lunch at the Oberoi.'

She leant across and touched my hand. 'Then you must go by yourself. It is very important. The palace was built by a small-time maharaja and ex-thug – a minor warlord really – but he had poetry in his veins. The monsoon pavilion is open-sided and made of marble. It has a huge concealed water tank in the roof once filled by elephants hauling leather buckets up from a special reservoir. Beside the pavilion there is a marble swing and an exquisite Hindu garden – a night garden, filled with white flowers which show up in the moonlight.'

'But it's all an illusion,' said Sanjay.

'That is exactly why it is so wonderful!' his wife said. 'In a rainless land he created his own illusory monsoon. On the appointed day he ordered flowers to be plaited into the ropes of the swing and then led his family into the monsoon pavilion. All at once water from the tank flowed down the walls, a thousand fountains played and, hidden up in the false ceiling, servants banged huge iron balls together to simulate thunder. The air became cool, running water could be seen and heard everywhere and, as his daughters rode on their monsoon swing, the illusion was complete.'

I stared at her, transfixed. 'I'll go tomorrow,' I said.

13 JUNE

A car, ordered late the previous evening, turned up on time at 7 a.m. It was an elderly Hindustan Ambassador driven by a tall, fleshy, stolid man who, as he negotiated Delhi's gladiatorial roundabouts – its users impetuously engaging in combat even at that hour – made it clear that he knew his business. I had engaged him because foreigners couldn't then hire self-drive cars in India, and buses to Deeg were infrequent and unreliable. For much of the way we would follow the Grand Trunk Road that ran towards Agra and the Taj Mahal.

The heat haze and desert dust, in daylight, formed a dense grey mist that obscured the sun and restricted visibility to a hundred yards. As the car rocked in a wind seemingly ducted through blast furnaces I thought of the British Army Engineers who, in 1830, began walking from Calcutta to Delhi to conduct the Grand Trunk Route Survey. Their party consisted of Indian troops with muskets to fight off dacoits and wild beasts, two sweating coolies who pushed the recording wheel, an official to reset the cyclometer and more coolies carrying tents, supplies, theodolites and compasses. One of the Engineers summed up the experience in verse:

> *The wheeling months go round*
> *And back I come again*
> *To the baked and blistered ground*
> *And the dust-encumbered plain*
> *And the bare hot-weather trees*
> *And the Trunk Road's aching white;*
> *Oh, land of little ease!*
> *Oh, land of strange delight!*

The traffic moved nose to tail at a brisk pace. In the township of Hodal, a settlement of red brick and thatch houses set among young eucalyptus, the Dabchick Restaurant had opened for business. We passed a hovel calling itself the English Wine Shop and a sign saying 'Gaunchi Main Drain Weak Bridge Ahead Caution'. A road gang's notice warned of 'Material on Berms'. The driver said, 'There are four things motorist needs in India: good brakes, good horn, good reflexes and good luck.'

Some instinct made me reach into my bag and extract the orthopaedic collar they had given me at the National Hospital. I recalled, word for word, John Morgan-Hughes's warning that another whiplash injury could put me in a wheelchair and now, quite suddenly, had the strongest conviction that something was about to happen.

The driver gazed at me wide-eyed in the rear-view mirror.

'Are you quite well, sir?' he asked.

I told him I had a small neck problem and, nodding, he turned his attention back to the road. Two minutes later the bonnet of the car in front suddenly snapped into the air. Its unsighted driver stopped abruptly and so did we, but the vehicles behind carried on and a trip-hammer sequence of three shockingly violent blows sent us cannoning into the car ahead. It was a dark blue Hindustan and we tossed it clean over a foot-high verge. In the silence that followed I noted wavelets of clear liquid surging across the road. The wind etched tiny cat's paws on it. Then the driver yelled, 'Petrol!' and scrambled out; a pair of jammed rear doors prevented me from following.

The landscape had been empty of people but now, in the Indian manner, scores of shadowy figures began looming out of the murk. The sight of two men with lighted cigarettes peering through my window encouraged me to attack the door again. I got it open by kicking, then vaulted clear like a tail-gunner leaving a doomed bomber. The windscreen of the vehicle behind, a jeep hybrid with its bonnet buried deep under our rear, had been wrapped around its occupants like cellophane packaging. Their faces, pressed to the glass, were animated crimson smudges leaking blood. A lorry, fringed and tasselled, its deserted cab gaily painted with surreal red fish and bearing the slogan 'Operators Good Transport Union Palwal', had welded itself to the jeep's rear. And, finally, projecting from beneath the tail of the lorry, was a mangled maroon saloon from which screams were coming.

My driver and I, too traumatized to do anything sensible,

watched dazedly as the crowd fell upon the trapped vehicles and prised the occupants free, laying them carefully on the central reservation where a bespectacled dental student carried out cursory examinations and announced that, contrary to appearances, none of the injuries was serious. A youth volunteered to fetch the police. Two women from the maroon saloon wept noisily while the driver of the Hindustan with the faulty bonnet catch sat on the ground holding his head in his hands.

I removed my orthopaedic collar which was getting some funny looks. The traffic began to flow again, bus passengers craning to look, a European in a chauffeur-driven Mercedes barely glancing up from his newspaper as he swished past. The dental student commandeered a passing van, ushered his patients aboard and departed at speed. My driver said he was going to find a telephone. We had left the worst of Delhi's heat fog behind and the landscape, glimsed through shimmering opaque air, was flat and arid. By the road I saw a lofty whitewashed wall with the words 'Fizz Drinks Pty Ltd Makers of Thril' painted on it, together with a movie-style poster showing a handsome, sleekly affluent couple beaming over a shared bottle. 'Hum Tum Aur Thril!' they proclaimed.

A man emerged from the Thril factory gate and beckoned to me. He was gnarled and stooped, with an unexpectedly youthful gaze. Having seated me on a wooden bench, he handed me a chipped cup of heavily sugared tea.

'Where are we?' I asked.

'Faridabad!' he said.

Members of the incoming day shift were treated to eyewitness descriptions of the accident. His reports, accompanied by gestures and sound effects ('Poong! Eeerrp! Whung!'), seemed to cheer everyone up. That morning they all went into work smiling.

I noted the approach of a stocky, responsible-looking man in starched shirt and trousers who introduced himself as the transport manager and led me gravely through the gate to the timekeeper's office, a concrete cubicle loud with the creak of an ancient ceiling fan. He put me in a chair and, in an eerie pantomime of my first examinations at the National, asked if I had any loss of feeling in my extremities. I said no. Was I spitting blood? No. 'Let me see you spit into your handkerchief,' he said. I did this and he nodded.

'Yes, the sputum is clear.' Then he held up a finger and, moving it back and forth, asked me to follow it with my eyes.

'What are you looking for?' I asked.

'Brain damage.'

'I don't think I've got that.'

He nodded. 'You will excuse me making such a fuss,' he said, 'but as transport manager I have to understand these matters. There are one million-plus lorries on Indian roads, many driven by lunatics. I must be qualified first-aider in case my own drivers have misadventure.'

The timekeeper, who looked like a matinée idol, brought me a copy of the *Times of India* and a glass of iced water. 'Boiled, no problem!' he said. I glanced through the paper, noting that the Controller of Stores and Purchases at Air India invited sealed tenders for a 'supply of good quality assorted Toffees for Inflight use on Annual Contract basis'. The monsoon was active over Konkan, Goa and Kerala, with thunder-showers reported in Assam and Meghalaya. That meant Cherrapunji had not yet received its tumultuous burst; the eastern arm seemed to be running late.

Another man offered me salted chickpeas in a brown paper spill, and asked permission to write his name and address – Sector 10, Housing Board Colony, Faridabad – in my notebook. He said he hoped we would become pen-friends. Others came to inscribe their names, most bringing snacks and drinks. The transport manager told me he had been a mechanic in the Indian Air Force and could still strip a Dakota engine with his eyes closed. He had visited Shillong in his air force days and thought it very nice. 'The poor peoples live below,' he said. 'There are most beautiful waterfalls.' But Cherrapunji he did not know. 'That is out of bounds, except when sometimes our planes crash there. They crash because of weather.'

'Where are police?' demanded the timekeeper. 'Here in Haryana they are always so slow.'

A small, frowning man approached bearing a glass of yellow liquid. The transport manager and the timekeeper received him with raised voices and a good deal of laughter but, stubbornly, he stood his ground.

The transport manager said, 'He has brought cow's urine.

Country people use it as general pick-me-up. He thinks it will rejuvenate your system after accident. He says it is fresh.'

I refused the urine and, rather ostentatiously, the small man drained the glass himself.

Then out on the road policemen appeared, stout and unsmiling, striding up and down the wrecked vehicles, swishing their lathis, shouting at those who had remained at the scene. I said I should make a statement but the transport manager shook his head emphatically.

'Intercede only if your driver is being charged,' he advised.

'They will take you to station and keep you for hours,' explained the timekeeper. 'Haryana police do nothing in a hurry. And if there is trial they will want you for witness. It is better to stay out of sight.'

A youth was sent to find out what was happening. He reported that the driver of the Palwal truck had been arrested and charged with careless driving. My driver appeared moments later, still shocked and distracted. He said another car was coming for me, driven by a friend.

'What will you do?' I asked.

His hands were shaking. 'I am waiting for my boss, Mr Singh,' he said, then turned abruptly and went to sit in the shade of the wall. When I went to follow, the transport manager tugged at my arm. 'Leave him. He is wishing to be alone.'

I returned to the timekeeper's office where, picking up a newspaper, I noted that my own hands had turned green. They gave off a pale glaucous glow and, astonished and fearful, I wet a finger and rubbed it on my shirt. No colour came off. I held them out to the timekeeper and asked if they seemed green to him.

'Green?' He examined them. 'No, not really.'

My hands also felt very stiff, my neck as though it rested in a clamp which was being gradually tightened. I thought of John Morgan-Hughes and wondered about the onset of paralysis. Could it happen by stealth, creeping up imperceptibly until the final tumblers fell into place and you awoke, one morning, with your limbs locked?

The timekeeper roused me from this reverie to say a car had arrived to take me to Deeg. Another Ambassador, it seemed even older than the mangled one still sitting out on the road; fernlike patterns of rust bubbled all over its worn, dimpled bodywork. My driver introduced his friend, whose huge, squared-off ears enclosed his head like bookends, and said his name was Dalip. 'He is doing me favour,' he said. 'This is not his usual work.'

'What is his usual work?' I asked.

'I am driving a hearse,' said Dalip.

'A *hearse*!'

'Yes, sahib.'

'That must be interesting.'

'Oh, yes, very interesting.'

He got into the car. I said goodbye to the kindly men of Thril who tumbled out through the gate and waved cheerily as we drove away. My hands seemed to have resumed their normal hue and I looked forward to seeing Deeg. Dalip barely spoke. Periodically, though, he was racked by yawns so convulsive that the car swerved.

'Are you tired?' I asked.

'Just a little.'

'Perhaps we should talk. What is the best thing about being a hearse driver?'

'Widows,' said Dalip. 'Yaarraghaa!' he went, yawning again.

Two hours later I made him stop and drink strong coffee. Then we left the Grand Trunk Road and motored through flat grey country ever deeper into Rajasthan, past a succession of dry stream beds with eddies and currents of sand blowing where water once flowed. Some had sun-bleached rags stuck on the banks, placed there by monks to prohibit fishing. A big six-wheeled army lorry barged past, horn going, leaving a boiling effusion of pale, choking dust. Its tailgate bore a sign showing a red cross over an uplifted hand; Dalip said it was to forbid people waving to the soldiers from following vehicles. We could see the flapping dust banner trailing across the landscape long after the lorry itself had vanished, and I was still idly tracking its progress when, quite suddenly, the car began to describe a veering, wandering course. Dalip was driving with his eyes closed, and his breathing had become deep and regular.

'Wake up!' I shouted, banging him on the shoulder.

He straightened and cleared his throat. 'Oh God!' he said, with a kind of moan.

'Do you want to stop and rest?'

'Not necessary,' he said, and stopped at once. Peering around he said, 'This is wrong road.'

We both got out. Then we saw two figures advancing towards us. The heat haze made them wraith-like but, as they drew closer, their shimmering forms were slowly transformed into a small boy and a naked man. He wore nothing but an expression of lordly indifference, and he halted beside us without appearing to notice we were there. He was tall and well fed, with his hair tied in a topknot and a truncheon-sized member hanging halfway to his knees. His companion, a kid of seven in tattered shorts, addressed Dalip in high, whiny Hindi while his master continued gazing absently over my shoulder.

Dalip interrupted the child to say, 'The naked fellow is a sadhu. The boy tells me that before renouncing the world he was a water bailiff.' He gave a kind of cackle. 'And, of course, they are asking for alms.'

'I'll give something if they'll tell us how to get to Deeg.'

We were so far off course the boy thought we must be going somewhere else. His directions were complicated and, midway through, I noted with a stirring of alarm that Dalip seemed to be paying no attention. Indeed, he looked so bored that I interrupted to ask if the boy spoke any English.

It was the sadhu who replied.

'Carry on down this road for two miles to security post. Go right until you are coming to village with big pond. Then go left. That is road for Deeg.'

The voice was fluting and reedy, the English rusty but correct. Intrigued, I asked him where he was from. He pointedly swivelled his gaze away as the boy addressed Dalip at length.

Dalip said, 'It is forbidden to put questions to the holy man. Anyway, he will not speak of the past; for him such a thing no longer exists. But the boy says his master once played cricket for the West Bengal Water Board. He made a century against a Slum Clearance Office team from Dhaka, but why he is telling us this I do not know. For some reason it is still important to the sadhu. And now I think we should give them some money and go. You must give it to the boy, not him.'

The encounter had made Dalip uneasy. It had also woken him up and he moved back to the car with uncharacteristic speed. As I handed the boy some rupees the holy man spoke again.

'One hundred and two not out,' he said. 'Three sixes, five fours.' Then he turned abruptly and continued striding on down the road.

Pigs roamed the narrow, hot streets of Deeg. The palaces of Brijenra Singh, Maharaja of Bharatpur, rose over the tumbledown little town like ornately iced cakes. Dalip left me at the gate. He said he had been here before. I explored the summer palace, abandoned by the maharaja's family in 1952 and now democratically opened to the citizenry. Scores had come to escape the heat and, here and there, I found them snoozing in its shadowy passageways and ante-rooms. Mine was the only foreign face around and, whenever I paused, some yawning figure would stir and, noting my interest, tell me what I was looking at.

Of all the great, rich rooms the best were the secretary's room and the chess room with its floor of black and white marble squares and its plump silk cushions ranged beneath a silk punkah. (The classic game of the monsoon had been dice, played wildly during the final month of the rains; in these circles palaces, estates and even kingdoms were lost on a single crazy throw.) Outside stood an odd little Mogul pavilion built to resemble a houseboat. Here, if and when the real rains came, the maharaja and his family sat to observe them, the giant doors thrown open so that their feet would be splashed.

In the mortuary room a man rose yawning from the dusty granite table used for washing the dead. He peered at me. 'Have you any English newspapers?'

'No.'

He stretched.

'Are you knowing anyone at the BBC?'

I said I knew a few people at the BBC.

Suddenly wide awake, he stared at me. 'BBC World Service is my lifeline. It always tell the truth. I listen to it daily.'

'I've broadcast on it a few times,' I said.

'How do you do!' He grabbed my hand and shook it. 'Let us drink some tea.'

'First I'd like to see the monsoon pavilion.'

'Of course. I will show you.'

He told me he slept here because it was cool, and, sometimes, he had extraordinary dreams, but all he really wanted to talk about was the World Service and the people who worked on it. For him I recalled their dedication and donnish demeanour (though the worn tweed jackets and scuffed shoes affected by the men were partly due to meagre wage packets; Britain can be careless about rewarding those who maintain its diminishing centres of excellence), and their surprising canteen, one of the best in London. That was to keep the foreign broadcasters happy. All foreigners – unlike the English – complain, but foreign intellectuals served indifferent food do so with a stridency that doesn't bear thinking about.

My friend's name was Ramesh. He had long arms and restless, deeply sunken eyes that never seemed to miss a trick. When we arrived at the monsoon pavilion, or *kesav bhawan*, they caught the sun and glittered like quartz.

It seemed to be built from weightless stone; the whole lovely edifice, one felt, changed its position according to the dictates of the prevailing wind. Five Mogul arches on a raised marble platform supported the flat roof, its water tanks disguised by ornamental friezes, the open concourse below containing groups of lounging people. Four broad stone channels ran towards the central arches, each studded with lotus-shaped iron fountains.

Ramesh said there were 3,000 fountains, installed by master plumbers held in such high esteem by the maharaja that he also consulted them on philosophical and military matters.

'Engirding the semi-octagonal quoins on which stand the noble arches,' he intoned, 'is a 0.91-metre canal separating the inner and outer squares of a graceful arcade and provided with a border of tiny jets. In the middle is a further row of fountains. The pipes above the arches set the spectacle of rains when water was released. And water pressure caused lithic balls to rotate and produce sound of thunder.'

'What are lithic balls?' I asked.

'Big stone balls, sir.'

We wandered around, admiring the airy arcades, inspecting the neighbouring concrete tank, empty now and at least an acre in size, its sides studded with 3,000 holes – each feeding a fountain.

'Into every hole a coloured dye was placed by divers swimming,' said Ramesh, 'red, green, blue, yellow and so forth, all colours of the spectrum.'

I tried, amid the white light and blasting heat of Rajasthan, to imagine this whole extraordinary affair in operation – water splashing from the fountains and streaming down the Mogul arches, the jets in the arcade canal discharging their cool polychromatic mist, small rainbows forming, thunder rumbling stonily overhead. To people trapped in never-ending summer this must have offered a glimpse of paradise.

We went to a mobile stall and bought glasses of weak tea. Ramesh said he was a part-time guide here, and began speaking of the difficulties of such a life, but I paid scant attention. I was thinking of the monsoon with a strange new intensity, wondering where it was, when it would come, pining for it; for the first time, I realized, I was thinking like an Indian. Then I heard Ramesh say, 'Fleet Street, perhaps even your own newspaper.'

I stared at him. 'What?'

'I would need British work permit too. With your BBC contacts this would be no problem. Oh! And woman to marry. I would prefer an Asian, of course, but she must be British national so that authorities will let me stay and pursue my career.'

I finished my tea. 'I'm very tired and I'm going to have a nap.'

'You can have my bed down in palace morgue,' he said.

'I'm going to the pavilion,' I said. 'I'll see you later.'

Drifting people made space for me. I felt weary after the events of the morning but also wondered whether, by sleeping in this place, certain unsuspected truths about the nature of the monsoon would be revealed. I lay on the floor with my bag for a pillow and was out within seconds.

A familiar, insistent voice intoned:

> *She left the web, she left the loom,*
> *She made three paces thro' the room,*
> *She saw the water-lily bloom,*
> *She saw the helmet and the plume,*
> *She look'd down to Camelot.*

I opened my eyes. Ramesh, grinning, squatted beside me, holding a green plastic portable radio.

> *Out flew the web and floated wide;*
> *The mirror crack'd from side to side;*
> *'The curse is come upon me,' cried*
> *The Lady of Shalott.*

He switched it off. 'World Service!' he said. 'I am thinking that is famous actor knight, Sir John Gielgud.'

I had been dreaming of my wife and daughter walking in Richmond Park, the sun filtering through the trees and touching their faces. That, and the sound of Gielgud reciting Tennyson, filled me with a wave of homesickness as strong as a fever. I looked around, remembering where I was. This place had nothing to do with me. It was a preposterous folly erected by some showman who would today have been running theme parks; I longed for the sounds, smells and sensations of the real rains. It was time to go.

'What about my job?' enquired Ramesh.

'Get into local journalism and send me some stuff,' I said. 'These things have to be done in stages.'

'How can I get into local journalism? I have no degree even.'

'You work at it. You knock on people's doors. You write pieces and keep submitting them until you get one published. In England, Ramesh, you have to do the same. There is no easy way.'

I handed him some money and he pocketed it wordlessly, anger and betrayal in his eyes; they had become bleak pin-pricks of light. Then he turned and walked away, clutching his radio, heading for his granite bed in the maharaja's mortuary.

Dalip stood under a tree talking to a middle-aged woman in a pale pink sari. He said she was a widow who just walked up and started chatting. 'Widows are liking me,' he explained. 'I know how to comfort them.'

'How do you do that?'

He started the car. 'You have to understand psychology of grief. It is 10 per cent talent, the rest common sense. We go home now?'

'Okay.'

Half an hour later, in open dusty country, he fell asleep. The car passed cleanly between two neem trees and came to rest beside the blackened carcass of a cow. Vultures staggered into the air with a bony clattering noise, gobbets of flesh hanging from their beaks. Later, by a roadside pump, we saw half a dozen women filling buckets and pitchers, their brilliantly coloured saris refracting the dusty light with a neon-like luminosity. Soon after that we got lost again. The landscape was empty and arid. A thought occurred to me.

'Have we any water, Dalip?' I asked.

'Water?' He seemed surprised. 'No.'

'We're not heading into the desert, are we?'

He frowned and gripped the wheel nervously. 'I do not know where we are heading. This is not my territory.'

Pollen records show that when the monsoon still fell copiously 6,000 years ago this had been a sylvan place of deep forests and large freshwater lakes. It supported a civilization based on primitive cereal agriculture, but now there wasn't a single blade of grass to be seen anywhere. Erosion had lifted much of the soil into the sky; quartz particles in the clouds dried the moist monsoon wind, even inhibited the formation of evening dew.

The few leafless, withered trees made me reflect on the frightening momentum of a desert on the move – though the Rajasthan, thought to be expanding at the rate of two inches each hour, was a tortoise compared with the hare of the African Sahel. That clocked up a daily prog ess of 38 feet, or slightly in excess of two and a half miles a year.

We came to a huddle of shacks standing by a pond with glistening mud at the bottom. A boy appeared with some fans made from peacock feathers. I bought one while a sad, dusty-looking man with a blue towel over his head tried to sell me his cattle.

'Three cows,' said Dalip briskly. 'He cannot feed them.'

'How can I feed cows?'

'Acha,' said Dalip, meaning okay, and spoke to the man in Hindi. The man shrugged.

'Please tell him I would like to help but it is impossible.'

'He understands,' said Dalip.

They talked for a moment, then the man squatted and began drawing careful lines in the dust with his finger. It was a map.

'It is too approximate,' Dalip complained, and questioned the man in a hectoring manner that embarrassed me.

Quietly, patiently, the man talked on, slowly expanding his map, adding a winding stream bed here, a house (indicating a police station) there, explaining it all in a schoolmasterly, almost pedantic way. I asked Dalip to talk me through it. He did this with bad grace but, in the end, we were both sure we knew how to reach the main road.

Later, heading west, we ran out of petrol.

An acrimonious exchange followed. Angrily I told Dalip that petrol was his responsibility, and that he must now go and find some. He asked where. Should he dig an oil well? The landscape had changed and our useless car sat halfway up the side of a shallow valley. Recollections of the map in the dust indicated there could be a small village at its head.

I urged Dalip to go and find it. I would stay and guard the car.

'No,' he said.

'Why not?' I was growing exasperated.

He frowned at his hands. 'This place is tiger sanctuary.'

'It's *what?*'

'Tiger sanctuary. That man told me. I will stay with car, you get petrol.'

'We both get petrol.'

'Then we are both being eaten. That is pointless.'

'Nobody will get eaten. They wouldn't put a public road through tiger countr,

'Tigers don't know it is public road. Anyhow, maybe now we have gone off public system. And car is my responsibility. So I must stay here.'

We sat glaring mulishly at each other. Then I heard a steady pattering sound approaching around a bend. 'Is that rain?' I asked, bewildered.

Dalip laughed. 'Sheep!' he said.

The flock, newly shorn, was five hundred strong and in the charge of three young shepherds who, as the sheep surged by like a clattering white tide, told us petrol was available two miles away. And they promised the road was safe from tigers; would they otherwise be bringing their animals along it? They had been to

Alwar for shearing and now faced the prospect of an 800-kilometre walk home to the sandstone city of Jaisalmer. But Dalip, afterwards, continued to fret.

'It is well known that tigers leave sanctuaries in drought conditions.'

'Well, I'm not sitting here all bloody night.'

'Then you must get petrol.' He spoke with cold logic.

I set off. The sun was westering now, redly incandescent in the dust, but it still carried a cruel sting. I recalled a recent report prepared by the Royal Meteorological Society which said that Rajasthan had suffered thirty drought years since records began more than a century ago. Only the Punjab, with thirty-three, and Saurashtra and Kutch, thirty-four, had suffered more, and the three areas had the highest statistical probability of more droughts to come.

I thought of the Queen's Lancers on their way to Aliwal in the Punjab in 1846. In a single day forty-three men dropped from their horses with sunstroke and, by nightfall, fourteen were dead; the officers on picket duty a mile from the camp site that evening lay inert under trees with wet towels around their heads. Major H. M. L. Lawrence, a political agent, advised that 'thirty yards of fine muslin rolled around a European cap or hat forms the best protection from the sun'; failure to take such precautions left your brains 'absolutely boiling'. The French botanist Victor Jacquemont found the summer temperatures 'incredible in every respect. As I sit writing I reject all garments except a thick turban of white muslin to keep my head cool, and a pair of breeches.'

I had no hat and, after a while, felt small surges of dizziness and nausea which began to affect my balance. Resting in the shadow of an obeliskal roadside bluff veined by heat cracks I took out my notebook with the idea of placing it on my head. But it fell open at a page on which someone had scribbled. 'Why do you never notice me?'

The writing was large, discursive and hurried. This particular notebook had been onstream since Bombay, rarely out of my sight. Sitting there on the perimeter of the Rajasthan Desert with the sweat stinging my eyes, I wondered who on earth had posed that sad little question. I moved on down the road, pondering her identity – it looked like a woman's hand – but reasoning that if I hadn't noticed her I was hardly in a position to make an accurate guess.

I passed a faded billboard saying, 'For the Fulfillment of Life Join the Indian Navy', and around the next bend came upon three houses and a large pond in which several buffaloes lay, their heads and horns protruding above the water like Viking helmets. A young woman, bare-breasted, with the hem of a golden sari thrown carelessly across her shoulder, squatted by the pond washing a bright brass pot. When she saw me she instantly covered herself and, head averted, hurried into one of the houses. Some children appeared, then a man with red, watering eyes.

'Have you any petrol?' I asked. 'Gasoline?'

He considered me for a moment, then nodded wordlessly and walked back to his house. A baking wind sprang up, filling the air with pale sand clouds that obliterated the sun. Two women in brilliant orange saris walked towards me, shimmering flames gradually assuming human form. The man returned carrying a shiny five-gallon tin. He said it contained three gallons but he wanted the tin back. He hitched one of the buffalo from the pond to a cart and we set off, swaying and creaking as though sitting in a small storm-tossed tree. He nodded at the buffalo, its stringy flanks and ribcage glistening with mud, and said, 'How much will you give me for this cow?'

'I'm very sorry, but I cannot buy any animals.'

We ambled on through blowing dust. Three more women, their saris mauve, crimson and leaf-green, passed on the verge, faces swathed, cloth-covered bundles balanced on their heads. I reflected that the more colourless the landscapes in Rajasthan, the more gorgeously robed were the female figures who inhabited them.

Dalip sat sleeping behind the wheel of the Ambassador. Malevolently I crept up, placed my mouth by his ear and roared like a tiger.

He went, 'Nnngghhrryyaaa!' and threw himself back across the seat.

I said, 'Put the petrol in the tank while I pay this man.'

The light was fading. The man told us of a hotel five miles away and we reached it in the dark – a sometime maharaja's hunting lodge inhabited by a tribe of silent, unsmiling servants. They seemed astonished when asked if any rooms were available. All the rooms were available. I specified cheap ones and told Dalip I would see him at dinner.

'I will eat alone,' he said with dignity.

There was no power so I used my candle to examine the framed English bird prints hanging beside my bed, mildewed yellow wrens and fading bearded titmice. The cavernous white-tiled bathroom contained a porcelain urinal of the kind found in Victorian public lavatories, made by John Bolding & Sons Ltd of Grosvenor Works, London.

A candle lit my way to dinner through public rooms adorned with the portraits of complacent, chubby-faced men sporting heavy moustaches, and the heads of the animals they had shot, mostly tigers. There were twenty tables in the dining room, all laid with starched white napery and heavy silver, and a dozen waiters to attend them, but I was the only customer tonight. A ruler-backed old man brought me brown Windsor soup and stood watching as I drank it. It was cold and oversalted, and my spoon clattered loudly against the plate.

'Where is the maharaja?' I asked.

He shrugged. 'Delhi.'

'What does he do in Delhi?'

'I don't know. We have lost touch. He is import–export of some kind.'

The main course was a small, leathery lamb chop and a few boiled potatoes. Picking at the food I asked when the monsoon would come.

'We have given up hope of monsoon,' he said. 'This year, probably, it will not come.'

'What will you do?'

'Wait and see.' He refilled my glass with water. 'Last week, I think, they are killing a child.'

I stared at him. 'What?'

'It is just rumour at the moment – that some peasants have cut throat of a small boy to pacify gods and bring rain. Maybe it is true, maybe not. But last time this happen, fifteen, twenty years ago, there was excellent monsoon. That child did not die in vain. Do you wish pudding?'

'No.'

'There is junket. Jelly even.'

'No.'

I picked up my candle and made the long trek back through the shadows to bed.

But sleep would not come, and it wasn't just the heat that made me sweat. There had been a similar story going around in the mid-1960s – perhaps the same human sacrifice that preceded the waiter's excellent monsoon – furiously denied by the Indian government but taken very seriously by an Indian journalist I knew in London. Thinking of the parched landscapes and weary, undernourished, despairing people I had seen today, I was half-inclined to believe it.

I ran that morning's accident through my mind and knew I had been lucky. But now my neck ached and my hands seemed encased in splints. Funny about going green; hysteria, probably. At Deeg it had been 120 degrees Fahrenheit in the monsoon pavilion and it seemed much the same now. Perspiration soaked my pillow and sheets; I was discharging so much fluid it may have raised the humidity around my bed, forming a tiny tropical micro-climate with small clouds gathering up by the ceiling. Perhaps there would be showers later, warm and salty. I thought of very, very cold beer. I thought of ice. I thought of the woman I had ignored.

An Englishman named J. M. Merk wrote this description of summer in the Punjab in 1880:

At sunrise, or soon after 5 a.m. houses must be closed, only a small door being left open for communication with the outside world. So long as the hot winds blow strongly and steadily, rooms may still be kept in some measure cool by means of 'tatties' or grass screens set up in front of the doorway, and continually sprinkled with water, or by the fan vanes which a servant keeps revolving and sprinkles with water; and at night the punkah is worked. Man and beast languish and gasp for air, while even in the house the thermometer stands day and night between 95 degrees and 115 degrees. Little by little the European loses appetite and sleep; all power and energy forsake him. Vegetation suffers equally; almost all green things wither; the grass seems burnt up to the roots; bushes and trees seem moribund; the earth is as hard as a paved highway; the ground is seamed with cracks; and the whole landscape wears an aspect of barrenness and sadness. The heat is truly fearful.

Far away, I heard a noise like the deep, ripping growl of thunder. After only a few heartbeats of lapsed time I identified it, with sudden delight, as the roar of a distant tiger. At peace, I finally fell asleep.

14 JUNE

I was awoken at dawn by the screech of peacocks. The light was a soft dusty grey. I asked for coffee and received a cup of hot water and a small jar of powder that had assumed the consistency of dried clay. I hacked and hewed with a spoon, eventually mining enough to make a black and bitter brew that was drinkable if taken with plenty of sugar.

Dalip's mood improved in direct ratio to our distance from Delhi. By the time we reached the outskirts he was in high spirits. There were police on every corner but he drove on, uncurious, glad to be home. He too had heard the story of the murdered child. The government, he said, was trying to hush it up, which meant it was probably true; these peasants, bound up in their ignorance, their animals and strange rural superstitions, were capable of anything. If one needed to intercede with the gods there were other methods available. He knew, for example, of classical musicians who could fill reservoirs by playing specially composed rain-making ragas beside them.

When we drew up at my hotel he switched off the engine, turned in his seat and gave me a big smile.

'Well, Dalip, thank you very much,' I said, preparing to get out.

The smile broadened. 'Watch, wallet, spectacles, testicles,' he said brightly. 'You have got everything?'

I looked at him resignedly. Dalip had fallen asleep at the wheel, got lost and run out of petrol. Because of Dalip I had been faced with the cost of overnight hotel accommodation for two. But the 100 rupees I handed him produced only small sighs and a muttered farewell. And he had the car going when I was barely out of it.

The clerk who gave me my key told me I should have stayed in Rajasthan. Last night terrorists using automatic weapons had murdered fourteen people in South Delhi. Many others had been injured; even small children were on the critical list. The killers were thought to be Sikh extremists, members of the Tiger Force of Khalistan. For forty-five minutes they had roamed the streets in a stolen Datsun, shooting indiscriminately. The clerk warned me not to go out. 'There is big police crackdown,' he said. 'They are stopping and searching everyone.'

It was a Sunday afternoon and I went to the hotel pool, sitting within earshot of two Delhi men in Italian designer swimming costumes who argued drowsily about the merits of English hand-made shoes; both, it seemed, had their personal lasts at fashionable Mayfair cobblers. Their wives and daughters wore rubies and lunched off iced Pimms and bowls of sugared almonds. They then rested. Only their eyelids moved, like lizards.

The heat was ferocious. Though the sun remained masked by the sand fog you couldn't walk on the poolside paving with bare feet. A blowtorch breeze came out of the desert, smelling faintly of sewage, and I suddenly knew I was going to faint.

I got to my room first and lay semi-conscious on my bed, sweating like a pig and hallucinating about the burst, hearing and seeing its arrival over Delhi, even smelling wet earth, grass and flowers. I wondered whether that fragrance might be chemically isolated and sold at perfume counters in 25 ml crystal flasks. Monsoon! The aroma India adores! Give it to your loved one this Christmas.

All at once I was fully alert and feeling very well. Perhaps the sweating had, like a sauna, removed various impurities from the blood. I had a shower, then went to the bar and put some back again, drinking two pints of cold beer straight off. That done, I began mentally preparing myself for my meeting, first thing in the morning, with Mr P. D. Gupta at the Ministry of External Affairs.

15 JUNE

Some instinct made me call first. I learned that Mr Gupta had just popped out to the Conference of Asian Foreign Ministers being held that week in Delhi. But the man I spoke to knew about my case and said it had been referred to the Foreigners Regional Registration Office. He gave me the address and told me I must go there and fill out the appropriate forms.

The city was in a strange, edgy mood. Many shops had closed in protest at Saturday night's killings. The assassins were still at large and people were calling for the resignation of Rajiv Gandhi. It took two hours to find the Foreigners Regional Registration Office, a nondescript concrete building tucked away anonymously among others. I was made to enter my name and many personal details in a large ledger before being allowed up a dusty stairway to the appropriate floor.

I found a room packed with grim-faced foreign supplicants queuing to be interviewed by two officials seated at adjoining desks. I filled out an extensive form and awaited my turn behind two giggling, merry-eyed Tibetan monks who wanted permits for Kashmir.

It took three hours to reach the interviewing official, a tired-looking man in a rumpled blue shirt. He glanced over my form, then handed it back, shaking his head.

'No,' he said.

'What do you mean?'

'I mean no. Is the word not known to you?'

'You have my file from the Ministry of External Affairs. I'm sure if you look at it you'll see . . .'

He gave me a brief smile. 'We have no file,' he said. 'And what you ask is impossible. At the moment Meghalaya, Assam and Nagaland are closed to foreigners. We are letting no one in.'

'But the people at the Ministry have applied to —'

'Ministry! Ministry!' he shouted. 'I am telling you go home! You cannot enter these places and that is that!' He flapped his hands at me and, leaving, I noted little sympathy in the faces of the other anxious, sweating applicants. In that place it was every man for himself.

*

I phoned the Meteorological Office and asked for an interview with Dr R. P. Sarker, the Director General. I wanted to talk to India's top weather man about monsoon matters but now it also occurred to me he might be a useful ally. Dr Sarker seemed relaxed and accessible; he agreed to see me that same day. As I arrived an antique Atco motor mower with a busted engine was being pulled across the Met Office lawns by a zebu bull. The gardener supervising the operation sat under a peepul tree reading an astrological manual. He said he was a Bachelor of Arts. Dr Sarker occupied a panelled, sunlit office at the top of the building. A crisp, likeable man with a surging enthusiasm for his subject, he reckoned the monsoon would arrive in Delhi on time, on 29 June, plus or minus the usual five-day leeway. He pronounced himself moderately satisfied with its progress to date; it would be a good, though not outstanding, monsoon.

How could he tell?

He beamed at me. 'Data! These days our preoccupations are global, remember. We are part of a multinational concern processing information from all over the world. What is the weather in London? We must know because, two or three days later, it may affect us. We track all the systems. In this office you will hear people discussing, oh, the pressure correlations in Australia, Buenos Aires and Tahiti, upper air flow patterns over the Soviet Union, the state of the icebergs around the Antarctic – the seventh Indian Met Office expedition is down on the ice cap now – temperatures in Northern Europe and so forth. All this material is required for statistical analysis in Delhi. What we are seeking is the Auto-Regressive Integrated Moving Average, or ARIMA, which is the most accurate means of forecasting we have.'

He spoke of an interesting connection between the El Niño current and the Southern Oscillations, called ENSO. (The fish-rich El Niño, flowing off the Peruvian coast, has become an important factor in the monsoon's predictive sequence; when it suffers from a deficiency of anchovies Dr Sarker must prepare for the worst.) India was an active member of the 160-nation-strong World Meteorological Organization WMO members, keeping in constant touch through the GTS, or Global Telecommunications System, had supported the foundation of the Summer Monsoon

Activity Centre, SMAC, set up in Delhi and staffed by monsoon specialists from all participating countries.

As he described the various monsoon projects in which they had co-operated – MONEX '79, MONSOON '77, ISMEX '73 and IIOE, or International Indian Ocean Experiment – I glanced at the honour board on his wall, the names of previous Directors General up there in gold, and wondered what they would have made of all this.

The first, H. F. Blandford, appointed in 1875, inherited a rough and ready reporting system established a century earlier by officials of the East India Company. They understood the huge economic importance of trying to predict the Indian weather, and all provincial medical officers and revenue collectors were ordered to keep records of local winds and rainfall. But they used primitive, non-standardized instruments which, notoriously, came without instructions, and their disparate readings cast little light on that most impenetrable of mysteries – the cause of the monsoon.

Blandford changed all that. He was the first in a line of remarkable India-based English climatologists fascinated by the monsoon phenomenon. For them it became a wholly absorbing preoccupation, a life's work which revealed mainly that the monsoon was a creature of incredible complexity and subtleness. Each veil lifted revealed a multitude of others. They perceived a chain of interlocking and interdependent mysteries, the meteorological equivalent of DNA and the double helix.

Blandford pursued it systematically. To acquire accurate data he set up the finest meteorological network in Asia; every day weather telegrams came in from all over India and Burma. He established mountain observatories and kite stations. He recruited bright young Indians and imbued in them his own sense of mission. And, though the answers to the monsoon mystery continued to tantalize him, he was, towards the end, at least asking the right questions. His monograph, *The Rainfall of Northern India*, became a classic of its kind while a textbook entitled *The Indian Meteorologist's Vade-Mecum* dominated the science of tropical meteorology for the rest of the century.

His successor, Sir John Eliot, pursued a policy of global co-operation that would have gratified Dr Sarker. India took part in the first International Cloud Year in 1897 and worked closely with foreign scientists like Teisserence de Bort, the Frenchman who discovered the stratosphere. It was Eliot who first published regular forecasts of monsoon rainfall (initially confidential and classified, for the eyes of senior civil servants only). His assistant, a young Cambridge mathematical physicist and Senior Wrangler named Gilbert Walker, took over Eliot's job and moved monsoon research several notches forward. In doing so he established himself as the giant of Indian meteorology.

Walker's curiosity was boundless. He looked for cause and effect everywhere. Was there, as had been suggested by Sir William Willcocks, Director General of the Reservoirs of Egypt, a link between monsoon rainfall and the flood waters of the Nile? Yes. Did deforestation influence the monsoon? No. Was sunspot activity (measured with blackened thermometers) a significant factor? Sometimes. Might there be a direct correlation between meteorological events in India and in places far, far away? Absolutely.

Walker astonished his colleagues by investigating barometric pressures in Sydney and Buenos Aires, and counting the icebergs in Antarctica. What on earth did this have to do with showers over the Western Ghats? A great deal, as it turned out. Walker was developing his Southern Oscillation theory – that high pressures over the Pacific Ocean will coincide with low pressures over the Indian Ocean, the presence of the latter during winter indicating a likelihood of heavy summer rains. It remains one of the pillars of monsoon science and, in a real sense, Dr Sarker and his colleagues, almost a century later, are carrying on where he left off. And Dr Sarker acknowledged this. 'Sir Gilbert is the father of monsoon studies.'

Before leaving I asked if I might count on his support in my Permissions quest. 'Unequivocally,' he said with characteristic generosity. 'Though I must warn you that it will probably do you little good. These matters are decided at a level much more rarified than mine.'

At this point I stopped keeping my journal on a daily basis. The Delhi bureaucratic machine ate up the days and made them meaningless. I waited – by the phone, on staircases, in corridors and ante-rooms – while following my file from official to official, building to building. It was now formally in the charge of Mr R. B. Baksh of External Affairs Press Relations, a rather stern, schoolmasterly man who occupied an office in a very long corridor; mysteriously, the number on his door bore no relation to those on either side. At our first meeting he confirmed that applications had been sent on my behalf to the state governments of Assam, Meghalaya and Nagaland but, to date, none had responded. His hands were tied. He wished me luck.

But Sanjoy Hazarika, the *New York Times* man in Delhi and himself an Assamese, told me the decisions would be made here in one of the Secretariat Buildings near Parliament House. Meanwhile I should pursue every avenue, speak to as many people as possible. His aunt, duty officer at Assam House in Delhi's diplomatic quarter, might be able to win me some support at state level. But he warned that the portents were not good. 'A friend from *National Geographic* magazine spent six weeks here trying to get permissions for Assam and Meghalaya, then gave up and went home.'

Mrs Hazarika, a sympathetic, merry-eyed lady, promised to do what she could. First, though, she would need my file number from External Affairs.

Using her phone I called Mr Baksh. He said, 'Your file number is secret', and hung up.

Mrs Hazarika sighed and suggested I enlist the support of another government department. 'Tourism, perhaps. Talk to Ramesh Chandra, Additional Director General at the Ministry.'

While waiting for an appointment with Mr Chandra I called on Peter Gregory Hood, who dealt with press matters at the British High Commission. He was affable but not encouraging. 'The official line is likely to be that there is serious civil unrest in these places which would expose you to risk. That is not a position which we could realistically challenge.'

The *Times of India* reported the imposition of an indefinite curfew in Meghalaya's capital, Shillong, due to a 'deteriorating law and order situation'. A clash the previous day between students and police had resulted in one death and twenty-six injuries. The mob, which had set fire to shops and vehicles, comprised members of the Khasi students' union protesting against the arrest of their presi-

dent, Mr Bull Lyndgoh. All Shillong's schools and colleges had
been closed and, with 'the overall situation in the town remaining
tense, police patrols had been intensified'.

In Assam two ministers were obliged to resign, one charged with
inefficiency, the other corruption.

On the Calcutta Stock Market pepper was up and jute down,
with twills, hessian and flourbags 'all dull due to lack of interest'.

Mr Chandra, at Tourism, offered sound advice. 'Forget about
Nagaland,' he said. 'They won't let you within a hundred miles;
Indian troops are getting shot there. If you withdraw that applica-
tion and concentrate on Meghalaya and Assam I will support you.'
He picked up a pen. 'What is your file number at External Affairs?'

'It's a secret,' I said.

He smiled, 'Well, you can tell me.'

'I can't. They won't even tell me.'

He put down his pen. 'Now that is going to make life very
difficult,' he said.

I followed a number of trails that suddenly dematerialized and
blew away. Sanjay Reddy urged me to see a businessman named
P. V. Biswas who had influence in Assam. Mr Biswas, a portly,
short-sighted man seated at an Edwardian roll-top desk, gave me a
glass of whisky and said his influence did not extend to immigration;
that was a grey area. But he scribbled a note to a retired politician
named Singh who showed me his splendid collection of
seventeenth-century Burmese Buddhas while regretting there was
little he could do. He, in turn, passed me on to a Mr Basheer, a
wealthy manufacturer of shirtings. His son, a mathematician, had
recently sat an entrance exam for Harvard and the result was
expected daily; somewhat distractedly Mr Basheer spoke to a Mr
Chakravarti, whose Assamese friends were more highly placed than
his own. Chakravarti, a charming, scholarly old man, peppered his
conversation with parables indicating that his Assamese friends,
though certainly highly placed, invariably took their instructions
from Delhi. But he promised to mention my case to his friend J. S.
Bhagat, a property developer who had the ear of 'fellows of
Cabinet rank'.

Nothing happened.

Then I called a colleague in London who knew Delhi well. He suggested I get in touch with Vijay Shankardass, a barrister who had been a contemporary of Rajiv Gandhi's at Cambridge. I rang Mr Shankardass, who listened carefully, promised to make a few enquiries and get back to me.

He was as good as his word. He had made an appointment for me with Mr D. G. Mehrotra, Private Secretary to the Minister of External Affairs. 'He wasn't actually there but I explained the position to *his* secretary,' said Mr Shankardass in his cool, cultivated Cambridge voice. 'Mehrotra is a very capable fellow and should be able to help, but I think you'd better take my own secretary, Radhakrishnan, with you. He can find his way around our bureaucratic maze blindfold. He'll be at your hotel at 9.30 in the morning.'

Radhakrishnan, a small, bustling, eager-looking man, took me down the great avenues and boulevards of New Delhi to Sir Edwin Lutyens's handsome red and grey sandstone Secretariat Buildings. Outside the Ministry of External Affairs entrance there were lines of soldiers and a peon with a yellow garden hose spraying the *khas* fibre curtains hanging over the door. In a vaulted Gothic stone reception area Radakrishnan vanished into a maul of clamorous men demanding attention from the clerks and emerged clasping our security passes. Mr Mehrotra occupied a sparse, uncluttered office with a large gold Buddha standing on a corner filing cabinet.

Greying and kindly, he told us he had flown in from Moscow at 2.30 that morning. 'But I am determined to keep up and running,' he said. He listened to me patiently. 'The chap who can resolve this problem is R. B. Baksh at Press Relations. I will call him.'

'I've already spoken to Mr Baksh,' I said. 'In fact, he's probably got my file.'

'I will call nevertheless.'

As he picked up the phone a large, distracted man wearing a waistcoat and rumpled cotton trousers burst in crying, 'Telegram! Telegram!'

Mr Mehrotra blanched and jumped to his feet but the intruder rushed out again before he could speak.

'That was Minister of External Affairs, N. D. Tiwari himself!' he said. With a sigh he returned to the phone and, eventually, raised Mr Baksh. After a brief conversation he hung up and sighed again. 'Please ring me at six o'clock this evening,' he said. 'By then I should have news for you.'

The Delhi Police were running newspaper ads saying, 'Don't spread panic and help the terrorists in achieving their aim of creating fear psychosis. Help Delhi Police to Help You.'

At six o'clock, though he must have been dog-tired, Mr Mehrotra was as courteous as ever. 'I have tried to expedite and conquer,' he said. 'I have been all around the houses and the result is thus: expedite yes, conquer no. Not yet. I have put the matter in the hands of a new man who must now start from scratch. It will take him six days. At least. Even two or three weeks possibly. Then I hope we shall have our result but, of course, I can guarantee nothing. These matters are not in our hands.'

'I think I might head back to London,' I said. 'And sit it out there.'

There was a brief pause. 'A tactical withdrawal? Not a retreat I hope.'

'Absolutely not.'

'Excellent! Actually, I think that is a sensible decision. Phone me each week and I will give you latest update.'

I put a call through to Air India. While waiting for someone to answer I noted an item in the *Times of India* entitled 'Pilot's Licence Exams in a Shambles'. It said that a number of the questions in the all-India qualifying examinations for senior commercial pilots were either wrong or incomplete. Sometimes the same question was asked twice; sometimes the questions contained insufficient data for the candidates to make their calculations. The pilots, as a consequence, were suffering from anxiety and apprehension.

I replaced the phone and called British Airways. They had a flight to London that same night and, miraculously, a free seat. Several hours later I boarded the packed Tristar and flew home.

In London my publisher gave me lunch at a smart Greek restaurant. He listened pensively to my news. 'On a scale of one to ten,' he asked, 'what is the most realistic chance of you getting to Cherrapunji?'

'Five,' I said. In truth, it was probably less.

He nodded and, by mutual consent, we talked of other matters, and the books other people were writing for him – all of which, I supposed, would come supplied with good, strong endings. The Cherrapunji ending was to have been as much for my father as for myself and I knew that, were our positions reversed, his stubborn Lowland Scots insistence on finishing everything he started would probably have got him there. But how?

Several days later, while describing the Cherrapunji painting to my daughter, it suddenly dawned on me.

He would have walked.

L. Geo. Lopez, the artist, had placed the village on the brow of a range of wooded green hills, the Khasis, which looked quite scaleable as I recalled, more of a scramble than a climb. According to my map the Khasis overlooked the border with Bangladesh. A railway spur ran from the Bangladeshi town of Sylhet to Chhatak, a border village less than twenty miles from Cherrapunji, and a crossing from Chhatak certainly looked feasible. If the front door of a house is locked, my father would have said, try the back.

I went for a twenty-mile hike around Richmond Park to prove I could do it, then took a friend from the Bangladeshi High Commission to lunch. He was a charming, urbane man who had been at Oxford with at least two members of the British Cabinet, and he saw through my casually devious enquiries at once.

'My dear Alex!' he said, laughing. 'Don't even think about it. The Indians are shooting at illegals. It's become a major problem for them. So many of our people are slipping over to escape Bangladesh's poverty trap that the Khasi tribals are rioting in protest. Those hills are crawling with troops, and if they don't get you, the Khasi mobs will.'

I stopped thinking about it.

Other friends suggested various means of gaining access to Cherrapunji, mostly of a robust, paramilitary nature which greatly amused them but were not helpful to me. I became despondent, and possessed of a growing conviction that I would never get back to India.

Then one fine, windy London afternoon Mr Mehrotra called out of the blue on a crackling line and urged me to return. Two hours later Vijay Shankardass did the same, implying in his elliptical jurisprudential way that things were finally moving. 'The auguries suddenly seem favourable for Shillong,' he said, 'though I'm afraid the Cherrapunji application remains controversial; I see problems there. By and large, though, it's probably the right moment to come back and fight your corner.'

I arrived in Delhi on the first day of Parliament's Monsoon Session. It was an acrimonious, stormy affair devoted to charges of bribery, or 'kickbacks', in the purchasing of Bofors guns and German submarines for the armed forces; the Opposition had even staged a *dharna*, or demo, in the well of the House. Despite 'spells of shouts and counter-shouts' and a rebel who 'screamed to the full extent of his lung power' they did not debate the monsoon itself which, according to the *Economic Times*, was behaving in a disturbingly erratic fashion: 'It has upset kharif sowing in different parts of the country. Paddy, jowar, maize and bajra are likely to be adversely affected. With less than 40 per cent of the districts in the country receiving normal to excess rainfall, is 1987–88 going to be the fourth successive year of below average monsoon?'

A former Finance Minister said, 'Every one of my Budgets was largely a gamble on rain.'

The Reddys called at my hotel for a cup of tea. 'We are all exhausted,' said Sanjay. 'The monsoon has absconded and things are absolutely dire. There are power cuts all day long and we can't use air-conditioning between six and ten at night. And now, to cap it all, there are supposed to be a dozen British and Canadian terrorists roaming the city with Kalashnikov machine guns. We haven't been told what they're doing here. All we know is that they're clean-shaven and the police are on maximum alert.'

'Gatherings of more than five persons have been banned,' said Mrs Reddy, still beautiful despite the weariness in her face. 'So has the shouting of slogans.'

I laughed. 'Where's the monsoon got to?'

'God knows,' said Sanjay. 'Down south somewhere. It just refuses to move.'

Mrs Reddy said, 'We haven't even seen the pied-crested cuckoo. It's meant to fly over Delhi a fortnight after it crosses the coast. Now we're holding the Teej festival in which maidens on flower-decked swings are supposed to celebrate the monsoon's arrival. But the poor girls are swinging in temperatures of 100 degrees and getting sunstroke.'

'Alex, there are very bad floods in Assam,' said Sanjay. 'Did you know?'

'No.'

'The army are up there with boats. At least thirty people have been drowned and thousands are marooned. I'm afraid it could affect your application.'

'Are they still rioting in Meghalaya?'

'They were last week.'

'Jesus.'

'Keep the faith,' he said. They glanced at their watches, gulped down the last of their tea, then went roaring away on the Enfield Bullet.

With a sinking heart I called Vijay Shankardass. He said an appointment had been made with Prasad Rao, officer on special duty at the Ministry of External Affairs, for two o'clock the following afternoon. Mr Rao was at last back from leave and should have news for me.

Before dinner I went to see the hotel soothsayer, a portly old man inhabiting a small office in the basement. He wanted payment in advance, in dollars. I asked if I would be travelling soon to Assam and Meghalaya, in the north-east.

He glanced at my palm and, sucking abstractedly at a hollow tooth, said, 'Nobody is going to those places any more. You should fly back to England. Who wants to stay in Delhi?' All he wished to speak of was power cuts and water shortages. The capital's water pressure was feeble; the human heart could pump harder. 'If, like me, you reside on upper storey it will not fill your tank even.'

In the Maharaja's Lounge a bald, elderly violinist in black tie and tails was playing to an attentive audience of well-turned-out Delhi folk. He had a highly polished scalp and thick spectacles which hugely magnified his eyes, and he was so bad he was funny.

Was he doing this, privately, for laughs? 'Flight of the Bumbly Bee!' he announced, before embarking on a series of noises so shockingly discordant that the Delhi folk looked at each other in astonishment. Then, catching my eye, he gave me a faint, ironic smile. I headed off to dinner, suddenly very glad to be back.

Prasad Rao occupied an office in Shastri Bhavan, a sprawling, tenement-like building in Dr Rajenda Prasad Road. Four friendly clerks told me that Mr Rao was in a meeting. It lasted an hour and, when he emerged, Mr Rao was not in the best of tempers.

His office contained a large map of India and some rather good pictures – semi-abstract figures and landscapes. Kicking off his sandals he hunted around his crowded desk for my file. Then, rubbing his feet together, he began reading aloud. 'The Government of India has considered the request of Alexander Russell Frater to visit Assam, Imphal and Shillong. Permission to visit Assam and Imphal is denied, but he may visit Shillong only for a period of seven days. Signed Amanda Prasad (Miss) for Ministry of Home Affairs.'

He closed the file and looked at me.

'What about Cherrapunji?' I asked.

'No.'

'Where do we go from here?'

He shrugged. 'You could see the fellows at Foreigners Regional Registration Office. They might change this ruling.'

'I've already been there. Twice.'

'Well, so be it.'

'Mr Rao, what's my file number?'

He frowned. 'I cannot give you that. It is confidential.'

'You could give it to them.'

'Impossible.'

He was bored and distracted. More important matters required his attention. Suddenly furious I said, 'I'm not leaving this sodding place until you've told Foreigners Registration I'm coming over. *And* given them my file number.'

Frowning, he fished in his pocket for a bunch of keys and unlocked his ancient telephone. The conversation was brief and carried out in a low voice, but I heard him say, 'Order number one-five-zero-one-three-oblique-seven-one-oblique-eight-seven-dash-F-dash-E.' Then he said, 'Acha!' and hung up.

'They are expecting you at 4.30,' he said. 'Oh, and you'd better take this.' He handed me a lilac form inscribed with my name. Smiling he said, 'It's your Shillong Permission. Well, cheer up! It's more than any of us thought you'd get.'

My motor trishaw ran into impenetrable traffic. Sitting there, feeling hope trickle out with the perspiration, I wondered why one of the apparent aims of India's bureaucracy seemed to be the creating of chaos where none had existed before.

I found myself recalling the New Hebrides and its Condominium arrangement. The overall effect had been much the same. The sharing of power by Britain and France meant the duplication of every aspect of their rule. The islands coped with two sets of coins and postage stamps, two legal systems and two administrations in which every official was twinned on the other side. These officials, divided by language and mutual antipathy, rarely met. The only exception was a venture called the Joint Court supervised by a British judge, a French judge and a neutral president appointed by the King of Spain. The King's nominee was a stout Spanish aristocrat named the Count de Buena Esperanza, whose friend and fellow-countryman, the Count of Andino, was appointed public prosecutor; a Dutchman got the job of registrar. The president spoke little French, no English, and was deaf; but since none of the Bench could understand what the native witnesses were saying anyway, it scarcely mattered. Maurice called the Condominium system Pandemonium and wrote pamphlets with titles like *Under Two Flags; a Hopeless Experiment and a Grave Scandal*. He would have felt at home here.

I arrived at the Foreigners Regional Registration Office five minutes before closing time. The official who had interviewed me before was preparing to go home and advised me, quite kindly, that my Cherrapunji application was hopeless. 'I thought we had seen the last of you,' he said. 'Go back to England and get on with your life. Kiss your wife. Cherish your children. There is nothing for you here.'

The *Times of India* ran a leader on the drought entitled 'A Frightful Prospect' which, noting that only ten out of a total of thirty-five meteorological regions nationwide had recorded normal or excess rainfall – not a drop had yet fallen on Rajasthan – raised the terrible spectre of famine and starvation.

The letters page carried eloquent testimony to the public's growing concern. Mr A. Mathan wrote:

I am sure no Delhiite would like to hear the jingle, 'Rain, rain go away', even from the mouth of an innocent child, with the mercury still touching 40 degrees C during day-time. We desperately need the rains now. The bounties of Nature and the gifts of the Creator are taken for granted by us till such a time when they are held back. It is then that we tend to grumble and think of the various blessings in life that are accepted as part of our normal routine by us.

And S. S. Gadkari complained about the standards of weather reporting in the Indian press: 'The newspaper coverage of the non-arrival of the monsoons was very inadequate. Frankly, the common man is more worried about his discomfort on this account and the relief that rains will bring, rather than about all the political news flashed in the headlines.'

That morning Vijay Shankardass flew to London with his family. His secretary, Mr Radhakrishnan, called to say that, before leaving, he had spoken to someone 'very high up'.

'How high is very high, Mr Radhakrishnan?'

'I cannot divulge that.'

'It wasn't one of his old Cambridge contacts, was it?'

He chuckled. 'Sir, sir! You must not press me! But I have a message: speak to Gupta!'

'When?'

'Now, sir!'

Mr Gupta was brisk and friendly. 'Ah, yes! The man you must talk to is Prem Prasad at Home Affairs,' he said. 'Today if possible.'

But Mr Prasad had gone home early. 'Call back tomorrow,' his secretary advised.

In the morning I learned that Mr Prasad was unwell and would not be coming to the office.

Mr Gupta told me to call Prasad's boss, Satish Chandra, a permanent under-secretary. His decision would be final.

Mr Chandra told me, courteously, that he had never heard of me or my case but promised he would look into it. At midday a youthful-sounding man from Mr Chandra's office asked me to call on Ms Prem Gulati at a government office near the Khan Market. 'Entrance Number One,' he said. 'She knows you are coming and will issue permit and stamp passport. Oh, and don't forget to take your Shillong Permission.'

'But why?' I asked.

'Aren't you the chap wanting to visit Cherrapunji?'

'Yes.'

He chuckled. 'Well, you can go.'

Racing into the ramshackle building I barely noticed a heavy build-up of cloud in the west. Entrance Number One was the Department of Security and, on the floor of the thronged lobby, a pock-marked scribe in a Nehru cap squatted before a typewriter, taking dictation from a small, squinting man, working with terrific speed and concentration. The lights went out. I seized the ledger from a protesting clerk, lit matches and entered the copious personal data required before they would let me up the stairs. Another clerk handed me two more forms, long and detailed, and told me to fill them out on both sides. I did this, striking many matches, at a small table on which an unattended baby slept.

Several dozen silent, sweating foreigners were packed into Ms Gulati's dark and airless office. A composed, matronly woman in a green sari, she sat working by the light of two flickering candles stuck in a saucer. Glancing up past an African shouting, 'Punjab! Punjab!' she beckoned me forward.

'Yes?'

Ms Gulati interrupted my explanation. 'I have been expecting you. But first your Shillong Permission must be photocopied. There is a place downstairs, in an alley behind this building. The cost is minimal. Leave your passport with me. When you return it will be ready.'

The manager of the photocopy booth said, 'Power cut. You must wait.' He spoke distractedly, preoccupied by a strip of black sky visible over his alley. When lightning went snaking across the roof tops he whooped and shouted something to the knife-grinder in the booth next door, but his words were lost in thunder. Then the electricity came back on and, clutching my photocopied Permission, I raced back to Ms Gulati's office.

It remained dark. She sat calmly among her shadowy supplicants in a pool of candlelight and, smiling, handed over my passport and invited me to read what she had written. Holding it close to the flames I saw the words, 'Permitted to visit Cherrapunji for three days via Shillong, Signed Prem Gulati, Documentation Officer, Ministry of Home Affairs', and the large Government of India stamp that made it pukka.

'Thank you very much,' I said.

'The permit starts from tomorrow. You will have to fly in through Calcutta.'

'Yes.'

'When will you go?'

'Now. Tonight. As soon as I can get a seat.'

'Can you get a seat?'

'That's the least of my worries.'

She laughed. 'Good luck!'

The lobby of Entrance Number One was empty, the typewriter sitting unattended in the middle of the floor. Everyone had rushed out into the street where, to the accompaniment of blaring car horns, they were all dancing together – the clerks, scribe and armed security men, the hundred people who, moments earlier, had been standing in here yelling for attention.

I put my passport in my pocket and stepped into the warm, streaming rain to join them.

Chapter Eight

�֎

I took a trishaw to the Cox and Kings travel agency near Connaught Place, urging the driver up to ambulance-chasing speeds. Water sheeted through the missing floorboards as he went bucketing off towards the capital's business district.

Power had failed there too. The airline offices lay in darkness, computers down, all trading suspended. That didn't augur well but I knew there were people at Cox and Kings adroit enough to find me a last-minute place on a crowded plane. From time to time during the course of the past weeks I had popped in to report on progress and ensure that my open tickets to Calcutta and Shillong were still valid. They plainly thought I would never make it but now, after pondering my Shillong Permission and Cherrapunji Amendment by the light of a hurricane lantern, they went to work.

The lantern was turned up till it smoked. Someone made strong tea. Then they got on their telephones, speaking to contacts, asking favours, calling in debts and, within the hour, booked me on to the last Indian Airlines Airbus of the day to Calcutta. The seat had originally been promised to a German mountaineer, but earlier he had fallen two hundred feet off some Himalayan rock-face and would, instead, be flying home to Frankfurt on a stretcher. A booking was also made on the Vayudoot Fokker Friendship going from Calcutta to Shillong at 8.30 the next morning.

Two hours after it started, the rain stopped. The atmosphere, heavy and oppressive, seemed faintly tainted by the sweetish, carrion smell of dead marigolds.

The Airbus lurched and bumped through heavy cloud and rain-bearing winds. The captain apologized for the ride. 'It is due to the wayward monsoon,' he said, 'which, as you know, finally got to Delhi after record delay. I must tell you, however, that my colleagues at the airport Met Office suspect it was not the proper onset. Today's showers were caused by a monsoon trough moving south-west from foothills of Himalayas but it was not well defined and may not sustain itself. So far, in this freak year, it is all God has granted us, but we must be grateful for His bounty and pray for more to come. Enjoy your flight tonight!'

The passengers, mostly businessmen, listened with rapt attention. My neighbour, a sallow auctioneer in a Nehru cap, sighed. 'Yet again the Devil holds an umbrella over Delhi,' he said. 'Has monsoon begun or has it not? When it behaves uncertainly, start-stop, stop-start, everyone becomes depressed and anxious. This mood affects everything, even business confidence and the stock exchange.'

On 17 July 1901 the Viceroy, Lord Curzon, wrote to his wife:

> Darling sweet Kinkie:
> We have had a curious weather week. For after the monsoon seemed to have begun 8 days ago in earnest, it suddenly slackened off, we had whole days without rain & anxious telegrams began to pour in from all parts of India. Now as I write, 10.45 p.m., it has just begun to rain again, and the latest reports are more favourable. What an awful thing it would be to have another famine. I shudder at the thought of it.

My neighbour took a pinch of clove-scented snuff and said that on 21 March, the day of the equinox, he had read confident predictions of an unusally bountiful monsoon.

'From the Met Office?' I asked.

'No, no, from certain top astrologers.'

Did the equinox relate, in any traditional way, to the monsoon?

He shrugged. 'The equinox sees the onset of the southerly winds that will eventually bring it, so I suppose it marks the monsoon's emotional start. The tenth day after the equinox is a very auspicious day for planting coconuts. I have watched my gardener doing this. He holds each nut to his heart and prays before placing it in the ground. Already, you see, he is dreaming of rain.'

We spoke of the great heat being experienced far beyond India. An Anatolian gunsmith, maddened by temperatures regularly exceeding 50 degrees Celsius, fell upon his neighbour's howling dog and bit it repeatedly.

Elsewhere in Turkey sixty people drowned after jumping into the sea to cool off.

The auctioneer sighed. 'We have yet, thank God, to reach such extremes here.'

Elsewhere in India, though, people awaited the rains with mounting anxiety. 'A special Shiva Lingam made of 28 kg of mercury,' said the *Times*, 'was installed in Rajkot for week-long prayers on Saturday "to appease the rain god". The "yagna" is being held at the Lal Bahadur Shastri ground. Pro-vice chancellor of the Saurashtra university, Mr Labubhai Trivedi, who is one of the organizers, said the mercury was "converted into solid state" through Vedic methods.'

The ordinary citizens of Rajkot, denied access to this high-tech wizardry, held daily demos and prayer meetings to 'propitiate the rain god'. In some places these were often ordered by government decree. Two years earlier in Karnataka the Minister of Agriculture commanded that prayers for rain be said throughout the state. To keep costs down, it was claimed, he first invited financial estimates from various leading temples, mosques and churches. The prayers yielded only passing showers and, afterwards, his opponents claimed that contracts had been awarded to the holy men who submitted the most competitive tenders, rather than to those with proven track records in the specialized field of precipitation through prayer.

To appease the rain god Varuna in Tamil Nadu a wedding of donkeys was celebrated with full religious solemnity. The 'bride' wore a colourful silk sari, the 'bridegroom' a silk dhoti, and a priest conducted the service according to Hindu rites.

In Jamnagar on 1 August 1986, at the behest of local religious leaders, sirens blew at 11 a.m. Work stopped and traffic halted as all 300,000 citizens prayed for five minutes. A spokesman said, 'The entire population stood united. We hope the rain god heeds us and brings us some relief from our pressing problems of withering crops and shortage of drinking water.'

The following day in Hyderabad eighteen-year-old Swaroopa Rani was installed as oracle during the Bonalu rain-making ceremony.

The girl, dressed in a red sari, her face and hands gleaming yellow with tumeric, mounted a wet pot and went into a trance as worshippers shouted 'Mahankalamma ki jai!'

The oracle answered questions from the gathering. She said the Goddess was not 'angry' with her people and, blessing them, asked for roasted dal and jaggery after the promised downpours materialized.

Lakhs of people participated in the colourful festival. Mr S. M. Haq, Deputy Police Commissioner, broke the traditional coconut as the procession stopped off at the Station House.

We flew on through the darkness, away from the rain and turbulence. Varanasi passed below, its lights brilliant in the clear air, a stray moonbeam catching the Ganges and making it ripple with silver. Peter Mundy, one of the first Britons to travel exhaustively through India, arrived here during the 1631 monsoon. 'In tyme of Raines,' he reported, 'it overflowes the Bancks the distance of 8 or 9 miles, the banck of the hither side somewhat highe, and the Countrie for 10 or 12 course very fruitefull, pleasant, peaceable and well governed.'

When the monsoon arrived over Varanasi it brought with it a season of scholarship and contemplation. Unable to travel because of swollen rivers and impassable roads, an army of wandering sadhus descended on the place and, in return for food and shelter, held classes. Each evening large crowds would gather in certain temples and houses to hear them teach. Sometimes the crowds included other sadhus who would take issue with the speakers, and their debates, held before an enthralled audience, their voices raised against the din of rain on the roof, might last long into the night. Varanasi, during the monsoon, became a great market-place for the exchange of religious and spiritual ideas.

The auctioneer said, 'Does that still happen? I don't know. But it might also be argued that the sadhus are staying put to avoid killing lesser creatures. When the monsoon comes the world is suddenly full of new life – insects, worms, tiny living things – and we risk harming them by placing a foot on the ground. Even a blade of grass is sacred; I can plant a wet seed and, when the shoot produces three leaves, treat it as a living god. I will even do a puja to it.' He looked at me. 'If you take this attitude to its logical extreme then a truly devout Hindu would not venture out of his house. I have heard of people who have actually stayed indoors for that very reason. Such devotion would be rare these days, though the thought is always there at the back of our minds. It certainly is in mine.'

'But you're 30,000 feet off the ground.'

He took off his Nehru cap, scratched his thinning scalp and put it back again. 'Perhaps the aeroplane itself is killing insects.'

'Not this high.'

'But during take-off and landing, certainly.'

Disembarking at Dum Dum Airport, Calcutta, he touched my arm and pointed; against the apron lights a trembling galaxy of swarming insects glittered like cosmic dust. I caught a taxi to the Ashok Airport Hotel, a few minutes away down a pot-holed road. The taxi's dashboard bore the legend 'Hypothecated to Bank of Madura' painted in an amateurish hand. At the Ashok they had closed the restaurant. Tired and hungry I remonstrated with the man at the desk. What kind of airport hotel was this that made no provision for passengers who flew in after 10 p.m.?

He frowned at me. 'If you are wishing to make complaint you must follow proper complaint procedure,' he said.

I left him. In the bar a weary-looking, middle-aged waiter went to the kitchen and made me delicious chicken sandwiches. He served them with a bottle of iced Kingfisher beer, then said good-night and went off duty.

My room smelled musty. There were cigarette burns on the furniture and exotic stains on the walls. From somewhere I could hear the faint strains of dance music. Rain pattering stonily against the window induced a melancholy so profound I lay there, wondering about it. I was aware that the circumstances – the darkness, the dance music, the rain – seemed familiar, and then it came to me. Late one night a couple of years earlier I had been awakened by the telephone in a Danish seaside town by the Kattegat.

It was my sister, calling from New Zealand. She was with our mother who, only weeks before, had been diagnosed as suffering from cancer. When the news came through I had flown out to see her and found her in remarkably good spirits. The doctor gave her at least six months and she told me she wanted to re-visit the New Hebrides, especially Paama. She had always detested the islands, somehow blaming them for my father's death; but now, quite unexpectedly, she spoke of an invitation I had brought from Paama several years before. I arranged to return shortly and take her there.

My sister sounded very calm. She said our mother was slipping away. It had all happened very quickly. She had gone into a coma and, though now briefly conscious, couldn't speak. She would place the phone by our mother's ear so that I could talk to her.

It took a ·moment for this to sink in. I felt disbelief, shock, bewilderment and then a bizarre, panicky kind of stage fright. What form of words would be suitable? What was the last thing one was supposed to say to one's mother?

'Tell her how much she means to you,' my sister advised.

We were not a demonstrative family and I had never said such things before. As I began my monologue rain pattered on the window and, somewhere in the Danish hotel, dance music was being played. Once, at the other end, I heard a faint rasping noise, but otherwise my mother remained silent. I spoke of our forthcoming trip to Paama, and of my father too, and then heard my sister's voice telling me I could stop. Our mother had lapsed back into unconsciousness and she remained that way, I learned in the morning, until she died four hours later.

Her Paama invitation was issued in 1980, shortly before the islands received their independence from Britain and France. The *Observer* had sent me to the New Hebrides to write a feature, my first visit since childhood, and I found many changes. The people, now intensely politicized, were split into pro-British and pro-French parties, the former led by black Presbyterian ministers, the latter by black Roman Catholic priests. Their rancorous, suspicious, recriminatory exchanges were mischievously encouraged by London and Paris, and the sour atmosphere made me even sadder than the disappearance of our old house and hospital, victims of weather, termites and time.

I wanted to spend a weekend on Paama. I sent a message and then, one Saturday morning, set off to the island of Epi aboard a small Air Melanesiae plane piloted by a couple of French youths. They staved off the tedium of the trip by finding some really interesting storms to fly through, but at Epi, where I transferred to the Paama launch, the weather sparkled. During the crossing the boatman offered me sugar-cane and switched on his transistor radio. We listened to the news headlines from Vila in Bislama, or pidgin – 'Nasonal Developmen Bang blong evriwan' ('The National Development Bank is intended for everyone') and 'Kopra Bod blong yumi se Jif Minista' ('The Chief Minister says we must have our own copra board') – and watched a veil of smoke billowing from Lopevi's sculpted ash-white summit; the groves of nut trees among which Maurice built his three churches still flourished at its base. Paama began filling the horizon, smaller than I remembered but prettier, and washed in soft buttery morning light.

We entered Liro Bay, where Maurice and Janey had floated their furniture ashore. A dense press of people packed the beach. As the launch drifted to a halt they began singing 'There Is a Green Hill Far Away' and an elderly lady came splashing out with a sun parasol and an enormous bunch of flowers. I jumped down and received the flowers standing knee-deep in the shallows. Holding the parasol over my head she indicated that we must not move until the service was over. An island pastor in a white linen suit and clerical collar intoned a prayer of thanks for the safe return of 'the man soltwater', which can mean pirate, invader or, in certain cases, long-lost traveller.

A second hymn followed. My lady companion and the boatman knew it by heart and sang vigorously, though my silence drew puzzled, speculative glances; could this mute stranger really be the grandson of Maurice? His voice would have been heard out beyond the shipping lanes.

The pastor gave a short address, welcoming Sandy, son and grandson of famous men, after an absence of thirty-nine years. Thirty-nine years! How did they know? Young Sandy's last act on leaving Paama had been to plant a coconut which, he would be pleased to hear, had grown into a healthy palm still bearing fruit and called 'Sandy's tree'; I had no recollection of ever having done any such thing, and listened with growing bewilderment and some apprehension. Tomorrow being the sabbath, Sandy would take morning service in the Rev. Maurice's church, and then attend a feast in his honour to which everyone was invited. And now he would step ashore so that all could greet him.

Steered by the old woman I waded to the beach and, for an hour, flowers clasped in one arm, the parasol shading my head, stood shaking hands with the people filing past. The pastor, and a group of merry young men called the elders, escorted me to my coconut tree and joined me beneath it for a formal photograph. At the tiny government guest-house the elders' wives brought a lunch of rice, yams and fish cooked deliciously in coconut milk. Their husbands, oblivious to the women waiting silently outside for the empty pots and plates, were hungry for information about my family, poring over photographs of the children, asking many detailed questions. What were their best subjects at school? What were their favourite Bible stories? What were the names of the ministers who had baptized them?

Later they showed me the remains of the mission house, blown down in a hurricane, and handed me a small stone which formed part of the kitchen wall. I noted that a few of the Swatow orange trees remained, gnarled but still fruitful.

They took me to the hospital my father had built, run by a taciturn old man who had been one of his students. It was a cool, graceful little building, more of a home than an institution, shaded by palms and scented with flowering trees. The elders said these had been planted by my mother.

We returned to the guest-house for dinner, the pastor and elders enlivening the meal with talk of the Sunday service. When I pointed out that I was wholly unqualified to conduct it, and could

not in all conscience say a public prayer, they chuckled and let me
into one of the secrets of South Pacific Presbyterianism: delegation.
I could appoint others to pray, but must do one Gospel reading
and preach the sermon.

Over roast pork, curried fish, corned beef fritters, sweet potatoes
and wild spinach cooked by the wives seated outside in the darkness
we chose the hymns and readings. As they quibbled amicably over
who would take the prayers I suggested we ask the wives in to join
us; perhaps one of them might wish to say a prayer.

The elders dismissed this idea as eccentric, and the conversation
grew more general. They told me about the life Maurice had
'saved' them from. Before his arrival the men practised cannibalism,
wore *nambas*, or straw penis gourds which held the sexual organ in
a permanently erect position, and were permanently spaced out on
kava.

Kava was, and on the other islands is still, prepared by the
women. They chew the root of the *Piper methysticum* plant, spit the
mess into a pot, then make themselves scarce. (Women are not
permitted to witness the men drinking; if one accidentally stumbles
upon a kava ceremony she must brace herself for the traditional
punishment, inflicted on the spot – a single whack on the head with
a heavy kava root.)

The stuff looks like milky tea and is non-alcoholic, but a single
dose packs the punch of four large whiskies and hits you four
minutes afterwards. Unlike alcohol, it produces a profound melancholy in the drinker, who becomes silent and drowsy, his eyes
sensitive to light, his ears to noise. It is intensely addictive and,
though the mind remains clear, temporary paralysis may occur in
the lower limbs.

When Maurice arrived the kava drinkers spent many hours
staring at stones, each containing the spirit of some plant or object
important to the tribe. There was the yam stone, the banana stone,
the coconut stone and the pig stone. The elders said Maurice,
pitying the poor savage Paamese who sat worshipping stones,
reached out his hand and raised them up to a state of grace.

Then they talked about the French. I heard familiar stories of
their duplicity, deviousness and blatant cultural imperialism, their
insistence that the inhabitants of French-controlled islands must

know French history, language and literature. 'In the rain forest the children read Zola!' said one. The elders sounded just like Maurice, who had detested the French, and even told me the kind of story Maurice had delighted in telling – about a greedy French trader on Malekula who arbitrarily doubled his prices and, within the hour, found himself contemplating bankruptcy. Could I guess why?

I shook my head.

'His customers collected up all their money,' said one elder, 'every last centime . . .'

'And threw it into the sea!' said another.

Later, when they had gone, I listened to the sleepy rumble of the surf and wondered about Maurice's continuing hold on this place; even his prejudices remained intact. Many of the other islands 'civilized' by his fellow-Presbyterians had now returned to their former ways, the men once again wearing the penis gourd, drinking kava and contemplating stones.

(On Tanna the previous week I had visited a lapsed Presbyterian community where the men worshipped a Duke of Edinburgh stone. They dreamed that he would soon renounce his present wife and come out to be their chief, or Big Man; I had seen an airfield hacked from the bush for his aircraft and met the three solemn, bare-breasted teenage girls who would be his new wives. The giant penis gourd he must wear had already been mailed to Buckingham Palace, and his framed portrait occupied the centre of a flower-bedecked shrine; the Duke's stone was the largest and most sacred in their compound.)

On Paama, though, I saw little change. Maurice had fashioned a society which, even forty years after his departure, continued to reflect his perceptions of what a decent society should be – the thrifty, God-fearing kind found today inhabiting any decent Glasgow suburb. How had he done it? He certainly liked the Paamese, preferring their company to that of anyone outside his immediate family; they, perhaps, felt a similar affection for him. *We had some laughs.* It was what he often said after returning from their functions, meetings or parties. *Aye, we had some good laughs.* Perhaps, in the final analysis, it wasn't necessary to look much further.

Four hundred people turned up for church, appearing through the trees and down the forest paths, a standard attendance. On the wall behind the pulpit were two pictures, a modest-sized print of Jesus and an enormous, ornately framed likeness of Maurice, hanging there like a boardroom portrait of the company chairman. I read from the First Epistle to the Corinthians – 'Though I speak with the tongues of men and of angels, and have not charity, I am become as sounding brass, or a tinkling cymbal' – because it was a favourite passage of my mother's and, later, delivered a political address, a plea for unity based on a couple of verses from John, Chapter 14. The congregation sat in judgement, all right, but handed down no verdict. That was left to the thirty children assembled on the floor around the pulpit who, as I spoke, lay comfortably on their backs, fast asleep with their mouths open.

Afterwards, at a feast of sucking pig roasted in an earth oven, the elders presented me with palm mats and intricately embroidered pillowslips. I was embraced by two weeping, half-blind crones who had been my grandparents' house-girls, and urged by many to return soon with my mother. A number of women spoke to me of the things she had done for them during her visits, of the quiet way she had taught them self-respect and a pride in their sex.

One said, 'Tell her I want to see her painting flowers again. She could make them grow on the paper and I liked to sit and watch her.'

I promised to pass that on. After the feast it began to rain, a warm, familiar childhood downpour from broken cloud resembling fracto-nimbus. The coals in the abandoned earth oven hissed and spat, going out just like the great rain-making fires of Kerala. My Paamese friends seemed happy and relaxed.

Thinking about them in the bedroom at Dum Dum they seemed to have become almost part of my Indian journey – though that fusion was nullified by the sudden recollection of a sharp little post-feast earth tremor on Paama. It had shaken fruit from the trees and caused laughter among the crowd. Perhaps I remembered it now because Maurice wished me to keep my priorities intact. I was in Calcutta, chasing the monsoon, with heavy Indian rain beating at the windows. I realized the dance music had stopped and, finally, drifted off to sleep.

In 1831 Lieutenant Thomas Bacon of the Bengal Horse Artillery wrote, 'During the season of the monsoon, Dum Dum, and the whole neighbourhood, are so completely inundated, that a small dingi may be paddled from the cantonment to the salt water lakes, or to the Sundurbunds, and thence into the open ocean, which is distant something more than one hundred miles.'

At 7.30 I reported to the tiny Vayudoot counter at Dum Dum for my 8.30 flight to Shillong. My mood was jubilant. Twenty-four hours earlier I had more or less abandoned all hope of ever seeing Cherrapunji. but now dazzling perspectives were suddenly opening up. That very afternoon I would be in Cherrapunji where, I knew, the monsoon was now fully established and on song. I thought of the picture on my nursery wall. I thought of my father. Might he be aware of where I was going? Did he realize one purpose of the journey was to tie up some old, unfinished family business?

The Vayudoot counter stood empty but for a team of carpenters erecting partitions in the area behind. I caught the eye of a man sawing plywood and, shouting above the racket, told him I wanted to check in for Shillong. He gave me a brief, puzzled look, then got on with his work. Several minutes later an elegant young clerk in a well-cut linen suit wandered up. He wore an Old Etonian tie and he told me the flight to Shillong had been cancelled.

'You should have been on early flight to Gauhati,' he said. 'It went at 5.30 and could be diverted to Shillong if required.'

'But my ticket says 8.30 departure. And it was issued by your head office in Delhi yesterday.'

He considered the ticket. 'Delhi should have known. That 8.30 service hasn't operated for nine days. They told us to cancel. Shortage of aircraft.'

I stared at him. 'So what shall I do?'

'You come back tomorrow at 4.30 a.m. I will put you on 5.30 flight to Gauhati and request Shillong diversion.'

The clerk frowned at the carpenters. 'What a din these fellows are making.' He amended my ticket with a flourish and handed it back. 'Would you like some tea?' he asked.

'All right.' My anger and disappointment began dissipating almost at once. India was teaching me a passive acceptance of the inevitable that had begun to make me faintly uneasy.

We went to an empty restaurant where a man with a broom came to take our order. 'Toast also?' he enquired.

'Yes, bring toast,' said the clerk. Then he smiled at me. 'Pardon my curiosity, but I am wondering why you are going to Shillong. It is not a place visited by foreigners.'

I told him about Cherrapunji and the monsoon. I also mentioned that I had now lost a day out of the three allocated to me by Ms Gulati.

'But you can put the time to good use here in Calcutta,' he said. 'We have monsoon also. It has arrived already but so far, touch wood, we have not had the terrible floods of last year. On 6 July then we were paralysed by blinding rain – 4.25 inches in twelve hours.'

Calcutta, I reflected, had known worse. In 1831 Lieutenant Bacon wrote that 'The heavens did not cease, during a space of one hundred and forty hours, to pour down without intermission a deluge of water.'

The clerk continued, 'The airport was closed due to waterlogging. No trams or buses ran on any routes so people had to walk home waist deep in water.' He gave me a sombre look. 'A number were never seen again.'

'Why?'

He said, 'When the flooding began many citizens rushed into the streets and ripped up the manhole covers to drain their houses. The missing people were pedestrians who fell through the open manholes. Plop! Gone, swept down into the sewers. To this day their numbers are not known.'

'My God.'

'You should talk to someone about the monsoon. For us it causes nothing but trouble.'

The sweeper brought our tea and toast. I went to pay but the clerk stopped me with sternly up-raised hand. 'Absolutely not,' he said. 'This repast is on Vayudoot.'

'Who would talk to me about the floods?'

'Our mayor, Kamal Kumar Basu, a famous Marxist and scourge of the Delhi government.'

I laughed. 'I can just walk in and chat to the Mayor of Calcutta?'

'Why not?' said the clerk. 'Everyone else does. He has an open-door policy between midday and one o'clock. You will have to wait your turn but he will see you.'

I finished my tea. 'Where did you get that tie?' I asked.

'From a gents' outfitters just off Shakespeare Sarani,' he said. 'Oddly enough, my aunty who works with refugees saw an identical one last week. It was in a second-hand clothing bundle sent from England.' He tossed some coins on the table. 'By Oxfam.'

Under a benign morning sun Calcutta's 270 grimy square miles looked cleansed and renewed. The monsoon rains had sluiced the streets and washed the buildings. Greenery was springing up. Seen from Dum Dum it seemed to sparkle, a garden city far removed from the 'surfeited muckheap' that Kipling so detested. But as my taxi neared the centre the old Calcutta began to assert itself. Traffic lights had broken down. The street community of homeless pavement dwellers and gaunt cattle wandered through the huge jams and tailbacks, a haze of exhaust fumes overlying everything like thin blue cloud. The congestion was worsened by the approach of a thousand striking metal workers marching behind a brass band. They crossed an intersection manned by three frantic, wildly gesturing policemen who seemed to be dancing to the music. Then the band and strikers broke ranks, the musicians still playing as they squeezed past the stationary vehicles, but competing now with the racket of horns blown in unison by disaffected motorists.

'God! God!' my driver muttered. He was very hyped up and nervous.

Calcutta people are different from other Indians. There is a weird sort of gaiety about them, as though they teeter on the edge of the apocalypse and are determined to squeeze more out of each passing day. Other Indians say the place is already out of control, that Calcutta and civic order are mutually contradictory terms. It represents the future which, should their anarchic, free-wheeling natures ever be let off the leash, awaits them all.

I paid off the taxi and continued on foot to meet the man charged with the city's governance.

The Mayor's secretary sat at a curved black desk set with an inlay of ornamental swastikas. Behind him hung a calendar from the Jadob Electric Company and a framed print of a Greek warrior addressing a crowd of earnest women beside the Parthenon. He noted down my name and waved me into a crowded ante-room furnished with black leather chairs and sofas. The supplicants were a cross-section of the citizenry, well-fed merchants, students, a couple of legal-looking men in suits, poor people from the bustees, all on their best behaviour and listening, wide-eyed, to the drama coming from the Mayor's office. A meeting was in stormy progress. A strong, autocratic voice shouted, 'No! That is not what I told you. Does no one listen? I said today. Today! That is no excuse. Go and get it! Get it now!'

A sweating, anxious man came blasting through the door and vanished into the passageway.

'Who said so?' yelled the Mayor. 'Who told you that? Well, I have news for him. He has exactly two minutes to get here and give account of himself. Two minutes! I am counting!'

Another aide shot through the ante-room and everyone exchanged appreciative glances. Here was the leadership Calcutta needed, a proconsul who ruled like a medieval nawab.

Kamal Kumar Basu dealt swiftly and efficiently with his callers. Though at the back of the queue I was summoned within the hour and invited to join him at a great polished table. His staff sat on sofas, frowning over documents or gazing abstractedly at a glass cabinet displaying Communist Party memorabilia – medals, letters, a small bronze head of Lenin. The Mayor, a lean, greying, clear-eyed man in a white shirt and dhoti, heard me out and then raised a hand.

'Get Sengupta, Drainage and Sewerage!' he ordered an aide. To me he said, 'It is better if you talk to my specialists. Of course we have a problem with monsoon flooding and, at this moment, I am trying to persuade central government in Delhi to give us money to make the city safer in the rains. Indeed, a report will be on the PM's desk within the next three months. One of the points it will make is that our last major sewer was laid in 1896. By the British. They built Calcutta as a great colonial capital, the second city of the Empire after London. Lord Curzon called it a European city set down upon Asiatic soil and that is really the heart of the problem. They built it for themselves, fine public edifices, cathedrals, churches, pleasant suburbs. They gave no thought to the millions of Indians who also lived there; no proper infrastructure was provided and, even then, it was notorious for its squalor and deprivation. Kipling hated it. Now the population has increased fourfold and, to make matters worse, we have a huge influx of migrants and refugees – 40 per cent of our present number. This flood of impoverished peasantry means we are a city in name only. Even around the business area rustic values and lifestyles predominate; country people live in shacks behind the office blocks and, of course, on pavements all over town.' He looked at me soberly. 'When the monsoon arrives our antiquated system cannot cope. Their lives become a torment of misery.'

Mr Sengupta popped his head around the door. I said goodbye to Kamal Kumar Basu and followed the Member, Mayor in Council for Sewerage and Drainage, Calcutta Municipal Corporation, to another office. There tea and biscuits were served and colleagues summoned by telephone – D. K. Sanyal, a plump, bespectacled executive engineer ('Drainage!' he said, shaking hands), and P. K. Ghose, assistant chief engineer to the municipality.

I asked about monsoon flooding the previous year. Mr Sengupta said, 'The rain paralysed the city totally and we all became its victims. More than 100,000 people were accommodated in 160 relief camps. For a period of seven days at least 277,000 had to be supplied with food, drinking water and medical help. To try and ease the situation we hired 200 extra portable pumping sets, opened manhole covers, desilted gully-pits and cleansed *nikashi* drains. Total cost of the operation was 58 million rupees.'

'Did many people vanish down the manholes?' I asked.

The men glanced at each other. 'That is a common Calcutta horror story,' said Mr Ghose, who was small, dark-skinned and intense. 'And it would be foolish to deny it has never happened. But not, I think, in the numbers you have been hearing about.'

Mr Sanyal said, 'The scale of our problems is enormous. The British built our sewers – they're the same age as London's – but designed them for a much smaller community. In those days it was considered acceptable to have three hundred people occupying an acre of land in Calcutta.'

'He means three hundred Indians,' said Mr Sengupta, drily.

'Now, thanks to the refugees who have been flooding in ever since Partition,' continued Mr Sanyal, 'we have areas where there are 4,500 people to the acre. We're still stuck with the old drains and sewers, and do not have the resources to improve them. What is required, in a flood situation, is a synchronized operation of pumping units and desilting networks that will push excess water through the storm drains and out into the River Hooghly.'

'There is a positive side, however,' said Mr Ghose. 'When disaster strikes, everyone pulls together. Each year, well before the burst on 15 June, we hold monsoon planning meetings at the town hall, chaired by His Worship. Thirty-eight department heads attend; so when the floods come, everyone knows what to do. The police, fire fighting department, Irrigation and Waterways, Civil Emergencies, Telephones, Electricity – all have their roles. The medical services are on full alert. Fleets of speedboats are ready to rush homeless to shelter.' He smiled. 'Calcutta suddenly becomes a very vigorous place.'

'Our councillors personally go out and give leadership,' said Mr Sanyal. 'I have seen the Mayor, even the Governor of West Bengal himself, walking chest deep carrying women and children to safety. Mr Sengupta too.'

Mr Sengupta allowed himself a modest shrug. Then he said, 'These disasters cleanse everything, you know. They flush away the rats.'

Mr Ghose said, 'For the PM we are preparing a special report. It is entitled *Calcutta – City of Joy* and it itemizes our sewerage and drainage requirements. Better storm flow, for example. New pump houses.'

'Renovation of trunk sewers,' said Mr Sanyal. 'A new treatment plant including digester; construction of new manholes and gully-pits; work on Tally's Nullah which now carries effluent from Tollygunje and South Suburban Units into the River Hooghly and causes pollution.'

'Improved solid waste management and night-soil service,' said Mr Sengupta. 'The city produces 2,600 tons of garbage every day; people throw all their rubbish into the street and leave the *mazdoors* to sweep it up. When monsoon arrives it clogs the drainage system.'

Mr Sanyal said, 'So we need litter bins, hand carts, extra brooms and mechanical sweepers. And incinerators to burn the infectious hospital waste now routinely chucked out with domestic garbage.'

'We have a very large cattle population in Calcutta,' said Mr Sengupta, 'together with untold numbers of dogs and cats. They all die in the streets, and we are telling Delhi that their carcasses must be disposed of scienuifically.'

'Delhi will also hear about our night-soil problems,' said Mr Ghose. 'All our privies and septic tanks are cleared and de-sludged by hand – a medieval practice which simply cannot go on. Mechanical cesspool emptiers must be provided.'

Mr Sanyal said, 'One of our aims is to assist penniless bustee dwellers who, inevitably, are the real victims when monsoon comes.'

He nibbled a biscuit. We drank our tea in silence. I said, 'What are the chances of Delhi listening?'

Mr Sengupta sighed. 'Frankly, they resent our old glory. Calcutta was the Indian capital until 1911, and central government is still wary of us. From time to time Delhi experts come to make reports but nothing more is ever heard from them. Now things have reached such a state that they must take notice.'

I said, 'But you've had no flooding this monsoon?'

'Not so far,' said Mr Sengupta.

'Touch wood,' said Mr Sanyal.

'We are all watching the forecasts,' said Mr Ghose. 'In a land that may drown, the weather man is king.'

I thanked these decent men for their time and went back into their vibrant, polluted, anxious city.

Kipling stayed at the Great Eastern Hotel in Old Court House Street while carrying out journalistic assignments for the *Civil and Military Gazette*. It has been frequented by journalists ever since; four were lunching at the table next to mine, three local men and a visiting Australian. The Aussie wanted to talk about affairs of state, about the Gandhi dynasty and the future of the Congress Party, but he couldn't get a word in edgeways because the Indians were arguing about mangoes.

One proclaimed, 'The Alfonso is peerless. It has the most wonderful spicy taste and a texture similar to the peach. It is—'

'No, no!' said a colleague. 'The Langra, the lovely one-legged Langra, is indisputably greater. Its sweetness is legendary. The flesh is so piquant, the aftertaste better even than a Tokay wine.'

The third said, 'I get rose petals in the Langra.'

'But you get rose petals in the Alfonso,' said the first. 'Also a hint of honeysuckle. And may I remind you that Alfonso is the official Harrods mango?'

The others laughed. 'That means only that it travels well,' said one. 'Like frozen mutton.' He added, 'I also get rose petals in the Daseri.'

'Ah, the Daseri! Yes, a Daseri from a good garden is not a bad mango but it is over now. It is really pre-monsoon.'

A waiter joined in. He said, 'Gentlemen, we have Safedas on pudding trolley.'

The Indians looked at him with interest.

'Ripe?' asked one.

'Ripe?' intoned the waiter. 'Sir, they are perfection. God has intended them for eating this very day.'

The baffled Australian sipped his beer. 'You blokes are worse than a bunch of bloody wine buffs,' he said.

'Arthur, this is a serious matter,' said the man who had started the argument. 'We are speaking of the most noble fruit on earth. It is one of the jewels in India's crown, bequeathed to us each year by the monsoon, and it arouses strong passions in all of us. You must have a Safeda for your pudding, though bear in mind that it is not one of the truly great mangoes. It is large and very sweet—'

'Sugary, even,' said a colleague.

'Yes, sugary. But lacking flavour. Certainly lacking those wonderful, subtle flavours you get with the Langra.'

'Or the Chausa,' said another, but this was greeted with derision by his colleagues; even the waiter allowed himself a faint smile.

'The Chausa is as large as the Safeda but that is the only similarity. Really, it is about as exciting as a potato.'

One proclaimed, 'For my money the Kalmi is the most delicious of all.' To the Australian he said, 'It is a small sucking mango. You rub it firmly between the hands to break the fibres, then you cut off the top, like a boiled egg, and simply suck out the contents. The taste is simply exquisite.'

'You can eat them in the office,' said a colleague, 'and while I am certainly very partial to the Kalmi I still say that the Langra is the mango of the true *aficionado*. I know Langra freaks who go back each year to buy their fruit from particular gardens . . .'

'From particular parts of particular gardens,' added a colleague.

'From particular trees in particular parts of particular gardens,' said the other.

One said, 'My grandfather once planted a Langra tree but, before he could eat the fruit, he had to marry it to another tree. A tamarind. Custom decreed it.'

'I know about that custom,' said a colleague. 'The jasmine was also considered a suitable bride for a mango.'

'The marriage was celebrated with a great feast. Two hundred people came. My grandmother had to sell her jewellery to pay for it. But it was a fantastic party and it meant that, when the tree finally bore fruit, it could be relished to the full.'

'In Jubbulpore,' said one, 'a man who made a tank dared not drink from its waters until he had married it to a banana tree planted specially on the bank.'

The Australian, visibly steeling himself, began talking about politics. His companions sighed softly. I called for my bill and left.

I went to look at the monumental structures erected by a homesick British community needing symbols of continuity and reassurance – St John's Church (containing the 1692 grave of Job Charnock, the city's founder), St Paul's Cathedral, the white marble Victoria Memorial, a Government House modelled on Lord Curzon's Derbyshire home, a High Court modelled on the Ypres town hall and the huge Writers' Building which once housed the East India Company's army of scribbling clerks. The only great British monument I couldn't see was the sewers.

In 1862 the British architect James Fergusson arrived in Calcutta and cast a professional eye over the buildings. He found that the British in India had succumbed to a Gothic craze; the Doric pillars proliferating everywhere served merely to 'obstruct ventilation without keeping out the heat'. The cathedral was 'Strawberry Hill Gothic', its flat roof 'supported by a diagonally-trussed beam such as we use in railway stations', its glassless Perpendicular windows 'disfigured with green painted Louvre boards to keep out the sun. We have done strange things in this country, but nothing quite as bad as this.'

Government House looked attractive but was too low. The town hall, with its Doric porticoes, seemed pretentious. Astonishingly, none of the buildings had been designed with the climate in mind. 'It is the misfortune of Calcutta,' Fergusson concluded, 'that her Architecture is done by amateurs – generally military engineers – who have never thought of the subject till called upon to act, and who fancy that a few hours' thought and a couple of days' drawing is sufficient to elaborate an important architectural design.'

This meant that successive viceroys and their families, stuck in their low, airless Government House, had to endure the same discomforts as everyone else. When the monsoon arrived Lady Canning complained that the atmosphere inside was 'like an orchideous-plant hothouse'. Her husband's dispatch boxes took on 'the appearance of a bottle of curious old port – white and fungus-y'. The place was invaded by insects. Crickets and grass-hoppers crawled into her clothes; there were one-inch black beetles and two-inch cockroaches everywhere, and so many creatures alighted on the dining-room table that she had to place improvised lids on the wine glasses.

For Fanny Eden the worst aspect of the monsoon was the snakes which 'took possession' of Government House. Bats crashed around in her bedroom at night and, on one occasion, a monkey broke in, smashed some china and stole a parrot belonging to her French maid. Evil-smelling civet cats scrambled up the pillars into her quarters while, at midnight, jackals crawled out of the drains and howled in the shrubbery. And perched on the parapet were a hundred six-foot-high adjutant cranes, scavengers said to pluck dead babies from the Hooghly and swallow them whole.

Thomas Babington Macaulay wrote that insects and undertakers were the only living creatures which seemed to enjoy the monsoon climate – though it was, he tartly noted, 'better than the House of Commons'. The humidity assaulted everything. 'Steel rusts; razors lose their edge; thread decays; clothes fall to pieces; books moulder away, and drop out of their bindings; plaster cracks; timber rots; matting is in shreds.' Macaulay maintained his equilibrium with apples and ice imported from the United States (they sent him novels as well) and huge jugs of lemonade.

Honoria Lawrence, an inveterate diarist visiting Calcutta in 1837, noted how Europeans without access to American ice kept their houses temperate:

> On the windward side are hung mats, called tatties, made of the fragrant kuss-kuss grass. They are constantly kept wet. The air that passes through them is delightfully cool. But the most important article of furniture in the Indian house is the punkah, an oblong frame of light wood covered with canvas and painted white. [It is] moved by a long string from the middle, which is constantly pulled.

A conscientious punkah-wallah could set up his own tiny wind system.

> The candles and lamps on the table must have glass shades to screen them from the perpetual breeze of the punkah. If you shake pepper on your plate at dinner, you must hold up your hand to prevent the punkah from blowing it all in your face. When you are writing, if you do not lay a weight on the corner of the paper, the punkah whisks it up against the pen.

Jemima Kindersley, wife of a Bengal Artillery officer, relished one particular aspect of the Calcutta monsoon:

> What I always behold with reverence and awe, and at the same time with pleasure, is the lightning; not an evening passes without it; it is not that offensive glare of light I have been used to see, but a beautiful fire, which plays among the clouds, and passes from one part of the heavens to another, in every direction, and in every variety of vibration.

Fanny Parks loved the sounds of the Calcutta rain which 'fell in torrents all night; it was delightful to listen to it, sounding as it was caught in the great water jars ... Today it is so dark, so damp, so English, not a glimpse of the sun, a heavy atmosphere, and rain still falling delightfully.'

*

I went to the Botanical Gardens, founded by the British in 1786, and the place where Lady Canning – when she wasn't travelling on the sumptuous state yacht with its marble bathroom – came daily to sketch the flowers. I sat in the shade of a great vaulted banyan. It towered overhead like a Gothic nave and was full of the squawk and chatter of mina birds. Thinking of the old Calcutta, my head full of English voices, I became aware of real English voices coming from somewhere up in the tree. I caught the sharp whiff of a substance being smoked, bhang or resin, and heard isolated snatches of talk. A woman said, 'He wants to go in across the Arakan Yoma mountains from Bangladesh', and a man said, 'Brian's going to try that? Jesus, he really is out to lunch.'

I couldn't see them; the branches where the couple lay were sturdy, cambered and curved, enclosing them like the bow of a galleon. Hating the furtiveness of eavesdropping I moved on, arriving at a grove of mango trees where the air was cool, dark and scented. It was lovely in there, a shadowy pavilion made drowsy by the cooing of doves. I recalled that mangoes planted for the common good – like these – were once held to be sacred. Even the dew and rainwater dripping from their leaves could not be touched. It was a libation for the soul of the benevolent man who, perhaps a century earlier, had created the garden to provide travellers with fruit and shade. I thought of an old Indian saying – 'The leaves of a green tree are a library teaching us the wisdom of the Creator' – then, feeling a quiet, unexpected, almost transcendental happiness, thought of Rabindranath Tagore. He had written:

In one salutation to thee, my God, let all my senses spread out and touch this world at thy feet.

Like a rain-cloud of July hung low with its burden of unshed showers let all my mind bend down at thy door in one salutation to thee.

Like a flock of homesick cranes flying night and day back to their mountain nests let all my life take its voyage to its eternal home in one salutation to thee.

I was drinking coffee at a refreshment stall by the gate when two young Brits wandered up and bought samosas.

I asked them how they liked Calcutta.

'It's great,' said the girl, who had serious brown eyes and a quick smile. 'There's so much going on. And the people are really interesting and funny.'

'Though you don't hear many jokes from the pavement dwellers,' her friend said drily. His hair and beard were thin and straggly, his bony nose sunburnt.

'I mean we keep meeting these people who want to put the world to rights,' she said. 'Intellectuals. The guy running our hotel in Sudder Street is a Marxist writer. And the cashier wants to make films. Last night we sat up arguing till two in the morning. They argue a lot around here.' She frowned. 'I know Calcutta's pretty ghastly in some ways, but I like it.'

'Molly's a romantic,' said the young man. 'She wants to stay in India for ever. She wants a marble palace and a big, shadowy Indian garden. By a lake. Don't you, Mol?'

'Yes,' said Molly, smiling. She said, 'The Nawab of Cambay had the kind of place I fancy, a beautiful little summer palace where water was piped up the marble columns to eight fountains on the roof. The cashier told us about it last night. He said in the evening the fountains came on and trickled down through screens of scented grass and jasmine. On hot summer nights you could create your own little monsoon, with everything cool and fragrant.'

I told her about Deeg and its 3,000 fountains. She took a pen and notebook from her jiffy bag and wrote it down. Then she asked me what I was doing in India. I told her that too, and she said, 'You mean you're actually following the monsoon?'

'I'm trying to.'

She gave me a serious speculative look. 'Could we come along? What do you think, Nick?'

'I wouldn't mind,' said the young man, slowly.

'I love the rains,' she said. 'They're . . . voluptuous. They make the air very soft. The days are fragrant and dreamy. And I love the nights when the-rain has stopped. There's magic in the air. Sometimes the moonlight's so bright you can actually see the individual flowers on the trees.'

'The trouble is,' I said, 'tomorrow I'm flying up to a place where you need a permit that takes six weeks to get.'

'Oh!' she said. 'Well, it was just an idea.'

We chatted for a few moments more. The shadows lengthened and Nick stole a glance at his watch. 'They shut the gates at dusk,' he said.

'You're not going back into the gardens!' I exclaimed.

Molly laughed. 'All our gear's there,' she said. 'Hidden in a banyan tree. We spent most of the day in it and tonight that's where we're going to sleep.'

Watching them slip through the gate it occurred to me that some things stayed constant. India might be an independent sovereign state freed from the constraints of British rule, but now the descendants of the Britons were coming back and, like many of their forebears, adoring the place. Molly, possibly in the teeth of her expectations, found herself bewitched in Arcadia. As a romantic ideal, turbulent, impoverished India could still weave its spell, and the key to it all – the colours, the moods, the scents, the subtle, mysterious light, the poetry, the heightened expectations, the kind of beauty that made your heart miss a beat – well, that remained the monsoon.

Behind our island house grew a mature frangipani with sturdy slate-coloured branches. Other frangipanis grew nearby, carpeting the ground with white and gold blossoms that gave off tiny vortices of fragrance when trodden on. There were also massed banks of hibiscus, bougainvillaea, poinsettia, wild orchids and tiger lilies which filtered and deepened the light, lending it the pellucid quality of stained glass. That was also a very Arcadian spot.

My father made a tree house in the frangipani, wedging boards between the lower branches and lashing a piece of sailcloth to the upper. Its perspectives were circumscribed by flowers and leaves; orange butterflies with the wingspan of pigeons drifted by. From time to time he would clamber up too, usually bringing glasses of lime juice, and occasionally talk about himself in a way he hadn't done before or since, speaking of a Glasgow he barely remembered, of his own childhood on Paama and his schooldays in Australia. I often sensed worry, usually caused by money troubles.

The Mission paid him £100 a year. He couldn't keep a family on that and had to borrow from local Tonkinese traders who charged fabulous rates of interest. The crunch came when my mother, very ill, required a hysterectomy. He wrote to the Mission begging for an advance on his salary so that he could send her for surgery in Australia. They wrote back saying no, he must learn to stand on his own feet, and the day he received that brutal letter was, effectively, the day they lost him. Throughout the war he worked single-mindedly for the islanders and the troops, but afterwards he quit and refused all further communication with the Mission.

In the tree house I first saw my father as an ordinary man with the same kind of fears and uncertainties that, years later, I would try to keep from my own children. I found it disconcerting, this hint of human weakness. It destabilized me, and whenever possible I would change the subject and get him on to weather.

That was different. There, selfishly, I could relax and enjoy myself, believing my father was doing the same. And perhaps he was. At moments like this he always rose to the occasion.

Here he told me about the glory phenomenon, sometimes experienced by people in the mountains where their shadows fell on banks of cloud or mist. Diffracted light met the reflected light inside the moisture droplets and caused a bright corona, or halo, to appear around the head of the beholder. Curiously, if a number of people standing side by side were all casting their shadows on the same cloud – the shadows being called Brocken spectres – you saw only the glory around your own head.

He told me about Flachenblitz, or rocket lightning, and about the corposants known as St Elmo's fire which streamed brightly from ships' rigging, weather cocks, even human hair. A thunderbolt was not a solid object, but a huge heat discharge which blasted oaks by boiling their sap. I learned about the ephemerides of the stars and the way moonlight could sometimes cause iridescence in thin, lenticular bands of cloud, colouring them unearthly pastel shades of pink and green. My father knew a lot about rainbows, this being a region particularly rich in them. He told me that sea-spray rainbows tended to be smaller than freshwater ones, due to the effect of dissolved salt on the refraction. He said that a morning bow usually preceded rain while an afternoon bow followed it; sometimes, in showery weather, you saw only a brief fragment or

two. I had witnessed these myself, and knew that sailors once called
them wind dogs.

Among the pedestrians waiting for the lights near Howrah Bridge
were a group of mourners carrying a body on a litter. The corpse,
that of a distinguished-looking man in his late fifties, grey hair
neatly combed, was banked with marigolds. When the lights turned
green his friends marched him purposefully across the road and
quickly vanished into the crowd.

I returned to the Ashok simply because it was well placed for the
early morning check-in at Dum Dum. In the bar I told two
Calcutta businessmen about the mayor and the money he was
trying to raise for his sewers. One laughed and said, 'I will tell you
why Delhi is so reluctant to comply. Half of it will end up in
people's pockets. Calcutta is like that. I know my employees steal
from me and I know how much – 5 per cent of the profits. So I
must build that figure into all my calculations. It is the system
here. And if I stopped I would get no co-operation. But I am a
small businessman and my people know they can go only so far.
With government money the sky is the limit. All those contractors
and subcontractors! All those favours! All those "commissions"! It's
a gold-mine and precious little would finish up underground.'

Shortly before 10 p.m. it began raining – real monsoon rain backed
by thunder. I went out to the entrance to watch. The headlights of
cars drawing up at the hotel looked as feeble as oil lamps. Giant
puddles were spreading at a rate that caused their edges to ripple
and eddy. A few inches above them a canopy of bouncing droplets
hung in a state of gravity-defying suspension, a glittering silver
cloak that could almost be seized by a corner and whisked inside.
    It was the first proper monsoon rain I had seen for six weeks –
the Delhi showers didn't count – and I felt an absurd sense of
contentment. My satisfaction was heightened by the knowledge
that I had finally met up with the monsoon's eastern arm. The
connection had been made. This rain had come all the way up
through Thailand and Burma but it didn't seem the least bit
travel-weary. On the contrary, it fell with tremendous weight and

energy, and I knew it would be falling ten times harder at Cherrapunji.

The *Times of India* said, 'The Capital and its neighbouring areas are likely to reel under fresh spell of heat wave from tomorrow. According to meteorological department sources, and despite partly clouded sky, the situation "drastically" changed today.' So the Delhi rains had indeed been a mocking flash in the pan.

I read an article entitled 'Spectre of Drought in Many Regions'. Sitting in my room, listening to the rain falling copiously on a city which it periodically flooded, I learned that standing crops in many areas were showing signs of 'moisture stress', the milk yield of cattle had declined, and there were critical shortages of drinking water. In Gujarat they had lost all their paddy, cotton, pulses, bajra and maize. 'Many talukas have not had a drop of rain, and 10,402 villages are being supplied with drinking water through tankers and bullock carts.' Rajasthan faced its fourth successive drought. Fears had been expressed for the Tamil Nadu *samba* crop. The tube-well water in Haryana had turned brackish and was useless for irrigation and drinking; the shortage of potable water, in fact, had now become acute.

The only states to have enjoyed 'a good monsoon', by comparison, were West Bengal, Sikkim, Orissa, Assam – and Meghalaya.

Elsewhere India faced the prospect of a monsoon so meagre that, experts were hinting, it might be the worst of the twentieth century.

Famine remained the real spectre that haunted India. In 1631 Peter Mundy had witnessed starving people searching the excrement of animals for undigested grain. He saw women roasting their children and travellers being attacked for their flesh. 'A man or woman no sooner dead but they were cut in pieces to be eaten.'

Two hundred years later Major-General Sir W. H. Sleeman came upon a district in which

every village had its numbers of the dead and dying; and the roads were all strewed with them. At Sagar ... hundreds were seen creeping into gardens, courtyards, and old ruins, concealing themselves under shrubs, grass, mats or straw, where they might die quietly, without having their bodies torn by birds and beasts before the breath had left them. Respectable families ... took opium rather than beg, and husband, wife and children died in each other's arms.

Though Lord Auckland, holed up at Government House in Calcutta, complained of being profoundly bored by the terrible 1834 famine, other Britons recognized the need to act. By 1868 the administration had devised a famine doctrine, its object to 'save every life'. But the early efforts of those charged with the task were not always lauded; Lord Lytton, the Viceroy, noted peevishly that the first famine relief camps in Madras seemed 'like picnics ... and the people in them, who do no work of any kind, are bursting with fat'. Outside the camp, however, Indians continued to perish.

In 1880 the formidable Famine Code was issued by a special commission sitting in Calcutta. Famine prevention measures were to be largely a matter of engineering. Villages would need ponds to store monsoon water; irrigation channels must be dug, rivers tamed by embankments. A tunnel was driven through the Western Ghats to carry water from one side to the other. The Upper Ganges Canal took water from the sacred river on a remarkable cross-country journey that led through hills, across one Himalayan torrent bed (half a mile wide in spate) and under another. Railways were crucial for rushing food to afflicted areas and thousands of miles of track were laid. An annual sum of 15 million rupees was set aside for famine insurance.

It was a remarkable scheme but, in the final analysis, the crises had to be dealt with by the men on the spot – the officers of the Indian Civil Service. In 1874 Herman Kisch, the 23-year-old son of a London surgeon, was given charge of

an area of 198 square miles. When my establishment is complete I shall have under me three clerks, 12 sub-superintendents and 24 messengers. I am supposed to make myself personally acquainted with every village. In one that I visited the condition of the villagers was such that I thought it necessary to have them fed on the spot with cooked food, rather than trust to their reaching alive the nearest store.

It is impossible to describe to you the condition of some of the children; after what I saw there I can readily conceive a skeleton from an anatomical museum being able to walk; unless I had seen it myself I could not have believed that anyone could live with so thin a covering to the bones.

Within a fortnight of his arrival young Kisch, exhausting the relays of horses and elephants on which he kept charging about, had erected fifteen storehouses for government grain and dragooned 15,000 able-bodied villagers into emergency relief projects. All received a small wage. Calcutta abhorred charity, so self-help was the order of the day; if a man could labour for his rice, then Victorian sensibilities decreed he should do so. In the space of only a few weeks they built five dams, forty reservoirs – designed to hold water 'all the year round' – and four huge central warehouses each able to accommodate several million pounds, or a million rupees' worth, of grain.

Kisch's optimism paid off. The monsoon arrived in early June (torrents coming off the hills knocked over two of his dams) and soon 'every day thousands of carts, bullocks, horses and mules' were arriving at the warehouses laden with rice and obliging him 'to run about like mad to see it stored'.

He and thousands of other young ICS men like him fought tigerishly to save lives. Each death was a personal affront and the infrastructure they created meant that, slowly, the terrible shadow of famine began to recede. Their work, now largely forgotten, remains a triumph of humanitarian engineering and one of the greatest gifts ever bestowed on India by the British.

What made it wholly extraordinary for me was that they got the monsoon's measure and then, in a sense, tamed it. Only a people with the energy, optimism and towering self-assurance of the Victorians would have ordered the reorganization of a phenomenon attributed directly to God.

I was starting to feel the edgy excitement that comes with the anticipated climax of any journey. Thinking of Cherrapunji, trying to imagine what it would be like, I picked up the phone and called the Baptistas in Bombay. It was done on the spur of the moment. They had been directly involved with the beginning of the trip and now I somehow wanted their blessing for the end. In truth, I didn't believe I would get through but, within seconds, Aloysius answered on a line clear as a bell.

'My dear chap!' he said. 'Long time no speak!' He remembered me, and his voice seemed full of warmth and interest. 'Are you at the Taj? Come to dinner.'

'I'm in Calcutta,' I said.

'Oh God! Is it raining?'

'Bucketing down.'

'I'm having a barbecue. And I've got real Scotch – half a dozen bottles of Black Label. A few friends here.'

'How's Rita?'

There was a silence. Then he said, 'Rita's not actually with me at the moment. She, uh, she's staying elsewhere. But she's well! Yes! Tiptop! More gorgeous than ever, in fact.'

'Give her my love when you see her.'

'Of course! She will be thrilled.'

'Aloysius, I was just calling to say I'm going to Cherrapunji tomorrow. You remember telling me about it in London? They've finally given me a permit and I'm setting off in the morning.'

He laughed. 'When you come back to Bombay you can dine out on that for months. But how will you get there?'

'I'm flying to Shillong.'

'I have friends in Shillong! You must see them. Dileep and Iris Patel. Their number is in my desk somewhere. While I am fetching it talk to Shashi. The vulcanologist. You met him at Bunny Gupta's party in Goa. Shashi!' he cried. 'Come and say hullo to Alex. He's the monsoon man from England and tomorrow he's going to Cherrapunji.'

Shashi took the phone. His voice was so thick I could almost smell the Black Label fumes. He told me Aly and Rita were having a trial separation. It was her idea and the signs were she would extend it almost indefinitely. Aly's migraines had come back. Sometimes they were so severe he even talked of returning to the Nervous Diseases hospital in London. Meanwhile, what did I make of Calcutta?

I said it was shocking and stimulating in equal measure.

'Some day,' he said, 'that whole damned place is going to blow up. Like one of your grandfather's volcanoes. It will probably happen during the monsoon when all those wretched people who live on the streets finally take matters into their own hands. Mark my words, it will be catastrophic, the Partition riots all over again.'

Aloysius returned with the Patels' phone number in Shillong. I asked about his migraines. He said they came and went, the triggers apparently claret, chocolate and cheese; these, regretfully, he must now deny himself. We chatted for a few minutes, then wished each other well and hung up.

But Shashi's analogy of the volcano haunted me for the rest of the evening. The greatest eruption that Maurice ever witnessed – it formed the corner-stone of his book – was in December 1913 when Mount Benbow on the island of Ambrym, just across the water from Paama, turned into not one but six contiguous volcanoes. The epicentre lay directly under Ambrym's fine new hospital, which was vaporized and transformed into a column of compressed steam that went roaring up for 20,000 feet. (Moments earlier the medical staff and patients had set off across the bubbling, boiling seas in an open boat; but a hundred yards offshore they were almost capsized by a submarine volcano emerging to turn itself into a 330-feet-high island.)

Maurice had been out in his launch, bringing people off the steaming beaches. A few months later he returned with a party of officers from HMS *Sealark* to conduct a survey, trudging across an ash plain to the twelve-fathom lake that now stood on the site of the hospital. Benbow still grumbled, periodically shaking the ground and emitting a 12,000-foot column of black smoke. Hundreds of blow-holes steamed and spat, while the lava columns dotted over the flow had assumed the shape of primeval chimneys. Nothing grew there.

But Shashi had got it wrong. It wasn't Calcutta that faced desolation. It was those huge, hungry areas of India where the monsoon had failed.

A curious, gritty optimism pervaded Calcutta. I remembered that the city council had entitled its report for Delhi *City of Joy*. I took this to be just another typical example of public relations nomenclature, ironic and provocative, but now I knew it implied something else. For the people on the streets it was a haven. They were in Calcutta by choice, victims of starvation or persecution elsewhere, and would rather be here, living rough, than in the places from which they had fled. And though the unceasing flow of refugees compounded the mayor's many problems, still he let them come.

I thought of the panicky, parsimonious way Western nations dealt with the dispossessed, and realized that Calcutta displayed a generosity of spirit that put the rest of us to shame.

The city was indestructible – despite the excess rain that kept sousing and rotting its foundations.

Y. P. Rao believed the rain was brought by transverse wind waves coming out of the Bay of Bengal. An estimated ten of these upper tropospheric troughs sailed over the city each month, accounting for 81 per cent of its rainy days and activating ten thunderstorms; each coincided with the transit of the troughs' coldest parts. Elsewhere in India, though, the skies remained empty, while the suffering people below tried to invoke clouds by ancient, well-tested means – thousand-strong choirs of red-robed women holding candles and chanting, 'Om, shakti, Parashakti! Om, shakti, Parashakti!', processing musicians playing rain-making medleys on timpani and strings as their acolytes burned camphor, rural priests officiating at the weddings of frogs and singing sacred, rain-making songs in their high, quavering cloud-seeding voices.

The people who would not be singing this year were the ones who usually did – flower-bedecked village girls skylarking beneath the mango trees on flower-bedecked swings. Perhaps next summer their rain-welcoming songs would, once again, float out across the green, dripping land.

> *Swing, swing, Rani Raja, till the flowering of the rose.*
> *Swing, swing, Rani Raja, till the flowering of the marigold.*
> *Swing, swing, Rani Raja, till the flowering of the* champa.

Chapter Nine

Taxis were not hard to come by at 3.45 in the morning. A dozen stood parked outside the hotel, their drivers asleep in the rear seats. My driver told me they virtually lived in their cars and, each night, competed for places near the larger hotels in case a fare materialized during the hours of darkness. 'When do you see your families?' I asked.

'My family is in Chittagong.' He spoke sadly. 'I am visiting them once a year.'

Only a few lights burned in the Dum Dum departure hall and the Vayudoot check-in desk stood empty. I was absurdly early and slumped, yawning, on a bench. At 4.30 my friend the clerk turned up, looking as elegant as ever. He seemed surprised to see me. 'Good morning!' he said. 'And what brings you forth at this ungodly hour?'

'The flight to Shillong,' I said. 'You booked me on it yesterday. It goes in an hour.'

He carefully threaded a gardenia into his buttonhole. 'It goes in four hours,' he said. 'The 5.30 flight today is for Gauhati and Tezpur. The Shillong departure is now 8.30.'

'You told me the 8.30 to Shillong had been cancelled.'

He smiled at me. 'Yes, and it will be cancelled again tomorrow. But today it has been reinstated. You are going with my friend Captain Ravi. There is one other passenger only so you will have plenty of room.'

Wearily I offered to buy him breakfast. He said he had to await the three passengers, all army officers, booked on the 5.30 to Gauhati. In the empty restaurant the same sweeper laid down his broom to bring me tea and toast. Waiting, I heard a Tannoy message advising that the Aeroflot service to Hanoi would be departing shortly. 'Passengers should keep boarding passes handy,' intoned the lady announcer. Then she sneezed and exclaimed, 'Bless me!'

Dawn revealed puddled runways reflecting a clear persimmon sky; as the sun rose the puddles began steaming gently. Through the miasma I spied an elderly Fokker Friendship parked far away. At 8.15, accompanied by the clerk and my fellow-passenger – a watchful, heavy-set Sikh who looked like a military man in mufti – I was delivered to it in a van. Jumping out, I noted that the aircraft's skin displayed the seasoned patina of old armour. A sultry, buxom, dark-skinned girl waited expectantly at the head of the steps but the clerk brushed past her calling, 'Ravi! Ravi! You have company!'

The pilot, handsome and youthful-looking, popped his head around the flight-deck door. 'The damn hydraulics have gone,' he said. Beside him stood a bald, anxious old man with a crimson caste-mark painted on his forehead.

'There is leak,' he told us in a small, whispery voice.

'This is Ground Engineer Gopalan,' Captain Ravi said. 'He is coming with us to make running repairs.'

I was comforted to note that the Sikh plainly regarded this as a routine occurrence. Unmoved by the news he strode off down the cabin, selected a seat and immediately immersed himself in a newspaper.

Captain Ravi didn't seem unduly bothered either. 'It means that we cannot raise undercarriage until pressure builds up after take-off. That will take twenty minutes or so.'

'Mr Frater is from England,' said the clerk. 'He is coming with you to witness the full pageant of monsoon at Cherrapunji. Can he occupy third seat?'

Captain Ravi pointed to a worn metal step giving access to the flight deck. 'That unfolds to form third seat,' he said. Then he pointed at a stout red pin protruding from the door frame above it. 'And that is the manual hydraulic control which Gopalan has just inserted. Clearly we cannot raise step while that is in position but, if you don't mind standing, you are welcome to stay. Later you can have my seat.'

I laughed.

'Of course, why not?' He glanced at his watch, then addressed the co-pilot, a beefy youth scarcely out of his teens. 'Tell the tower we're ready to go.'

The clerk cried, 'Happy landings!' and departed. Our two venerable turbo-props began to whine and, propped in the flight-deck doorway, I witnessed the take-off and slow climb away to the east of Calcutta. 'We'll be cruising at an altitude of 11,000 feet,' said Capain Ravi, 'on a heading of zero two zero. In eighteen minutes we shall reach NOMIX – an imaginary line drawn along the Bangladesh border. That is when we'll think about trying to retract our wheels.'

Gopalan stood behind me, popping fennel seeds into his mouth and suffusing the air with the smell of liquorice. He gave a nervous little nod. 'Undercarriage up over Bangla. Good, good, I concur.'

'This aircraft,' said Captain Ravi, 'is twenty-seven and probably the oldest Friendship still flying.'

According to the route map, he and his vintage machine passed, each day, within twenty miles of Cherrapunji; what, I asked him, were the particular problems of monsoon flying?

'Well, mist or torrential rain wiping out a strip seconds before you touch down,' he said. 'Gusting crosswinds; we can take 20 knots but more than that you have a major skidding risk. Cloud. Cu-nim anvils occur as high as 55,000 feet. More than half the severe turbulence reported over India during the year is caused by monsoon cu-nim. It shows up on the weather radar – the stronger the cell the stronger the signal.'

The young co-pilot wore his shirt unbuttoned almost to the waist. Now, with a faint jangling of gold chains, he stirred. 'Lightning,' he said.

'Yes, though the bark of a strike is worse than its bite. There is a terrific bang and a bump which always scares the passengers. It poses no real risk but can cause temporary blindness in the pilot. That only lasts a few minutes but can be quite frightening the first time.'

'I am still frightened when we both go blind together,' said the co-pilot.

Captain Ravi turned. 'Gopalan, share out your fennel!'

Sheepishly the engineer handed around his seeds. Captain Ravi, chewing, said, 'Flight controls made heavy by rain. At the end of a long day you suddenly realize how weary you are; a pilot must be very fit for monsoon work. The prevailing wind comes always from the right, and sometimes it's so strong you can't turn the aircraft into it. Then you have to devise a way of getting where you want to go by only turning left.'

'Line squalls,' said the co-pilot.

'Yes, but mainly during the period immediately preceding the monsoon. They contain 100-knot winds and always appear around Calcutta at four in the afternoon; going in to Dum Dum can be like riding a surfboard through breakers. Line squalls are also common in Meghalaya, where we're going now, though there you can get them around the clock.'

We droned on towards the NOMIX line. Dhaka gave us permission to cross and, once over, there was tension on the flight deck as Gopalan pushed home his makeshift hydraulic bolt and Captain Ravi tugged at the undercarriage lever. We heard a clunk as the wheels retracted and locked into position; then Gopalan, smiling for the first time, went to persuade the sultry stewardess to put the kettle on. Passing to the east of Madhupur Jungle we picked up the Brahmaputra on the radar, a ghostly, perfectly miniaturized rendering of the river depicted for us long before we actually reached it.

Then, puzzlingly, the landscape ahead began to dematerialize. The pale greens and browns were gradually replaced by a swelling effusion of light which turned to quicksilver and then assumed the shining milky blue of Arctic ice. I pondered this glittering realm and the fact that, at 11,000 feet, we would soon be entombed in it.

'What's happening?' I asked.

'Floods,' said Captain Ravi. 'Caused by monsoon rain and a snow-melt surge in the Brahmaputra. From now on, until we leave Bangladesh at a point just west of Cherrapunji, we will fly over this. It is very beautiful, is it not? I like the way the water reflects the sky and the cloud shadows form little islands. But down there two hundred people have drowned, a million are homeless and a million tons of rice have been destroyed. Dhaka has asked the world for food and fifty speedboats with which to distribute it but, so far, they have had little response.'

Gazing down at this peaceful inland sea, its surface scored here and there by the wakes of small craft, I realized we were passing across the part of the world most consistently punished by the monsoon. Regular inundations called *kal Baisakhis* deposit water direct from the sky, while more water cascades from Himalayan foothills eroded by overgrazing and trees felled for firewood. Now Bangladesh is at risk each year and, though dams and watercourses were planned to restrain this terrible seasonal tide, so far little had been done.

The flooding scourge arrives from the north. From the south, raging up out of the Bay of Bengal, come the cyclones. The monsoon's most feared engines of destruction, they kill indiscriminately and in the kind of numbers normally associated with a nuclear holocaust; the one that struck Bangladesh in 1970 slaughtered half a million. (The kinetic energy generated by a tropical storm is equivalent to an explosion of 360 megatons.) In 1900 Sir John Eliot, India's old weather wizard, published his *Hand-book of Cyclonic Storms in the Bay of Bengal* which established that the early phase of the summer monsoon provides conditions favourable for their formation. An estimated 15,000 died in May 1985 when a cyclone sweeping up the Sandwip Channel into southern Bangladesh towed a giant tidal wave behind it. Inevitably, an outbreak of cholera followed. One harrowing report in the London *Daily Telegraph* said, 'As the bloated bodies of children lay nearby, health officials on the island of Urir Char used one needle to inoculate about 300 people. "We cannot change the needle. We cannot afford it. God will give them resistance," said Surgeon Commander Nural Islam of the Bangladesh Navy.'

Then, to compound the country's misery, extensive flooding followed and inundated the area we were overflying now.

'It was a terrible time,' said Captain Ravi. 'In the space of just three days the whole nation had become a disaster zone. Sometimes, passing over here, we would see our passengers weeping.' He sipped the strong black tea the stewardess had brought us. 'I flew over the coastal areas as well. What devastated them was not just the cyclone, but the storm surge it brought with it. That's the tidal wave – a sudden rise in sea level you sometimes get when the cyclone comes ashore. It's caused by onshore winds, falling pressure, coastal geometry, sea-bed friction, many different factors. A friend at the Met Office tells me that they can now watch the storm tracks and forecast the size of the surges. He says this is saving lives.'

In 1569 the merchant Caesar Frederick found himself adrift in a Bay of Bengal cyclone which 'carried away our sayles, yards and rudder; and because the ship laboured in the Sea, wee cut our Mast over-boord . . . Sixtie men did nothing but bale water out of her . . . nothing but cast the Sea into the Sea.'

Then, at about four o'clock in the morning, a storm surge – Frederick calls it 'a great wave of the Sea' – carried the vessel up on to 'the fertilest Iland in all the world'. It deposited it high and dry a full mile inland. Almost at once, having welcomed them, the business-minded local community erected a large bazaar 'with Shops right over against the ship'. And there, for forty days, the bemused crew sated themselves on 'fine Rice, salted Kine, wilde Hogges and great fat Hennes for a Bizze a piece, which is at the most a Penie'.

The effect of the monsoon storm surge on shipping is well documented. Albert Hervey wrote in 1833 that near Calcutta 'a huge East Indiaman, of eight hundred or a thousand tons, was lifted out of the water and landed in the middle of a rice-field, several hundred yards from the banks of the river'. And two years later an Englishman occupying a mansion at Coringa on the north-east coast awoke one morning to find a length of timber protruding through his bedroom window. It was the bowsprit of a large, abandoned tea clipper which sat peacefully at rest in the garden.

The flood stretched away interminably. No clear horizon could be seen, though a faint band of radiance far ahead may have marked the point where sky and water met, or perhaps indicated merely that a further infinity of sky and water lay beyond. Then, over the nose, I seemed to discern the idea of a river, a broad, looping, muddy affair displaying just enough speed and surface tension to impose itself on the drowned world through which it passed; it was spanned by a long green bridge, a surreal, purposeless structure now partially submerged and foaming like a weir. But the scene appeared familiar and, like someone identifying a landscape from a grainy snapshot, I realized I had seen it on the radar.

'The Brahmaputra!' I said.

Captain Ravi nodded. 'But only just.'

The Fokker droned on. Beside the islands cast by cloud shadows there were real islands, small hills protruding above the water with villages set on them. I saw one ahead and several degrees to the right. 'Can we go and look at that?' I asked.

'Sure.' Captain Ravi climbed out of the flight deck and stretched. 'Take it over yourself.'

I slid into his seat. He pointed to a bakelite switch on the autopilot console. 'Turn that to the right.'

I turned it and the Fokker banked.

'Further.'

The Fokker banked more steeply.

'You're on course. Now you can straighten up.'

I clicked it back to the vertical and we soared straight over the top of the village, a collection of red roofs and coconut palms among which, even from this height, I could see people waving. Another appeared several miles off our port beam. 'Switch left?'

'Sure, sure, switch left.'

Gopalan appeared with the sultry stewardess in tow. Neither seemed surprised at the crew change. The stewardess carried a pencil and a secretarial shorthand pad and, as Gopalan shouted out readings from the instrument panel, she carefully wrote them down. The co-pilot spied another settlement and jabbed a finger. It was crowned by a church with a baroque bell tower, and looked like a tiny Italian hill town. I spent twenty minutes quartering the flood and then relinquished the seat to Captain Ravi.

He pointed. 'Meghalaya!' I saw a citadel of granite-coloured cumulus towering fifty miles ahead. 'You know what it means? Abode of the clouds. They're always there, sitting over the hills, almost part of the structural integrity of the place. It's the only Indian state you can reliably pick up on the weather radar.'

The co-pilot called up the Assamese town of Gauhati where the Fokker was bound after dropping me off at Umroi, the tiny mountain strip that served Shillong. Gauhati, a fully instrumented airport, reported eight kilometres visibility and one okta of cloud at 3,000 feet, but had no knowledge of the weather at Umroi.

'Wind sheer can be a problem here,' said Captain Ravi. During the monsoon you get up to 30 knots coming from any point of the compass, and you remain at risk until the aircraft has stopped. The strip lies deep in a valley which often fills with cloud like, well, milk being poured into a bowl. This, and heavy rain suddenly wiping out visibility, can turn some landings into real suicide attempts.'

'What's the likely weather today?' I asked, suddenly worried. 'Will we get in?'

He shrugged. 'We won't know until we're twenty miles out. Umroi has very primitive radio facilities.'

'Umroi has a kind of crystal set,' said the co-pilot.

That awesome citadel of Meghalaya cumulus sat over a range of hills so unimaginably green they seemed radioactive. The rising terrain ahead glistened in the morning sun, its wild, vibrant, primeval viridescence almost colouring the undersides of the clouds.

'The Khasi Hills,' said Captain Ravi. 'The world's wettest.' He pointed to the right. 'Cherrapunji is that way, but today it's out of sight and locked in solid.' He peered into his Bendix weather radar and pronounced the oncoming cloud benign.

Meghalaya's clouds gave us a boisterous, turbulent welcome before parting to reveal a lovely perspective of rolling highland country embellished by dense copses, shadowy clearings and white-water streams plunging along so vigorously we could almost hear them. We could almost smell the wildflowers too. We couldn't see them, but these wooded hills and secret valleys gave off a queer, soft, starlight luminosity that might have been emitted by fields of lilies beneath the trees. We were flying over an abandoned, over-grown garden, and it wasn't hard to imagine a seed planted at dawn blooming before dusk.

We entered the Umroi valley from the south-west. It looked clear, though ragged shards of cloud were starting to spill down its eastern slopes. The pilots had been unable to contact the aerodrome manager and now, tense and alert, they monitored the sky as closely as combat fliers watching for enemy fighters.

The co-pilot pointed at the cloud piling in from the east. Captain Ravi grunted. He said, 'And there's a heavy localized shower down there, approaching the strip at about four o'clock. Can you see it?'

'I see it,' said the co-pilot.

The shower, a smoky acre-sized edifice several hundred feet high, was moving across the valley floor at the speed of a galloping horse.

Then the aerodrome manager came through on the radio. He sounded breathless.

'What's the wind, Umroi?' enquired Captain Ravi.

'Zero five zero at seven knots.'

To me he said, 'The government is doing nothing to improve these small fields in the north-east. They have no aids, no facilities. Umroi hasn't even got a phone, and his radio is from the Stone Age. Sometimes it seems better just to open my window and shout.'

He pondered the valley. The descending cloud formed itself into a thick mist which began bearing down on the runway. 'Where's Gopalan?'

Gopalan was standing by my shoulder. 'Here, Ravi!'

'Let's do the undercarriage. I must go in quickly.'

Three green dashboard lights indicated that the wheels were lowered and locked. Captain Ravi went skimming down the valley wall like a swallow, racing the mist and rain to the runway threshold. It was a wild, exhilarating ride, made with surging engines and many small, abrupt course changes. The strip, visible across a rushing forest canopy, began diminishing as the rain squall reached its further end and hastened along it. Green birds exploded from the tree tops and passed inches beneath our wheels.

The mist, chasing the Fokker out to the left, was closing fast on the threshold.

'Oh, God,' muttered Mr Gopalan.

The co-pilot sat up very straight.

I sensed we were in the hands of one of the best monsoon pilots in India. This man understood the monsoon's vagaries, and possessed the experience, skill and cunning to deal with them. It had declared its hand and now he would match it.

The Fokker thudded down seconds before it was enveloped by rain that thundered on the fuselage and cascaded over the windshield, drowning even the howl of reverse thrust being applied. Mindful of the dangers of skidding, he used the brakes cautiously. We rolled to a halt in semi-darkness and zero visibility.

'Nice one, Ravi,' I said.

He turned, grinning from the excitement of the chase, and said, 'All in a day's work, my friend.'

By the time we parked, the shower had moved on up the valley, and so had the mist. Ravi said, 'There are still riots in Shillong, you know. Watch yourself.' I shook hands and sloshed across the glistening apron to a tiny terminal where an overweight army officer in a khaki sweater and gaudy tartan scarf looked at me in astonishment. 'Transit passengers must stay on plane!' he barked.

'I'm not a transit passenger. I'm getting off here.'

'That is not possible. You have no Permission for this place.'

I showed him Ms Gulati's handwritten entry in my passport. He stared at it, shaking his head. 'Cherrapunji! You cannot go there.'

'Delhi says I can.'

'Acha, always Delhi says, but what is Delhi knowing? I am man on spot and I am telling you Cherrapunji is off limits.'

I stood before him in a bare, cell-sized room. He sat on an upright chair which creaked when he moved, emphasizing his weight and plumply spherical unmilitary shape. Beneath it lay a girlie magazine, open at a full-page photograph of a naked Nordic blonde with eyes closed and legs parted. He saw me looking at it and, despite the deafening paroxysm of creaking it caused, quickly pushed the chair back and went to place his large, wet, muddy boot on the picture.

But he couldn't bring himself to do it.

With a small expulsion of breath, part moan, part hiss, he stood and walked to the door. He called and an elderly corporal, whiskery and sweet-faced, ducked into the room. The officer snapped at him in Hindi, then turned back to me. 'Your Shillong Permission expires in thirty-six hours. That means you must catch Fokker back to Calcutta tomorrow. If you are not on it I will have you arrested.' He handed me my passport. 'This man will escort you to the office of Deputy Commissioner in Shillong. You must report to him. And you will hear what he has to say about this Cherrapunji Permission.' He flapped his hands at us and, picking up my bag, I followed the corporal out of the terminal.

Shillong lay 31 kilometres away along a winding, ascending road.

We made the journey in a country bus with a radiator that leaked like a busted tap. Twice we stopped at tea houses so the driver could cadge water, once at the foot of a steep gradient where everyone jumped off and pushed. The countryside was very beautiful, soft light gleaming on emerald fields veined by small rushing streams. The corporal spoke no English but smiled kindly and seemed to enjoy the ride. At one halt he plunged into a bazaar and returned with dried watermelon seeds. Nibbling them, I surveyed the passing scenery and wondered whether the Deputy Commissioner would really cancel my Cherrapunji Permission.

The town stood among firs and pines on the summit of a broad hill. Leaving the bus at the depot the corporal and I continued on foot. Now he seemed tense and urged me to move quickly, glancing around like a man fearing ambush. There were many police about, all walking in pairs and swishing their bamboo lathis. But the citizens they policed paid them no heed; the Khasis, small, stocky, tough-looking, treated them like ghosts, looking through them and talking around them. The only cop I saw them acknowledge was a young constable with a bandaged head. He was greeted with derisory laughter and mocked by a crowd of Khasi girls; his colleagues, observing this, glowered and pantomimed vengeance, swinging their lathis like scythes.

Our trek through this old British hill station revealed that at least one of its imperial structures remained intact. The Anglican church was such a perfect example of nineteenth-century English ecclesiastical architecture that I felt a pang of homesickness. Wapshot must have known this place – though, as a hardline Glasgow Presbyterian, he had probably never set foot inside; he would have regarded it as an enemy laager in which braying, claret-swilling vicars in dresses nurtured their unsound theology and dangerous territorial ambitions. But it looked pretty, nevertheless, and strikingly similar to a church I visited sometimes in London.

The Deputy Commissioner was not in his office so the corporal led me to his bungalow a quarter of a mile away. He wasn't there either, and a servant indicated that the DC's present whereabouts remained a mystery. A fine rain began to fall. The corporal, in a quandary, didn't know what to do but I did. We had spent an hour scrambling around this precipitous little town seeking the

Deputy Commissioner, and I felt that if he wished to see me the initiative now lay with him. Captain Ravi had given me the name of a hotel and, with the help of a passing policeman who spoke a little English, I told the corporal I wished to go there.

The Pinewood turned out to be a pleasant, homely building, its deep verandas facing a carefully tended garden. The manager stifled a laugh when asked if he had a room but, before inviting me to choose any key from his board, wanted to see my passport and Permissions. 'Cherrapunji!' he murmured, pondering the entry like a rare, exotic stamp. 'When will you go?'

'As soon as possible.'

I offered the corporal tea but he shyly shook his head and slipped away. The manager said the hotel had been built early in the century by an entrepreneurial Swiss couple, M. and Mme Perouse, for vacationing planters from the Assam tea gardens. My room was cavernous, with a shadowy dressing room and bathroom adjoining, but dank and dirty. The manager pointed this out himself in a smiling, good-humoured way. 'Pretty filthy, eh?' he exclaimed. 'No water and power only sometimes; if you need water a peon will bring. Oh, and rats also.'

'The peon will bring rats?'

He chuckled and clapped me on the shoulder. 'Come! I will open the bar.'

We drank Black Label beer as, holding the glass delicately between finger and thumb, he described the problems of running a hotel amid regular civil disturbances – no staff, no guests, no supplies, no communications, nothing. He warned that there was an 8 p.m. curfew, rigorously enforced; anyone found on the roads after that risked a broken head and imprisonment.

'This particular curfew has been in force for a week,' he said. 'It was brought in because of the anti-foreigner riots we are having. Most of the anger is directed at Bangladeshis and Nepalese who walk in here, thousands of them, and steal land and jobs. But no foreigner is very popular just now.' He drained his beer. 'So for Cherrapunji it is necessary to use a taxi. It is 112 kilometres return and you must come back before sundown; the road is dangerous in the dark. I will arrange this now, with a trusted driver.'

'Is it raining there?' I asked.

He laughed. '*Raining*! At Cherra? You know most of its rain falls during this month, July. So far they have had 366 inches. That is 30 feet.'

'A couple of years ago they had 40 feet.'

'In 1876 they got 75 feet. More. Some days these were 40 inches. No wonder the people are a bit loopy; it is water on the brain. The strange thing is, Shillong is only 56 kilometres away, yet we get only five feet per annum. I am a Delhi man, actually, and there five feet would be a godsend. Already they are announcing this will be worst monsoon for a hundred years.'

I said I had been in Delhi two days earlier, when the phoney burst electrified the city, then left it dejected.

He nodded. 'A senior Department of Finance official has declared there will be no further rain there until 18 August, when Jupiter becomes retrograde and Saturn reverses; now Jupiter is directional. Mars, until 31 August, is in advance of sun so the rain will be small like dew in the morning. But when sun moves ahead of Mars he expect the Delhi rains to be copious.'

Then he jumped up and sent a runner to fetch me a taxi.

The rust-pitted Ambassador was driven by a bony young man wearing broken sunglasses and terrific winged moustaches. A youth sat with him, to whom the driver spoke unceasingly in the soft, contrite voice of the confessional. The youth carried a bundle of green leaves which he fed to the driver one by one, but otherwise remained mute and listened intently to the monologue.

We headed west down an alley walled by scarlet rhododendrons, then south through the hills towards the Bangladeshi border. An intricate interlocking matrix of creeks and streams divided the landscape into a series of moated islands. When the car suffered one of its routine stalls the air was loud with the splash of running water. At Laitlyngkot, once a place of backyard iron forges where the air rang with the chime of hammers, we stopped at the bazaar for bananas and glasses of sweet tea. The descendants of the iron workers were stocky, composed, self-reliant people who looked you straight in the eye. Drinking my tea beneath an English yew I saw a bus approach, painted with crimson demons and the legend

'God's Gift None Can Blot'. It stopped and the several joining passengers attacked it like rock climbers, swarming on to the roof and settling back to light their pipes.

An Indian official begged a lift to Sohrarim, the next village. He was a soils analyst from Madras and said the Khasis, unable to burn their dead on ground waterlogged by the monsoon, preserved the bodies in local orange-flavoured honey. I told him I had first heard that story when I was five, the problem then being one of brimming graves in marshy burial grounds. He looked at me curiously. 'Was your family here?' he asked.

'No. A friend of the family.'

We passed a quiet, clear river with hornbeam trees on its banks and hornstone rocks in its bed. The road, walled on one side by coal-bearing sandstone, fell away on the other into deep, wooded valleys that reminded me of the Cherrapunji painting. I wondered if there were still tigers down there, and naked nomads pursuing them with bows and arrows. The soils analyst said the nomads were around, all right, but not the tigers. These days the nomads shot wild boar, sloth bears, barking deer and, of course, monkeys, which they ate in large numbers. There were also leopards and, from time to time, marauding elephants.

'In the forest near Rajapara a while back,' he said, 'a big tusker chased a woman to her house, kicked it to pieces and trampled her to death. Nothing could be done. Only one hunter in the village possessed a gun.' Here he gave a sudden high-pitched giggle. 'It was a *muzzle*-loader, from the nineteenth century. But, alas, he had neither shot nor shell to fit.'

Outside Sohrarim we passed a group of seated women who shouted and gestured. I took this to be a manifestation of social tension, but the soils analyst said they were merely shooing monkeys from their ginger garden. Then he left us and, still dogged by the sound of the driver's soft, unceasing voice, we set off on the final leg to Cherrapunji. The voice had become petulant, underpinned by a singsong note of complaint.

The country ahead began to open up. We tracked along a high grassy escarpment strewn with rocks and scrubby pandanus palms. It had a scoured, comfortless, wind-blasted look, though the walls of the vertiginous gorges tumbling away beneath were so densely forested that, under a hot sun, they seemed upholstered in lustrous green tapestry.

The sun shone brightly on the escarpment too. There wasn't a raindrop within twenty miles and, aggrieved, I looked up at an empty summer sky. The gorges broadened into deep, jungly valleys, and I realized why there were no clouds above. They were all down below, veils of feathery cirrus, islands of domed cumulus, boiling through the valleys like a grounded tropical front. It was destabilizing to observe, this inversion of the sky and earth, but beautiful too. Small, perfect rainbows stood along the clouds' route, delineating their highway in lights, even charging them with a brief, glittering opalescence as they drifted by.

The driver suddenly paused in his discourse and pointed ahead. 'Cherra!' he said.

He changed gear and took the car slowly up a steep, winding incline. I craned to see and, at the head of the gradient, 1,300 metres above sea level, I finally laid eyes on the wettest place on earth.

It wasn't much to look at. I noted a cluster of low, discoloured hilltop buildings which, as we approached, opened to reveal a tiny bus depot and bazaar. Two battered vehicles boarding passengers and freight bore the 'God's Gift None Can Blot' legend. I jumped out and asked the driver to meet me back here in three hours, noting that many of the market people carried calico-wrapped backpacks suspended from headbands in the fashion of Himalayan porters. Into each headband a furled umbrella had been stuck, giving them a curiously horned appearance, like unicorns. The houses and tea shops were roofed with corrugated iron sheets worn thin as razor blades and crowned by tall tin chimneys; plastic bags had been lashed over the chimney tops to seal them against the rains.

I felt reserve, even hostility. No one smiled. And, though the villagers avoided my eye, I sensed their eyes on my back. The only person to speak to me was a small girl from whom I bought a handful of peanuts and a ripe orange; then she reached beneath her table and gravely produced, for my inspection, a tray of carved silver-bowled opium pipes.

Nearby I examined a display of coracle-shaped, raffia-worked 'knups' or sou'westers which, placed over the head and shoulders, afforded protection from the rain. I passed on, seeking the Cherrapunji umbrella seller, and found him crouching beside a flight of slippery stone steps. Emaciated, with sore red eyes, he was assembling a whole umbrella from the wreckage of several ruined ones, painstakingly fitting old, rusted ribs into a sprocket clasped between his toes. He was surrounded by bits of oiled silk, coloured and patterned fragments of nylon, and handles both orthodox and fantastic – the heads of ducks, spaniels, horses, rabbits and Red Indian chiefs.

'I'd like to buy an umbrella,' I said.

After all these weeks I still didn't possess one, and this seemed an appropriate place to make good the deficiency.

He didn't want my business. A rack of umbrellas, either new or reconditioned, stood propped behind his stool, but he waved a finger and shook his head. None was available. I knew the market people were watching because the whole place had gone quiet, and I persisted. Eventually, giving me an odd, fathomless look, he reached behind the rack and produced a silver-handled parasol, pink silk and trimmed with lace. It was a fragile European antique, probably made last century to shield some wealthy memsahib from the sun. Against forty feet of rain it would afford as much protection as a knotted handkerchief. I heard a faint susurration of laughter from the spectators behind and handed it back. He took it with a faint, ironic smile. I thanked him for his trouble and headed out of the market-place to see the rest of the town.

Cherrapunji occupied a spur of flat tableland three miles long and two wide. Waterfalls lined the wooded limestone cliffs at its back, foaming out of the trees into cloud-filled ravines. One fall was reputed to be the world's fourth highest, though so many were parading today that I couldn't isolate it from the others; no fewer than twelve sprang from the glistening, hundred-yard cliff face before me. The reluctance of the cloud to quit the ravines led me to think it might somehow be colluding with the falls, perhaps even taking nourishment from them. Each, after all, discharged billions of cloud particles a second which, when absorbed, added extra body to the swirling precipitation streaks and streamers that kept obscuring the view.

Whenever they parted, more waterfalls appeared. I may even have induced one; dimly, through drifting mist and at the precise point I suddenly willed it to be, I perceived a new cascade emerging from the rock. I had never seen so many, had never imagined that such a profusion of these lovely, diaphanous things could be congregated in a single area. The town, isolated inside this foaming wall, its northern limits demarcated by rainbows, rang with the exuberant sounds of tumbling water.

The southern limits of the spur dropped steeply away to the flooded plains of Bangladesh, now a glamorous Caribbean blue in the afternoon sun. Cherrapunji's lofty elevation gave me a grandstand view of the drowned country below, and I suddenly understood that, with nowhere else to go, the overflow from these hills went surging out across the undefended flatlands. That's what Cherrapunji's rain did. It assisted in the annual flooding of Bangladesh. As I stood pondering again the two sides of the monsoon coin, death and destruction on the reverse of life and continuity, a voice suddenly said, 'What are you doing here?'

I turned. A burly Indian in a rumpled khaki safari suit stood watching me.

'Just having a look around,' I said.

'Where are your papers?'

'Why?'

'Security. You are in a prohibited zone.'

I opened my passport at the Cherrapunji Permission and handed it to him.

He pondered it for some time, then gave it back, frowning. 'There has been a mistake,' he said. 'You are not allowed here.'

'Delhi says I am.'

'Unfortunately Delhi is far away. You must leave at once. Many illegals are coming in through Cherrapunji from Bangladesh. The people are angry and things are very tense.'

'Do I look like a Bangladeshi illegal?'

He cocked his head and said, unexpectedly, 'Perhaps a Bangladeshi illegal on a bad day. But they will not make the distinction; they are against all foreigners. They think you are here to steal from them.'

I told him my business and, after I promised to be gone two

hours before sunset, he relented. Then, strolling with me, he said the Indian government was proposing to fence off the whole of its border with Bangladesh.

'The fence will be a stout one, best quality steel, and it will run along the slopes here below Cherra. Maybe we will even electrify it, but we are having problems enough generating power for our own needs. And those Banglas are resourceful people, you know; they would probably run wires from the fence to light their damn houses.' He gestured towards the slopes. 'Just a few hundred metres below there is big climate change; the Cherrapunji people grow fantastic tropical fruit – oranges, grapefruit, magnificent bananas, the finest mandarins in the world.'

He left me beside the old British graveyard. A number of tombstones bore the faint, weathered legend, 'Died by His Own Hand'. Cherrapunji had been the first British hill station in the north-east, but its founders had not anticipated the oppressive effect of rain and isolation on the temperaments of young men sent out to administer it.

In 1850 Joseph Dalton Hooker, a Royal Navy doctor turned naturalist, spent the monsoon months in Cherrapunji. He found it

> as bleak and inhospitable as can be imagined ... there is not a tree, and scarcely a shrub to be seen, except occasional clumps of pandanus. The low white bungalows are few in number, and very scattered, some of them being a mile asunder; and a small white church, disused on account of the damp, stands lonely in the centre of it all.

The rainfall astonished Hooker. He noted that the first person to draw it to the attention of the outside world was a

> Mr Yule who stated that in the month of August, 1841, 264 inches fell, or twenty-two feet; and that during five successive days, thirty inches fell in every twenty-four hours! Dr Thompson and I also recorded thirty inches in one day and night, and during the seven months of our stay, upwards of 500 inches fell, so that the total annual fall perhaps greatly exceeded [the] 600 inches, or fifty feet, which has been registered in succeeding years!

(He was puzzled, though, by the curiously localized patterns of the rain; move your gauge a few hundred yards and it registered only half as much as before.)

But it wasn't the precipitation that encouraged him to remain in 'Churra Poonji'. It was the flora, 'an extraordinary exuberance of species' which, he alleged, was probably the richest in all Asia. 'We collected upwards of 2,000 flowering plants within ten miles of the station of Churra, besides 150 ferns, and a profusion of mosses, lichens and fungi.' He found 250 kinds of orchid, many terrestrial and flourishing in the damp woods and grassy slopes, and 25 species of balsam, both tropical and temperate. There were oaks, palms (14 kinds), bamboos (15 kinds) and 150 different grasses – remarkable, since the whole of India contained barely 400.

The site of the Cherrapunji settlement itself, though, was a wasteland, its wretched soil and ferocious climate – in winter, 'owing to the intense radiations, hoar-frost is frequent' – supporting little but the ubiquitous pandanus palms I saw around me now. Hooker was accompanied on his excursions by two of the station's resident officers, Lieutenants Raban and Cave, both dedicated amateur horticulturists whose attempts, far from home, to create their own English gardens he recorded. 'Very few English garden plants throve in the flower beds. Even in pots and frames, geraniums, etc, would rot from the rarity of sunshine.' They managed to raise a few petunias, nasturtiums, chrysanthemums and fuchsias but 'the daisy seed sent from England as double came up very poor and single. Dahlias do not thrive, nor double balsams. Now they have erected small but airy green-houses, and sunlight is the only desideratum.' (Healthy young apple, pear and peach trees, packed in moss, regularly arrived in Calcutta aboard American ice ships – the ice, sold in the market for a penny a pound, proved beneficial to those suffering from post-monsoon fevers – but they flourished, alas, only in the cool, temperate hill stations of the Himalayas.)

Now, making my way to the Mawsmai Falls, I thought of Raban and Cave and wondered whether they had finished up in that forgotten graveyard. If they hadn't resorted to suicide they may have been claimed by a climate which killed Europeans at random In 1690 the Rev. James Ovington wrote:

September and October, those two Months which immediately
follow the Rains, are very pernicious to the Health of the
Europeans; in which two Moons more of them die, than gen-
erally in all the Year besides. For the excess of earthy Vapours
after the Rains ferment the Air, and raise therein such a sultry
Heat, that scarce any is able to withstand the Feverish Effect
it has upon their spirits, nor recover themselves from those
Fevers and Fluxes into which it cast them . . . Which common
Fatality has created a Proverb among the English there, that
Two Mussouns are the Age of Man.

The small Cherrapunjee Presbyterian School (Est. 1930) stopped
me in my tracks. Though it stood locked and deserted, the shade of
Wapshot seemed to hover nearby. Had he founded, even built it? If
so, mention must have been made in his letters and I found myself
pondering the very structure that perhaps, far away and long ago,
my father had visualized in his mind's eye. Maybe he even mentioned it to me: 'Sandy, guess what. Wapshot is putting up the
world's wettest school!' Then he would have worried about its
structural integrity, the kind of foundations, roof and guttering
needed to protect the nippers from those batteries of firehoses
whooshing down from the sky. Being a practical man, the one
thing he probably never thought to discuss would have been the
syllabus; only my mother would have wondered about that.

I moved on, feeling that I had seen something famous, a lost
monument of which I had heard rumours but never clapped eyes
on till now.

The bungalows hereabouts, like those erected by the British, stood
hundreds of yards apart. One had a garden wall fashioned from
two halves of a Dakota's wing, another fencing from a Dakota's
tailplane. In several gardens I saw Dakota propeller bosses being
used as flowerpots; orchids seemed to thrive in them. Then I
remembered the kindly Thril transport manager at Faridabad
who, as a Dakota mechanic with the Indian Air Force, had served
on a base near Cherrapunji and recalled its high accident rate; I
guessed, though, that this recycled wreckage had less to do with his
handiwork than with the conditions pertaining here during the

monsoon. I imagined flying a Dak blind through sheeting rain, with turbulence coming off the hills and windshear roaring up the slopes from the plains of Bangladesh. It must have been a mortally dangerous combination. No wonder so many had crashed around Cherrapunji – more victims, their numbers unknown, to add to its tally of deaths.

The Mawsmai Falls were located on the outskirts of the settlement. On the bluff overlooking them stood a broken stone balustrade, a small, nostalgic echo of a great English estate at which, on fine evenings, the expatriates doubtless gathered to view the pretty cascades across the valley. Here they would have talked, counting the days until the next Home leave, discussing the Khasis (and possibly taking the Hooker line: 'Sulky intractable fellows, averse to rising early and intolerably filthy in their persons'), perhaps shakenly mourning the sudden passing, by gunshot, of a neighbour ('Did he seem dejected to you?') and endlessly comparing notes on how best to keep dry and warm.

Advice on what to wear was available even in London – flannel shirts, woollen undervests, trousers cut from American or Dutch Pepperill unbleached drill, merino socks, stout but comfortable boots, leggings, a waterproof one could ride in, a cashmere coat kept closed to the neck with pearl buttons, shanks and fasteners, and two yards of warm red flannel in case of a sudden chill to the liver. A woven Jaeger, or sanitary belt was held to be a great safeguard against dysentery. They were urged to sleep in flannel and carry umbrellas of strong silk or alpaca.

Beneath the falls Hooker found laurels, brambles, jasmines, oaks and, to his surprise, Khasi miners labouring in hidden coal-pits. Today the Mawsmai was flanked by numerous other falls. Plumes of white water sheeted off the green cliff, vanished into cloud, then reappeared in a foaming burn that went plunging down to nourish the tropical fruit gardens and top up the Bangladeshi flood.

Wapshot might occasionally have joined the expats here, though my impression was of a man not much given to social chit-chat; indeed, if he talked obsessively about the contents of his rain gauge the others may have found him depressing. And what would my father have made of Cherrapunji? Certainly he would have appreciated its similarity to some of the wilder parts of western Scotland, which he loved, and, provided he experienced a few of those famous forty-inch days, might well have regarded it as the trip of a lifetime. Now I had come in his place and, staring out at the falls, I tried to conjure him up. But I couldn't see the shy young doctor who once pitted his wits against the extremes of the tropical weather systems, and who would have pressed me hard for details of Cherrapunji and the Indian monsoon, shaking his head, laughing in that surprised, delighted way that I missed so much.

All I saw was the brave, tired man who knew he had a mortal heart condition and who, stubbornly rejecting the idea of retirement, suffered his massive, inevitable coronary two weeks after joining a new practice in New Zealand; it happened on the steps of an Auckland post office where he had called to mail an affectionate letter to my daughter. I imagined this father looking at me a little doubtfully, privately wondering whether the trip had really been a good idea. Travel writing, eh? Well, perhaps such things serve a purpose. But a need? Hmm. He had wanted me to be a doctor too.

Some youths were leaning on the balustrade, gossiping noisily, and now I became aware that they had fallen silent and were watching me. Two detached themselves and strolled over, umbrellas tucked under their arms, ragged shirt-tails protruding from worn, patched sweaters. One spoke English.

'What are you doing here?' he enquired.

'I've come to see the waterfalls.'

'Come from where?'

'England. London.'

'Are you Methodist?'

'No.'

'I am Methodist. My friend here is animist. He see God in the waterfalls. Where do you see God?'

'Well . . . inside my head, I think. But not very often.'

He nodded, and translated for his friend. The friend, who had a nervous disorder that made him twitch and start, spoke at some length.

'He is telling you he also see the spirits of dead ancestors around here. These are two great-aunts who lived in bottom village far below. One stormy night, after selling their potatoes at Cherra bazaar, they climb down high and precarious cliff ladder beside the Mawsmai – and tumble off.'

The friend spoke again.

'They were drunk!'

'That's a terrible story,' I said.

'Yes.' He gave a merry laugh.

'Your English is very good.'

'Of course. Every day I am listening to BBC World Service. And my teacher was taught by the Methodists. Welshmen. Thomas Jones, father of the Khasi alphabet, gave us our written language and started big fashion for literature in Cherrapunji. Now there are poets working all over the hills.' He nodded át his friend. 'He is a poet. He has written a very good poem about the great-aunts. It is called "Falling".'

I asked for a translation of 'Falling' but thought bemusedly: Welsh? Methodists? I never realized the Methodists had been in Cherrapunji. Would Wapshot have mentioned them in his letters? Undoubtedly, but news of their deeds had not been relayed to me. Perhaps my father thought I was too young to know; tales of Old Testament floods and honey-smeared corpses might be dull but they weren't controversial. I saw Wapshot in a new light. He had been a man under stress, competing day and night with the sonorous, persuasive Taffs and their buttery bardic voices; perhaps they had introduced rugby to the Khasi Hills as well. Poor Wapshot. He had certainly had his work cut out.

The boys were discussing their opening stanzas in low, eager voices when, abruptly, the sun went out and a bomb exploded a hundred feet above our heads. The flash and bang almost lifted me off the ground, but they barely glanced up. Casually unfurling their umbrellas they continued talking as, stunned, I watched the approach of the Cherrapunji rain.

A fountain of dense black cloud came spiralling over the hills, then rose steeply into the sky. It formed a kind of tent, apex high overhead, sides unrolling right to the ground. It was very dark inside but I could just discern, trooping towards us, an armada of shadowy, galleon-like vessels with undersides festooned with writhing cables of water. They gave off thundery rumbles and a noise like discharging hydrants, the rain descending in hissing vertical rafts of solid matter that lathered the earth and made the spokes of the poet's umbrella, under which I had taken shelter, bend like saplings.

Standing there, I recalled the words of Y. P. Rao. 'Observations of meteorologists who have visited the area suggest the phenomenal rains at Cherrapunji prevail over a short length of the range, up a small portion of the slope.' He believed they were lured into a unique orographic trap. The wet air, rushing up from the south, struck that small, sloping aspect, then found itself being ducted, willy-nilly, into a south-facing, funnel-shaped catchment opening in the hills – a limestone corral from which it could only escape by shedding its moisture.

I felt little of the excitement I had known when the burst arrived in the south. Those had been occasions for public jubilation. This was a routine matineé performance at Cherrapunji, awesome certainly but exhilarating only to earnest collectors of meteorological records; such specialists would now be watching, incredulous, as their gauges foamed like champagne glasses.

The rain left us enveloped in low, luminous cloud. The poet and his friend, summoned by their companions, left with the poem still untranslated. I set off back to the bazaar and, moments later, saw six men and a woman emerge from the Scotch mist and troop towards me in single file, all sporting closed umbrellas tucked into their headbands. After they had passed, the woman suddenly turned, ran back and placed a brown, speckled bird's egg in my hand.

That night, as I ate dinner at the Pinewood, a well-dressed, middle-aged Indian sat down uninvited at my table and ordered two Black Label beers. He asked how I had spent my day. I told him I had been to Cherrapunji. He wanted to know what I thought of the place. I said I had found it very strange, and asked him who he was.

'Oh, no one in particular. Just a taxpayer.'

'You're not the Deputy Commissioner?'

'God, no.' He gave me a fleeting smile. 'I understand you intend to write about Cherrapunji. What will you say?'

'I don't know yet.'

'It's mainly the rain that interests you. Am I right?'

'More or less.'

'Were you threatened at all?'

'Absolutely not.'

'Did you speak to anyone?'

'A cop. A couple of kids. Why?'

He hesitated. 'Well, we have a situation developing in Meghalaya which could, possibly, turn into something like the British problem in Northern Ireland.'

'You mean the illegals?'

'It goes deeper than that. We're really in South-East Asia now; with regard to race, language and culture these people are closer to the Thais, even the Khmers, than us, and they want a degree of autonomy we can't give them. Now they are becoming belligerent. There are rumours they may even be obtaining weapons from the rebels in Nagaland.' He smiled. 'And some of our most intractable malcontents are to be found, I'm afraid, at Cherrapunji. It's become a bit of a revolutionary hothouse.'

'I see.'

A waiter brought the beers. My companion lifted his glass. 'Mud in your eye!' he said, and talked of other things – London restaurants, the service on Air India, the effect of the curfew on Shillong's tiny red-light district behind the Delhi Hotel. 'The girls are bored and broke, poor things!' Then, as he got up to go, he said, 'You will, of course, remember to catch the plane tomorrow.'

I said the plane was very much on my mind. He nodded, gave me a final courteous smile and walked out of the room.

Several days later I arrived at my London office to find a letter waiting for me. It came from an official at the Indian High Commission and said that, after careful consideration by the authorities in Delhi, my request to visit Cherrapunji had been denied. The official expressed regret, and hoped that the news would not cause undue inconvenience or disappointment.

In the morning, with several hours to spare, I looked around Shillong in the company of an affable, educated young Khasi named Jerry. A friend of the Pinewood manager, he took me first to the Shillong Golf Club. At the clubhouse, a large, dim Home Counties bungalow built in 1927, I examined original prints hanging on the walls – 1920s golfing cartoons, a faded map inscribed 'The Old Course, St Andrew's 1921, presented by the Manufacturers of Dunlop Golf Balls' and, above the bar, a notice saying, 'Do not hold up the whole field. Please realize that behind you is a course full of thirsty blokes losing precious BEER TIME.'

We visited the Butterfly Museum, where many of the 500 species that inhabit the Khasi Hills were displayed and named for the lepidopterists who first netted them: Doubleday, Westwood, Cramer, Donovan, Gray, Butler and Hope. Mr Wankhar, the breezy curator, took me to meet the girls framing specimens bred on his butterfly farm for collectors around the world. He pointed out his best-selling lines. 'Nawab, raja, tortoiseshell, Indian fritillary. You wish to buy? I give you special price.'

Those jewel-like creatures should have been alive and out adorning the hills. I said no. At the State Museum there were giant oil portraits of Lord Keating, the first commissioner of Assam, and Edward VII in full coronation regalia. Other oils, mostly of grand English ladies in silk gowns and coronets, had not been identified and Dr Chattopadhyay, the deputy curator, asked if I could help. He was proud of his pictures, but their anonymity devalued them. Regretfully, I couldn't even hazard a guess.

Then, ever-mindful of the Fokker's 2.15 departure from Umroi, we hurried on to the bazaar, a warren of seething alleyways each the territory of a particular guild. The purveyors of pan occupied this alley, the spice sellers that, basket weavers the other. In the stinking, offal-strewn butchers' row, a youth swinging his axe like a woodsman severed the head of an amazed-looking buffalo and then, with a few slashing swipes, laid open the steaming stomach. His person streamed with blood – dried blood made his hair spiky, and teeth and eyes glinted in his blood-encrusted face.

The alley of the umbrella sellers contained well-stocked stalls run by men eager for my custom. I began negotiating for a plain black churchwarden's model, then realized this was my last day on the monsoon trail; startled, I followed Jerry to the alley of the archery suppliers. He told me Shillong's archery sweepstakes draw great crowds to the shooting fields, where bowmen fire a set number of arrows into a cylindrical bamboo-slat target at high speed. Bets are placed on the number that strike the target, and anyone predicting the final two digits of the total gets an eight-to-one return on his investment.

Then he said, 'I know an Englishman living in Shillong. Mr Tom Richmond. It's a pity you must go now. You would have enjoyed meeting him.'

This was extraordinary news. 'Do you know where his house is?'

'Of course.'

I had to check in at Umroi in two hours. It would take an hour to get there, and first I needed to return to the Pinewood to pack and pay my bill.

'Let's go and find him,' I said.

Twenty minutes later we stopped outside a small, two-storeyed wooden residence with blue door and window frames. Thomas Sebastian Richmond turned out to be a handsome, strong-looking man of seventy-five who welcomed me warmly and ushered me into a living room containing comfortable chairs, a piano, a custom-built, mirror-backed bar with curtains, two friendly golden retrievers and some bits of machinery. It smelled strongly of meat. 'I'm a West Cumbrian, from Seascale,' he said. 'I shot my first hare on the spot where that nuclear reactor thing now stands, and went to school just up the road, at St Bees. There used to be another Old St Beghian in Shillong, oddly enough, living not two golf shots from this very house.'

He threw open the curtains of the bar. 'Fancy a snort? It's all Indian, but the whisky's quite tolerable.'

I said it was a little early for me and, besides, I had a plane to catch.

Mr Richmond arrived in Assam in 1933, a young engineer tea planter, and first came to Shillong three years later. 'I had my appendix removed by the famous Dr Hughes at the Welsh Mission Hospital. In those days this was known as "the Scotland of the East"; most evenings Highland pipers played at the bandstand while everyone cried into their gin. It was dinner jackets every night, and when the Governor turned up you couldn't get plastered till he'd gone.' He polished his spectacles. 'Shame you have to rush off. We could have gone to see Carruthers. He's in Upper Shillong, but comes from Dumfriesshire and is doing very big things in chickens.'

Mr Richmond did things in the meat-curing line. 'Bacon, mainly. And, of course, loads of hams at Christmas. I've married a local girl and we have three sons, George, Tony and Bill. Bill's in the police and George runs the local Home Guard. I've still got a sister at home in Seascale and a brother somewhere in Pinner. We've lost touch now, but he used to be with Rowland Ward, the well-known taxidermists.'

I asked Mr Richmond how he coped with the monsoon.

'Boredom becomes a factor.' He nodded at the piano. 'This year I'm rebuilding and tuning that. It was absolutely clapped out when I got it but, by the time I'm through, it'll sound like a Steinway concert grand. Rebuilding old pianos is a very popular monsoon activity in Shillong. Every household has one, some two. In fact, there are more pianos per head of population here than anywhere else in India. Jerry, old son, can't I tempt you to a quick gargle?'

Jerry said he would soon have to get back to work.

'You can get some surprisingly decent stuff here. One of my chums, Mike Hunt, used to make an excellent cherry brandy and I sometimes lent him a hand. It was a famous brew, one of the things visitors always took home with them: orange honey, framed Khasi butterflies and Captain Hunt's cherry brandy. Then he diversified into the plum sort, and I reckon that's what killed him; plum brandy has a dangerously high wood alcohol content.' He beamed at me. 'Mike's sister married the bloke who owned all those barges at Port Said, know who I mean? *Famous*.'

Mrs Richmond, a shy, softly spoken Indian woman wearing a blue *jainsem*, brought coffee and biscuits but Jerry caught my eye and tapped his watch. At the front door Mr Richmond gestured around him. 'I built this place when I retired from my Assam garden in '58. Then you could bag snipe, woodcock and grouse not a hundred yards from here. On cold days you could even shoot the buggers from the privacy of your bedroom. But not any more.'

I promised to contact his sister in England, then shook hands and went speeding back to the Pinewood. I had exactly one hour to get to Umroi.

*

Jerry returned to his office. The hotel doorman offered to find me a cab, then reported that none were available. I felt a stirring of alarm, but moments later a clapped-out Ambassador taxi, bravely flying silk scarves from its door handles, delivered an air force officer to the Pinewood. As he jumped out I jumped in. The check-in time was now forty minutes away and I asked the driver to take me to the aerodrome as quickly as possible. A small, wizened man in a red plastic baseball cap, he too was accompanied by a youth who fed him leaves. The youth knew two words of English: 'No problem.' Within seconds, though, I knew we had a very big problem. The engine rattled like coins in a collecting tin and the driver was severely uncoordinated; he couldn't manage the gears, seemed baffled by the steering and grew dizzy when the forward velocity exceeded 25 m.p.h. At 20 m.p.h. he kept his eyes open, and sometimes on the road.

'Can't he go faster? I'm going to miss the plane.'

'No problem,' said the youth.

It began to rain, not heavily, but enough to make the surface slick. The Ambassador began to drift round corners sideways, even backwards, and caused oncoming road-users to honk at it. This angered the driver, who, sometimes finding himself facing in the same direction as the departing vehicle, honked furiously back. Whenever he used the horn a cheery red light fixed above the mirrorless rear-view mirror came on. Watching it blinking like an Aldis lamp on an empty stretch of highway I suddenly realized what was wrong.

'This man's drunk,' I said.

The youth slipped him another leaf. 'No problem,' he said.

We rolled to a halt beside a small, thatched repair shop where the driver, staggering, collected a spare tyre, bald as a beach ball, and slung it into the boot. I had to be at Umroi in twenty minutes and we weren't even a quarter of the way. He inserted a tape in his stereo and turned it up full – old Frankie Lane numbers played on a Wurlitzer. We pressed on at 20 m.p.h., the driver fidgeting with the controls, chewing leaves and chain-smoking tiny, inch-long cigarettes the youth kept rolling for him. Laden lorries and buses pulled out and passed impatiently, our red lamp twinkling as long, derisory blasts sent them on their way. Then, descending a gradient, the Ambassador went into a stately skid. Pivoting gently, it buried its nose in a high, muddy bank and triggered off a small landslide. We sat and watched the smoking bonnet slowly vanish beneath a cascade of stones and wet red earth.

The driver got out and fell flat on his face.

The youth said, 'No problem.'

And I started contemplating a term of imprisonment.

The Deputy Commissioner occupied a spacious office overlooking a shadowy garden. He looked up as I was brought in. 'Ah!' he said. 'Our illegal immigrant.'

My explanation took no more than a minute. He listened closely, a large, competent-looking man with tired eyes, then nodded, tapping his teeth with a pencil. Finally he said, 'Do you think there is any correlation between the moral and economic health of a nation and the way its cricket is played? I mean, back in the days when Britain was rich and governed by Christians, was there any of this arguing with the umpire, hurling away the bat, tantrums on the field and so on?'

'Well, there was the "bodyline" tour of Australia,' I said warily. 'That got pretty rough.'

He nodded. 'Harold Larwood. Bowling at their heads. Yes. But by then Germany had rearmed and the threat of war was beginning to loom. Also, with Mosley, Britain was experiencing Fascism domestically so perhaps bodyline was a symptom of a general unease, a feeling that the old order was about to change for ever.'

'I think Larwood just wanted wickets.'

'Possibly. But I also think the mood of the English party reflected the uncertainties at home. Their inflexible code of conduct, their . . . *bushido*, was abandoned. And now it's happening to us. Our economy is in a parlous state, our cricketers behave like a tribe of monkeys and the spectators are even worse. Once men played for India from a deep sense of national pride and commitment; it was like going into the priesthood. Today they play because it gives them access to money, overseas travel, hard liquor and fast foreign girls.'

'Sounds pretty good to me,' I said.

'I heard the other day that this will be the worst monsoon for a century. Its effect on the economy doesn't bear thinking about. As

for its long-term effect on the game, well, that could be catastrophic.' He sighed and opened my file. 'So how long do you want
to stay in Shillong? Two days? Four days? A week?'

'Another day should do it,' I said.

He amended my passport and handed it over with a smile. 'But
pound for pound,' he said, 'our monkeys can still beat the living
daylights out of your monkeys.'

I returned to the Pinewood. The manager looked frightened when
I walked in, and frowned over the amended Permission before
letting me have my room back. I called Mr Richmond but his
phone went unanswered. There was just enough daylight remaining
to venture up the Shillong Peak from where Joseph Dalton Hooker
had surveyed, in one direction, the Gangetic plain and, in the
other, 'the whole Assam valley . . . and the dark range of the Lower
Himalaya crested by peaks of frosted silver'. He calculated he
could see in total 'an area of fully 30,000 square miles, which is
greater than that of Ireland'.

The view today was obscured by a fine afternoon mist and I
sensed, rather than saw, the occasional flash and glitter of distant
ice. Those mountains marked the end of the monsoon's progress.
Here it was finally restrained and more or less walled up inside
India, its final days kept a private family affair. But climatologists
believe the mountains may also play a key role in its conception
and growth. The depth of the Himalayan snows could affect the
vigour of the young monsoon, even help govern the speed of its
advance all the way from Trivandrum. Heavy, late-melting spring
snow inhibits the heating of the highlands – particularly the Tibetan
Plateau – necessary for the generation of monsoon-forming winds
and jet streams.

Y. P. Rao had readings taken on the Silver Hut glacier halfway
up Mount Everest. He found that nocturnal radiation 'out to
space' from the snow surfaces took the temperature down to minus
25 degrees centigrade but then, during the day, high-intensity solar
radiation took it back up again to 20 degrees centigrade. Could
snow liquidize under such violent extremes? Was radiation modified
by the monsoon? The matter, Rao believed, required further study.

Heading back down to Shillong I thought of Sir George Everest, the Surveyor General of India who, in 1825, as a young captain in the Bengal Artillery, measured the Grand Meridional Arc of India. It was a complex trigonometrical survey using 'flags and masts with piles on all ordinary occasions, and blue lights in long distances'. Orthodox blue survey lights, however, were not available so Everest improvised, filling cups with oil, resin and cotton seeds, lighting them and placing them beneath upturned clay pots with holes knocked in the sides. 'I have, on occasion, taken an angle very satisfactorily between two of these small lights at a distance of thirty-one miles, long after day had so far advanced as to render it unnecessary to illuminate the wires of the telescope.'

Everest, shooting sextant measurements in the mountains from the back of an elephant, tirelessly doing his vertical angles at three o'clock in the morning – 'That method gives the fairest chance of overcoming the errors of terrestrial refraction' – came across a strange phenomenon. The dry season proved unsuitable for observations by daylight because a mist pervaded the atmosphere which could not be penetrated by telescope. After dark it was a different story. Then the 'mist is so completely pervious to night-lights, that for distances of forty and forty-five miles we can carve a passage right through it'.

When the monsoon set in, the reverse happened. The climate might be 'most fatal to health and comfort . . . yet the sky is limpid, beyond anything that can be imagined, *except when mists take place*'. At night, he couldn't see a blue cotton-seed light at five paces and wrote grimly of the anomalies produced by observations taken in dry and wet weather; aside from deciphering the laws governing terrestrial refraction – about which 'we shall never come to any conclusion' – India's opaque monsoon mists proved to be the greatest thorn in his side.

Twenty-five years later, in the summer of 1850, a group of young surveyors – Everest's protégés to a man – first glimpsed the mountain they would later name for him. It stood far away, a tiny finger of ice barely visible on the northern horizon. Yet, using the methods he had taught them (and allowing for the hazards of terrestrial refraction), they measured its stupendous height with such accuracy that, according to the most sophisticated methods available today, they were a mere twenty-seven feet adrift.

*

The only other person dining at the Pinewood was the air force officer who had turned up in that ruined taxi. I thought of inviting him over to compare notes but, from a distance, we could hear the sounds of combat between the police and a mob of curfew-breakers, and the officer sat hunched introspectively over his plate. I went to bed. Tonight, though, the peon had brought rats. They scuttled about the darkened room with the purposeful energy of new tenants and, by torchlight, I watched one climb into a shoe and compose itself for sleep. Only another shoe, thrown hard, forced it back to a corner where, to judge by some erratic tinkling noises, its companions were trying to get through to someone on the telephone.

In the morning I called Aloysius Baptista's friends, the Patels. Iris Patel said, 'We're very worried about Aly. He seems to be heading for some sort of breakdown. Did you know he wants to visit Cherrapunji?'

'No. I spoke to him only a couple of days ago. He didn't mention it.'

'He wrote us a very odd letter: it didn't sound like him at all, no jokes, absolutely no gossip and nothing at all about Rita. My husband thinks he's going through a personal crisis. Could that be?'

'It's possible,' I said.

'But *Cherra*? What does he expect to find there? And who on earth put the idea in his head?'

'Rita's father knew it from his air force days. She and Aly have both spoken about it.'

She fell silent. Finally she said, 'I think he's looking for Mecca.'

I thought, in truth, that he might be looking for his own country. I also thought the monsoon might be the key to the search; annually in Trivandrum, after all, the monsoon cure offered him a new lease of life. Travelling to the place where those same rains reached their crescendo would take him deep into India, and as far into himself as he wished to go. 'It would be an astonishing place to try and fly a glider,' I said, not entirely joking. I tried a clumsy imitation of Aly's mellifluous party-going voice but she wasn't amused. We exchanged a few pleasantries, then, by mutual agreement, concluded the conversation.

*

When I turned up at Tom Richmond's house he laughed. 'Heard you missed the plane,' he said. 'Why don't we take you out to the airfield? We could bring a picnic. Bill's coming over here anyway. So is Enid, his wife. Interesting girl, very bright. We can use the Jeep. Family outing.'

Bill, the policeman, turned out to be bluff and fit-looking, Enid a petite, pretty woman who had just completed a Ph.D thesis on the matrilineal aspects of Khasi society. Here inheritance was passed down the female side; a boy took his mother's name; land and property went from mother to daughter. 'The girl often proposes marriage,' said Enid, 'and the oldest sisters are traditionally the family heads and providers.'

'They're great litigants,' said Bill. 'Lawyers love them. Those sisters spend half their lives in court disputing each other's land claims.'

Tom helped himself to a little brandy from the bar. 'The old Assam–Bengal railway ran through my garden, you know, built on the bones of Irishmen, so they say. At night it was truly beautiful, all fireflies and bullfrogs.'

On the wall, beside a framed Lake District landscape, a tiger's head hung. 'Can't bag those any more,' he said. 'Not unless you're a policeman.'

Bill laughed. 'Now, now, Daddy. We only shoot on a public safety basis – man eaters, rogue tuskers and so on.'

'And the rest,' said Tom.

The picnic ready, we all piled into Bill's Jeep and set off for Umroi, Tom mourning the sudden demise of a fighting cock he had been nurturing. 'Magnificent creature, quite fearless, mad as a hatter. Cock-fighting is extremely popular around Shillong, though illegal. An old mate of mine, lived just down the road here, bred some particularly good and crazy fighters. He's passed away now. He went to Repton. He was six foot eight. It's funny, but all the Repton chaps I knew were unusually tall.'

We motored past a spot where a beer lorry had crashed a year earlier. Bill said so many passers-by had thrown themselves down to drink from the puddles, and in such quantities, that the senseless figures littering the highway made it look like a battleground.

'Illicit liquor is also a big problem here,' he added. 'My people spend a lot of time chasing bootleggers. It's good fun, actually. They bring the stuff to town in old American cars, Buicks and Chevrolets with huge eight-cylinder engines, which can go backwards as fast as they go forwards. You think you've got one cornered and he'll suddenly blast off at 100 m.p.h. *in reverse*. It makes them bloody difficult to catch.'

Halfway to the field, cloud blanketed the valley and rain fell so torrentially that, with visibility barely extending beyond the bonnet, we slowed to a crawl.

'The Fokker will never get down in this,' I said.

Tom said, 'Any minute now it'll all blow away again.' Even as he spoke, the cloud began vanishing up the valley like smoke being sucked into an extractor fan. He told me he had last seen England in the 1950s, and no further visits were planned. Now, as a soft, pewtery light gleamed on streams, tarns, a lake and sheep grazing on grassy hillsides, I guessed that in his mind's eye one vision of Cumbria had become fused with another.

We drove into a meadow beside the airfield. Bill poured cold beers while Enid handed around sandwiches, meatballs and small, delicious steaks fried in batter. Tom sat down to write a letter to his sister which I would post in London. The sun shone and those glittering Khasi butterflies swooped among the monsoon wildflowers.

Drinking Bill's beer and idly remembering the small New Hebridean island where, in a sense, all this had started, it finally dawned on me that the monsoon had been a vehicle intended to take me back as well as forward, parallel journeys going in opposite directions. And I knew the seed had been sewn not at the National Hospital, in the company of the Baptistas, but a year earlier when I received word of my mother's death in New Zealand. The loss of our second parent fixes us next in the firing line and makes life suddenly finite. It is the moment when we finally grow up.

The rains had helped me with that. I felt younger, stronger, better, curiously at peace. This monsoon may have been a distressingly bad one for much of India but because I – perhaps alone in all the land – possessed a brief to follow it, I had been rewarded in the way that traditionally it was supposed to reward everyone.

Out on the runway long blasts were blown on a whistle. 'They've sighted the plane,' said Tom.

The Fokker came wheeling out of the clouds, now regrouping at the head of the valley. When I walked into the terminal the overweight security officer who had threatened me with arrest gave a high, strangulated cry and jabbed a finger in the air; then, seeing Bill, he heaved himself erect and saluted. He ushered us into a tiny VIP room containing an overstuffed sofa and a framed photograph, badly faded, of the Prime Minister. He brought us tea and offered us pan from a silver box. He was solicitous, even twinkling. 'Your friend Captain Ravi on this flight,' he said.

Ravi hastened in a moment later, shook hands with everyone and gulped down some tea. 'What happened to you yesterday?' he said. 'We should go; there is weather coming.'

'How are the hydraulics?' I asked.

'Pretty good. The emergency pin is out of the door. You can have the third seat.'

I said goodbye to my friends. Tom said, 'My great-grandfather was George Richmond, the painter. Did I mention old George? He was famous, quintessentially the most English of artists, something to do with the way he used light.' He shook my hand. 'Well, old cock, have a gargle for me when you get back. It's summer now, isn't it? Have you been to Buttermere? There used to be a nice little pub there. Sitting outside in the evening you could hear just about all the birds in England.' And then I saw there were tears in his eyes.

On the tiny flight deck the young co-pilot sat peering around the valley. 'Hurry, hurry, hurry,' he murmured. Ravi drove the Fokker out to the threshold like a fire engine. 'Strap yourself in tight,' he said. He pushed the throttles forward before he was even aligned, accelerating into the turn, then bounding forward as the usual Umroi fog came rolling down behind and, in front, another black wall began closing on the runway. But this one rippled with tongues of flame and gave off small, eddying puffs of smoke. Above the racket of the engines Ravi shouted, 'They're shooting at us!' I stared wordlessly ahead. The base of the smoking, burning rampart scraped along the valley floor but its dome soared upwards to form part of the substructure of heaven itself. And it came from the south. I wondered whether this was a full-blown Cherrapunji *son et lumière* production, diverting through Umroi to show me something I would never forget.

We crashed into it ten feet off the ground. Huge internal vortices tossed us up another fifty. The rain drummed like buckshot and lightning fitfully illuminated the flight deck. Bottles were breaking in the galley and the stewardess, strapped in behind, cried out. For almost a quarter of an hour the Fokker, creaking and groaning, wings flexing like a planing gull's, went lurching and porpoising through the maelstrom.

Then, as if the monsoon had finally wearied of my presence and decided to spit me out, we burst into calm air and sunshine so blinding it made us blink. Before us the sapphire plains of Bangladesh were stippled with the shadows of benign clouds drifting through the huge, pale Indian sky. In a month the rains would withdraw, travelling down India the way they had come, the final showers passing across Trivandrum and then vanishing over the horizon in, perhaps, a valedictory puff of smoke.

I looked back for a last glimpse of Cherrapunji. But it lay beneath a lavender-coloured canopy that reached past the Himalayas and on, drawing the eye much further than it would actually go. It seemed to cover half the world, and I imagined that at long last the summer monsoon was flowing free, unimpeded by those mountain ramparts.

Ravi, steering carefully around the clouds, began talking to someone on the radio.

Even Siberia, I thought, might become a land of rice and mangoes, of green, glittering landscapes mirrored everywhere in water.

ALEXANDER FRATER

Tales from the Torrid Zone

PICADOR

Alex Frater, ex-chief travel correspondent of the *Observer* and master storyteller, takes us on a wonderful personal journey through the tropics in *Tales from the Torrid Zone*. Part memoir, part travelogue, the story is rooted in his birthplace, the tiny tropical republic of Vanuatu. From this obscure South Seas group he ranges over the hot, wet, beautiful swathe of the world that has haunted him ever since. He dines with a tropical queen in a leper colony, makes his way across tropical Africa (and two civil wars) in a forty-five-year-old flying boat, delivers a new church bell to a remote Oceanian island and visits scores of countries to learn about their history, politics, medicine, flora and fauna. The result is a witty, entertaining and immensely readable book from a multiple award-winning travel writer.

'Engaging. Moving and deeply affectionate . . . The range of material is delightful. [Frater] has a distinctive voice, the most essential weapon in the travel writer's arsenal, and he deploys it to express something universal'
Sara Wheeler, *Guardian*

'Into this long and entertaining narrative, which has the tone and texture of the stories one hears at sundown on a tropical veranda while nursing a tumbler of whisky, [Frater] has distilled a lifetime of experience . . . *Tales from the Torrid Zone* is Frater's love letter to the region'
Anthony Sattin, *Sunday Times*